Complete

TACHS!

**Test for Admission into Catholic High Schools
Study Guide**

Published by

Complete TEST Preparation Inc.

Copyright © 2013 by Complete Test Preparation Inc. ALL RIGHTS RESERVED. No part of this book may be reproduced or transferred in any form or by any means, graphic, electronic, or mechanical, including photocopying, recording, web distribution, taping, or by any information storage retrieval system, without the written permission of the author.

Notice: Complete Test Preparation Inc. makes every reasonable effort to obtain from reliable sources accurate, complete, and timely information about the tests covered in this book. Nevertheless, changes can be made in the tests or the administration of the tests at any time and Complete Test Preparation Inc. makes no representation or warranty, either expressed or implied as to the accuracy, timeliness, or completeness of the information contained in this book. Complete Test Preparation Inc. makes no representations or warranties of any kind, express or implied, about the completeness, accuracy, reliability, suitability or availability with respect to the information contained in this document for any purpose. Any reliance you place on such information is therefore strictly at your own risk.

The author(s) shall not be liable for any loss incurred as a consequence of the use and application, directly or indirectly, of any information presented in this work. Sold with the understanding, the author(s) is not engaged in rendering professional services or advice. If advice or expert assistance is required, the services of a competent professional should be sought.

The company, product and service names used in this publication are for identification purposes only. All trademarks and registered trademarks are the property of their respective owners. Complete Test Preparation Inc. is not affiliated with any educational institution.

Complete Test Preparation is not affiliated with the makers of the TACHS, who do not endorse this product.

We strongly recommend that students check with exam providers for up-to-date information regarding test content.

Published by
Complete Test Preparation Inc.
Visit us on the web at https://www.test-preparation.ca
Printed in the USA

Version 7.5 March 2018

About Complete Test Preparation Inc.

The Complete Test Preparation Team has been publishing high quality study materials since 2005. Over one million students visit our websites every year, and thousands of students, teachers and parents all over the world (over 100 countries) have purchased our teaching materials, curriculum, study guides and practice tests.

Complete Test Preparation is committed to providing students with the best study materials and practice tests available on the market. Members of our team combine years of teaching experience, with experienced writers and editors, all with advanced degrees.

ISBN-13: 9781772450934

Feedback

We welcome your feedback. Email us at feedback@test-preparation.ca with your comments and suggestions. We carefully review all suggestions and often incorporate reader suggestions into upcoming versions. As a Print on Demand Publisher, we update our products frequently.

Find us on Facebook

WWW.FACEBOOK.COM/COMPLETETESTPREPARATION

Contents

6 Getting Started
How this study guide is organized ... 6
The TACHS Study Plan ... 7
Making a Study Schedule ... 7

12 Reading
Reading Self-Assessment ... 13
Reading Part I - Vocabulary ... 15
Answer Key ... 17
How to Improve your Vocabulary ... 18
Reading Part II - Reading Comprehension ... 22
Answer Key ... 28
Help with Reading Comprehension ... 31
Main Idea and Supporting Details ... 33
Drawing Inferences And Conclusions ... 36
Point Of View And Purpose ... 38

41 Language
Language Self-Assessment ... 42
Answer Key ... 54
English Grammar and Punctuation Tutorials ... 57
Capitalization ... 57
Punctuation Tutorials ... 59
English Grammar Multiple Choice - Verb Tense ... 64
Common English Usage Mistakes - A Quick Review ... 77
Subject Verb Agreement ... 83

88 Mathematics
Math Self-Assessment ... 91
Answer Key ... 97
How to Solve Word Problems ... 101
Types of Word Problems ... 103
Fraction Tips, Tricks and Shortcuts ... 109
Decimal Tips, Tricks and Shortcuts ... 112
Percent Tips, Tricks and Shortcuts ... 113
How to Answer Basic Math Multiple Choice ... 114
Cartesian & Coordinate Plane and Grid ... 118
Pythagorean Geometry ... 122
Scale drawings ... 124
Quadrilaterals ... 125

129 Ability
Ability Self-Assessment ... 129
Answer Key ... 134

135	**Practice Test Questions Set 1** Answer Key	179
194	**Practice Test Questions Set 2** Answer Key	232
245	**Conclusion**	

Getting Started

CONGRATULATIONS! By deciding to take the Test for Admission into Catholic High Schools (TACHS®), you have taken the first step toward a great future! Of course, there is no point in taking this important examination unless you intend to do your best to earn the highest grade you possibly can. That means getting yourself organized and discovering the best approaches, methods and strategies to master the material. Yes, that will require real effort and dedication on your part, but if you are willing to focus your energy and devote the study time necessary, before you know it you will be opening that letter of acceptance to the school of your choice!

We know that taking on a new endeavour can be scary, and it is easy to feel unsure of where to begin. That's where we come in. This study guide is designed to help you improve your test-taking skills, show you a few tricks of the trade and increase both your competency and confidence.

The Test for Admissions into Catholic High School

The TACHS exam is composed of four sections, section one, Reading, comprises vocabulary, and reading comprehension, section two is English language. Section three is mathematics and section four is Ability, or IQ.

While we seek to make our guide as comprehensive as possible, note that like all exams, the TACHS® Exam might be adjusted at some future point. New material might be added, or content that is no longer relevant or applicable might be removed. It is always a good idea to give the materials you receive when you register to take the TACHS® a careful review.

How this study guide is organized

This study guide is divided into three sections. The first section, Self-Assessments, which will help you recognize your areas of strength and weaknesses. This will be a boon when it comes to managing your study time most efficiently; there is not much point of focusing on material you have already got firmly under control. Instead, taking the self-assessments will show you where that time could be much better spent. In this area you will begin with a few questions to quickly evaluate your understanding of material that is likely to appear on the TACHS®. If you do poorly in certain areas, simply work carefully through those sections in the tutorials and then try the self-assessment again.

The second section, Tutorials, offers information in each of the content areas, as well as strategies to help you master that material. The tutorials are not intended to be a complete course, but cover general principles. If you find that you do not understand the tutorials, it is recommended that you seek out additional instruction.

Third, we offer two sets of practice test questions, similar to those on the TACHS Exam.

The TACHS Study Plan

Now that you have made the decision to take the TACHS, it is time to get started. Before you do another thing, you will need to figure out a plan of attack. The very best study tip is to start early! The longer the time period you devote to regular study practice, the more likely you will be to retain the material and be able to access it quickly. If you thought that 1x20 is the same as 2x10, guess what? It really is not, when it comes to study time. Reviewing material for just an hour per day over the course of 20 days is far better than studying for two hours a day for only 10 days. The more often you revisit a particular piece of information, the better you will know it. Not only will your grasp and understanding be better, but your ability to reach into your brain and quickly and efficiently pull out the tidbit you need, will be greatly enhanced as well.

The great Chinese scholar and philosopher Confucius believed that true knowledge could be defined as knowing what you know and what you do not know. The first step in preparing for the TACHS is to assess your strengths and weaknesses. You may already have an idea of what you know and what you do not know, but evaluating yourself using our Self- Assessment modules for each of the four areas, Reading, Language, Mathematics and Ability, will clarify the details.

Making a Study Schedule

To make your study time the most productive, you will need to develop a study plan. The purpose of the plan is to organize all the bits of pieces of information in such a way that you will not feel overwhelmed. Rome was not built in a day, and learning everything you will need to know to pass the TACHS® is going to take time, too. Arranging the material you need to learn into manageable chunks is the best way to go. Each study session should make you feel as though you have accomplished your goal, or at least are a little closer, and your goal is simply to learn what you planned to learn during that particular session. Try to organize the content in such a way that each study session builds on previous ones. That way, you will retain the information, be better able to access it, and review the previous bits and pieces at the same time.

Self-assessment

The Best Study Tip! The very best study tip is to start early! The longer you study regularly, the more you will retain and 'learn' the material. Studying for 1 hour per day for 20 days is far better than studying for 2 hours for 10 days.

What don't you know?

The first step is to assess your strengths and weaknesses. You may already have an idea of where your weaknesses are, or you can take our Self-assessment modules for each of the content areas.

Exam Component	Rate 1 to 5
Reading	
Vocabulary	
Reading Comprehension	
Mathematics	
Basic Math & Arithmetic	
Algebra	
Geometry	
Ability (IQ)	

Making a Study Schedule

The key to a successful study plan is to divide the material you need to learn into manageable sized pieces and learn it, while at the same time reviewing the material that you already know.

Using the table above, any scores of 3 or below, mean you need to spend time learning, reviewing and practicing this subject area. A score of 4 means you need to review the material, but you don't have to spend time re-learning. A score of 5 and you are OK with just an occasional review before the exam. A score of 0 or 1 means you really need to work on this should allocate the most time and the highest priority. Some students prefer a 5-day plan and others a 10-day plan. It also depends on how much time you have until the exam.

Here is an example of a 5-day plan based on an example from the table above:

Ability: 1- Study 1 hour everyday – review on last day

Vocabulary: 4 - Review every second day

Geometry: 2 - Study 1 hour first day – then ½ hour everyday

Algebra: 5 - Review for ½ hour every other day

Reading Comp.: 5 - Review for ½ hour every other day

Using this example, reading comprehension and algebra are good, and only need occasional review. Geometry is good and needs 'some' review. Vocabulary needs a fair amount of work and Ability is very weak and need the majority of time. Based on this, here is a sample study plan:

Day	Subject	Time
Monday		
Study	Ability	1 hour
Study	Geometry	1 hour
½ hour break		
Study	Vocabulary	1 hour
Review	Reading Comp.	½ hour
Tuesday		
Study	Ability	1 hour
Study	Word Problems	½ hour
½ hour break		
Study	Geometry	½ hour
Review	Algebra	½ hour
Review	Reading Comp.	½ hour
Wednesday		
Study	Ability	1 hour
Study	Word Problems	½ hour
½ hour break		
Study	Geometry	½ hour
Review	Reading Comp.	½ hour
Review	Vocabulary	½ hour
Thursday		
Study	Ability	½ hour
Study	Word Problems	½ hour
Review	Geometry	½ hour
½ hour break		
Review	Reading Comp.	½ hour
Review	Algebra	½ hour
Friday		
Review	Vocabulary	½ hour
Review	Geometry	½ hour
½ hour break		
Review	Algebra	½ hour
Review	Ability	½ hour

Using this example, adapt the study plan to your own schedule. This schedule assumes 2 ½ - 3 hours available to study everyday for a 5 day period.

First, write out what you need to study and how much. Next figure out how many days you have before the test. Note, do NOT study on the last day before the test. On the last day before the test, you won't learn anything and will probably only confuse yourself.

Make a table with the days before the test and the number of hours you have available to study each day. We suggest working with 1 hour and ½ hour time slots.

Start filling in the blanks, with the subjects you need to study the most getting the most time and the most regular time slots (i.e. everyday) and the subjects that you know getting the least time (e.g. ½ hour every other day, or every 3rd day).

Tips for making a schedule

Once you make a schedule, stick with it! Make your study sessions reasonable. If you make a study schedule and don't stick with it, you set yourself up for failure. Instead, schedule study sessions that are a bit shorter and set yourself up for success! Make sure your study sessions are do-able. Studying is hard work but after you pass, you can party and take a break!

Schedule breaks. Breaks are just as important as study time. Work out a rotation of studying and breaks that works for you.

Build up study time. If you find it hard to sit still and study for 1 hour straight through, build up to it. Start with 20 minutes, and then take a break. Once you get used to 20-minute study sessions, increase the time to 30 minutes. Gradually work you way up to 1 hour.

40 minutes to 1 hour is optimal. Studying for longer than this is tiring and not productive. Studying for shorter isn't long enough to be productive.

Studying Math. Studying Math is different from studying other subjects because you use a different part of your brain. The best way to study math is to practice everyday. This will train your mind to think in a mathematical way. If you miss a day or days, the mathematical mind-set is gone and you have to start all over again to build it up.

Study and practice math everyday for at least 5 days before the exam.

For more information, see our How to Study Guide at www.study-skills.ca.

Reading

THIS CHAPTER CONTAINS A SELF-ASSESSMENT AND READING TUTORIAL. The tutorials are designed to familiarize general principles and the self-assessment contains general questions similar to the Reading questions likely to be on the TACHS, but are not intended to be identical to the exam questions. If you do not understand the questions, or the tutorial, or find the tutorial difficult, it is recommended that you seek out additional instruction.

Note that these questions are for skill practice only.

Tour of the TACHS Reading

The TACHS Reading section has two sections, reading comprehension and synonyms. Below is a detailed list of the types of reading questions that generally appear on the TACHS®:

- Drawing logical conclusions
- Make predictions
- Analyze and evaluate the use of text structure to solve problems or identify sequences
- Summarize
- Meaning from context
- Synonyms

The questions below are not the same as you will find on the TACHS® - that would be too easy! And nobody knows what the questions will be and they change all the time. Mostly the changes consist of substituting new questions for old, but the changes can be new question formats or styles, changes to the number of questions in each section, changes to the time limits for each section and combining sections. Below are general Reading questions that cover the same areas as the TACHS®. So, while the format and exact wording of the questions may differ slightly, and change from year to year, if you can answer the questions below, you will have no problem with the Reading section of the TACHS®.

Reading Self-Assessment

The purpose of the self-assessment is:

- Identify your strengths and weaknesses.
- Develop your personalized study plan (above)
- Get accustomed to the TACHS format
- Extra practice – the self-assessments are almost a full 3rd practice test!
- Provide a baseline score for preparing your study schedule.

Since this is a self-assessment, and depending on how confident you are with Reading, timing is optional. The TACHS® has 50 questions, and 20 vocabulary questions to be answered in 10 minutes and 30 reading comprehension questions to be answered in 25 minutes. The self-assessment has 15 vocabulary questions and 18 Reading questions, so allow about 10 and 20 minutes respectively to complete this assessment.

The timing is not exact, as the Reading section includes reading comprehension and vocabulary questions. For the entire section, there are a total of 35 questions to be answered in 50 minutes.

Once complete, use the table below to assess your understanding of the content, and prepare your study schedule described in chapter 1.

80% - 100%	Excellent – you have mastered the content
60 – 79%	Good. You have a working knowledge. Even though you can just pass this section, you may want to review the tutorials and do some extra practice to see if you can improve your mark.
40% - 59%	Below Average. You do not understand reading comprehension or vocabulary problems. Review the tutorials, and retake this quiz again in a few days, before proceeding to the practice test questions.
Less than 40%	Poor. You have a very limited understanding of reading comprehension and vocabulary problems. Please review the tutorials, and retake this quiz again in a few days, before proceeding to the practice test questions.

Reading Part I Self-Assessment Answer Sheet

	A	B	C	D
1	○	○	○	○
2	○	○	○	○
3	○	○	○	○
4	○	○	○	○
5	○	○	○	○
6	○	○	○	○
7	○	○	○	○
8	○	○	○	○
9	○	○	○	○
10	○	○	○	○
11	○	○	○	○
12	○	○	○	○
13	○	○	○	○
14	○	○	○	○
15	○	○	○	○

Reading Part I - Vocabulary

Directions: Choose the word that is most similar in meaning to the underlined word.

1. Her amazing talent wowed the audience during the contest.

   a. Ugly
   b. Extraordinary
   c. Plain
   d. Ordinary

2. Jean was furious when her little brother destroyed her favorite doll.

   a. Distraught
   b. Angry
   c. Annoyed
   d. Eviscerated

3. We will inquire about our scores on the pop quiz.

   a. Ask
   b. Complain
   c. Suggest
   d. Command

4. The car accident was an awful experience the victims want to forget.

   a. Terrible
   b. Pleasant
   c. Wonderful
   d. Unforgettable

5. Cinderella's wicked stepmother failed in the end.

   a. Understanding
   b. Happy
   c. Evil
   d. Supportive

6. The tourists enjoy watching the magnificent beauty of the ocean.

   a. Ordinary
   b. Unattractive
   c. Simple
   d. Beautiful

7. The race will begin in five minutes.

   a. End
   b. Start
   c. Finish
   d. Exceed

8. A thousand people can sit comfortably in the enormous auditorium.

   a. Mountainous
   b. Narrow
   c. Towering
   d. Spacious

9. The knight fought the enemies alone. He was very courageous.

   a. Cowardly
   b. Strong
   c. Independent
   d. Brave

10. The thieves broke the windows of the grocery store.

   a. Smashed
   b. Fractured
   c. Opened
   d. Fired

11. The sparkling diamonds are very expensive.

   a. Intelligent
   b. Expensive
   c. Shimmering
   d. Cheap

12. Many people prefer living in a peaceful neighborhood.

   a. Far
   b. Busy
   c. Quiet
   d. Noisy

13. Our visitors will come tomorrow.

   a. Visit
   b. Arrive
   c. Leave
   d. Stay

14. You should wear thick clothes to keep yourself warm during cold season.

   a. Wintry
   b. Warm
   c. Windy
   d. Humid

15. I had to <u>scream</u> his name so he can hear me.

   a. Whisper
   b. Sob
   c. Shout
   d. Spell

Answer Key

1. B
Amazing means the same as extraordinary.

2. B
Furious means the same as angry.

3. A
Inquire means the same as ask.

4. A
Awful means the same as terrible.

5. C
Wicked means the same as evil.

6. D
Magnificent means the same as beautiful.

7. B
Begin means the same as start.

8. D
Enormous means the same as spacious.

9. D
Courageous means the same as brave.

10. A
Break means the same as smash.

11. C
Sparkling means the same as shimmering.

12. C
Peaceful means the same as quiet.

13. B
Come means the same as arrive.

14. A
Cold means the same as wintry.

15. C
Scream means the same as shout.

How to Improve your Vocabulary

Vocabulary tests can be daunting when you think of the enormous number of words that might come up in the exam. As the exam date draws near, your anxiety will grow because you know that no matter how many words you memorize, chances are, you will still remember so few, and there are so many more to memorize! Here are some tips which you can use to hurdle the big words that may come up in your exam without having to open the dictionary and memorize all the words known to humankind.

Build up and tear apart the big words. Big words, like many other things, are composed of small parts. Some words are made up of many other words. A man who lifts weights for example, is a weight lifter. Words are also made up of word parts called prefixes, suffixes and roots. Often times, we can see the relationship of different words through these parts. A person who is skilled with both hands is ambidextrous. A word with double meaning is ambiguous. A person with two conflicting emotions is ambivalent. Two words with synonymous meanings often have the same root. Bio, a root word derived from Latin is used in words like biography meaning to write about
a person's life, and biology meaning the study of living organisms.

- **Words with double meanings.** Did you know that the word husband not only means a man married to a woman, but also thrift or frugality? Sometimes, words have double meanings. The dictionary meaning, or the denotation of a word is sometimes different from the way we use it or its connotation.

- **Read widely, read deeply and read daily.** The best way to expand your vocabulary is to familiarize yourself with as many words as possible through reading. By reading, you are able to remember words in a proper context and thus, remember its meaning or at the very least, its use. Reading widely would help you get acquainted with words you may never use every day. This is the best strategy without doubt. However, if you are studying for an exam next week, or even tomorrow, it isn't much help! Below you will find a range of different ways to learn new words quickly and efficiently.

- **Remember.** Always remember that big words are easy to understand when divided into smaller parts, and the smaller words will often have several other meanings aside from the one you already know

- **Be Committed To Learning New Words.** To improve your vocabulary you need to make a commitment to learn new words. Commit to learning at least a word or two a day. You can also get new words by reading books, poems, stories, plays and magazines. Expose yourself to more language to increase the number of new words that you learn.

- **Learn Practical Vocabulary.** As much as possible, learn vocabulary that is associated with what you do and that you can use regularly. For example learn words related to your profession or hobby. Learn as much vocabulary as you can in your favorite subjects.

- **Use New Words Frequently.** As soon as you learn a new word start using it and do so frequently. Repeat it when you are alone and try to use the word as often as you can with people you talk to. You can also use flashcards to practice new words that you learn.

- **Learn the Proper Usage.** If you do not understand the proper usage, look it up and make sure you have it right.

- **Use a Dictionary.** When reading textbooks, novels or assigned readings, keep the dictionary nearby. Also learn how to use online dictionaries and WORD dictionary. As soon as you come across a new word, check for its meaning. If you cannot do so immediately, then you should write it down and check it when possible. This will help you understand what the word means and exactly how best to use it.

- **Learn Word Roots, Prefixes and Suffixes.** English words are usually derived from suffixes, prefixes and roots, which come from Latin, French or Greek. Learning the root or origin of a word helps you easily understand the meaning of the word and other words that are derived from the root. Generally, if you learn the meaning of one root word, you will understand two or three words. This is a great two-for-one strategy. Most prefixes, suffixes, roots and stems are used in two, three or more words, so if you know the root, prefix or suffix, you can guess the meaning of many words.

- **Synonyms and Antonyms.** Most words in the English language have two or three (at least) synonyms and antonyms. For example, "big," in the most common usage, has about seventy-five synonyms and an equal number of antonyms. Understanding the relationships between these words and how they all fit together gives your brain a framework, which makes them easier to learn, remember and recall.

- **Use Flash Cards.** Flash cards are one of the best ways to memorize things. They can be used anywhere and anytime, so you can make use of odd free moments waiting for the bus or waiting in line. Make your own or buy commercially prepared flash cards, and keep them with you all the time.

• **Make word lists.** Learning vocabulary, like learning many things, requires repetition. Keep a new words journal in a separate section or separate notebook. Add any words that you look up in the dictionary, as well as from word lists. Review your word lists regularly. Photocopying or printing off word lists from the Internet or handouts is not the same. Actually writing out the word and a few notes on the definition is an important process for imprinting the word in your brain. Writing out the word and definition in your New Word Journal, forces you to concentrate and focus on the new word. Hitting PRINT or pushing he button on the photocopier does not do the same thing.

Reading Part II Answer Sheet

1. (A) (B) (C) (D)   11. (A) (B) (C) (D)
2. (A) (B) (C) (D)   12. (A) (B) (C) (D)
3. (A) (B) (C) (D)   13. (A) (B) (C) (D)
4. (A) (B) (C) (D)   14. (A) (B) (C) (D)
5. (A) (B) (C) (D)   15. (A) (B) (C) (D)
6. (A) (B) (C) (D)   16. (A) (B) (C) (D)
7. (A) (B) (C) (D)
8. (A) (B) (C) (D)
9. (A) (B) (C) (D)
10. (A) (B) (C) (D)

Reading Part II - Reading Comprehension

Directions: The following questions are based on several reading passages. A series of questions follow each passage. Read each passage carefully, and then answer the questions based on it. You may reread the passage as often as you wish. When you have finished answering the questions based on one passage, go right onto the next passage. Choose the best answer based on the information given and implied.

Questions 1 – 4 refer to the following passage.

Passage 1 - Who Was Anne Frank?

You may have heard mention of the word Holocaust in your History or English classes. The Holocaust took place from 1939-1945. It was an attempt by the Nazi party to purify the human race, by eliminating Jews, Gypsies, Catholics, homosexuals and others they deemed inferior to their "perfect" Aryan race. The Nazis used Concentration Camps, which were sometimes used as Death Camps, to exterminate the people they held in the camps. The saddest fact about the Holocaust was the over one million children under the age of sixteen died in a Nazi concentration camp. Just a few weeks before World War II was over, Anne Frank was one of those children to die.

Before the Nazi party began its persecution of the Jews, Anne Frank had a happy live. She was born in June of 1929. In June of 1942, for her 13th birthday, she was given a simple present which would go onto impact the lives of millions of people around the world. That gift was a small red diary that she called Kitty. This diary was to become Anne's most treasured possession when she and her family hid from the Nazi's in a secret annex above her father's office building in Amsterdam.

For 25 months, Anne, her sister Margot, her parents, another family, and an elderly Jewish dentist hid from the Nazis in this tiny annex. They were never permitted to go outside and their food and supplies were brought to them by Miep Gies and her husband, who did not believe in the Nazi persecution of the Jews. It was a very difficult life for young Anne and she used Kitty as an outlet to describe her life in hiding.
After 2 years, Anne and her family were betrayed and arrested by the Nazis. To this day, nobody is exactly sure who betrayed the Frank family and the other annex residents. Anne, her mother, and her sister were separated from Otto Frank, Anne's father. Then, Anne and Margot were separated from their mother. In March of 1945, Margot Frank died of starvation in a Concentration Camp. A few days later, at the age of 15, Anne Frank died of typhus. Of all the people who hid in the Annex, only Otto Frank survived the Holocaust.

Otto Frank returned to the Annex after World War II. It was there that he found Kitty, filled with Anne's thoughts and feelings about being a persecuted

Jewish girl. Otto Frank had Anne's diary published in 1947 and it has remained continuously in print ever since. Today, the diary has been published in over 55 languages and more than 24 million copies have been sold around the world. The Diary of Anne Frank tells the story of a brave young woman who tried to see the good in all people.

1. From the context clues in the passage, what does annex mean?

    a. Attic

    b. Bedroom

    c. Basement

    d. Kitchen

2. Why do you think Anne's diary has been published in 55 languages?

    a. So everyone could understand it.

    b. So people around the world could learn more about the horrors of the Holocaust.

    c. Because Anne was Jewish but hid in Amsterdam and died in Germany.

    d. Because Otto Frank spoke many languages.

3. From the description of Anne and Margot's deaths in the passage, what can we assume typhus is?

    a. The same as starving to death.

    b. An infection the Germans gave to Anne.

    c. A disease Anne caught in the concentration camp.

    d. Poison gas used by the Germans to kill Anne.

4. In the third paragraph, what does outlet mean?

    a. A place to plug things into the wall

    b. A store where Miep bought cheap supplies for the Frank family

    c. A hiding space similar to an Annex

    d. A place where Anne could express her private thoughts.

Questions 5 – 8 refer to the following passage.

Passage 2 - Was Dr. Seuss A Real Doctor?

A favorite author for over 100 years, Theodor Seuss Geisel was born on March 2, 1902. Today, we celebrate the birthday of the famous "Dr. Seuss" by hosting Read Across America events throughout the March. School children around the country celebrate the "Doctor's" birthday by making hats, giving presentations and holding read aloud circles featuring some of Dr. Seuss' most famous books.

But who was Dr. Seuss? Did he go to medical school? Where was his office? You may be surprised to know that Theodor Seuss Geisel was not a medical doctor at all. He took on the nickname Dr. Seuss when he became a noted children's book author. He earned the nickname because people said his books were "as good as medicine." All these years later, his nickname has lasted and he is known as Dr. Seuss all across the world.

Think back to when you were a young child. Did you ever want to try "green eggs and ham?" Did you try to "Hop on Pop?" Do you remember learning about the environment from a creature called The Lorax? Of course, you must recall one of Seuss' most famous characters; that green Grinch who stole Christmas. These stories were all written by Dr. Seuss and featured his signature rhyming words and letters. They also featured made up words to enhance his rhyme scheme and even though many of his characters were made up, they sure seem real to us today.

And what of his "signature" book, The Cat in the Hat? You must remember that cat and Thing One and Thing Two from your childhood. Did you know that in the early 1950's there was a growing concern in America that children were not becoming avid readers? This was, book publishers thought, because children found books dull and uninteresting. An intelligent publisher sent Dr. Seuss a book of words that he thought all children should learn as young readers. Dr. Seuss wrote his famous story The Cat in the Hat, using those words. We can see, over the decades, just how much influence his writing has had on very young children. That is why we celebrate this doctor's birthday each March.

5. What does the word "avid" mean in the last paragraph?

    a. Good
    b. Interested
    c. Slow
    d. Fast

6. What can we infer from the statement " His books were like medicine?"

    a. His books made people feel better

    b. His books were in doctor's office waiting rooms

    c. His books took away fevers

    d. His books left a funny taste in readers' mouths.

7. Why is the publisher in the last paragraph referred to as "intelligent?"

    a. The publisher knew how to read.

    b. The publisher knew that kids did not like to read.

    c. The publisher knew Dr. Seuss would be able to create a book that sold well.

    d. The publisher knew that Dr. Seuss would be able to write a book that would get young children interested in reading.

8. The theme of this passage is

    a. Dr. Seuss was not a doctor.

    b. Dr. Seuss influenced the lives of generations of young children.

    c. Dr. Seuss wrote rhyming books.

    d. Dr. Suess' birthday is a good day to read a book.

Questions 9 - 11 refer to the following passage.

Keeping Tropical Fish

Keeping tropical fish at home or in your office used to be very popular. Today, interest has declined, but it remains as rewarding and relaxing a hobby as ever. Ask any tropical fish hobbyist, and you will hear how soothing and relaxing watching colorful fish live their lives in the aquarium. If you are considering keeping tropical fish as pets, here is a list of the basic equipment you will need.

A filter is essential for keeping your aquarium clean and your fish alive and healthy. There are different types and sizes of filters and the right size for you depends on the size of the aquarium and the level of stocking. Generally, you need a filter with a 3 to 5 times turn over rate per hour. This means that the water in the tank should go through the filter about 3 to 5 times per hour.

Most tropical fish do well in water temperatures ranging between 24^0 C and 26^0 C, though each has its own ideal water temperature. A heater with a thermostat is necessary to regulate the water temperature. Some heaters are submersible and others are not, so check carefully before you buy.

Lights are also necessary, and come in a large variety of types, strengths and sizes. A light source is necessary for plants in the tank to photosynthesize and give the tank a more attractive appearance. Even if you plan to use plastic plants, the fish still require light, although here you can use a lower strength light source.

A hood is necessary to keep dust, dirt and unwanted materials out of the tank. Sometimes the hood can also help prevent evaporation. Another requirement is aquarium gravel. This will improve the aesthetics of the aquarium and is necessary if you plan to have real plants.

9. What is the general tone of this article?

   a. Formal
   b. Informal
   c. Technical
   d. Opinion

10. Which of the following cannot be inferred?

   a. Gravel is good for aquarium plants.
   b. Fewer people have aquariums in their office than at home.
   c. The larger the tank, the larger the filter required.
   d. None of the above.

11. What evidence does the author provide to support their claim that aquarium lights are necessary?

   a. Plants require light.
   b. Fish and plants require light.
   c. The author does not provide evidence for this statement.
   d. Aquarium lights make the aquarium more attractive.

12. Which of the following is an opinion?

   a. Filter with a 3 to 5 times turn over rate per hour are required.
   b. Aquarium gravel improves the aesthetics of the aquarium.
   c. An aquarium hood keeps dust, dirt and unwanted materials out of the tank.
   d. Each type of tropical fish has its own ideal water temperature.

Questions 13 - 16 refer to the following passage.

The Civil War

The Civil War began on April 12, 1861. The first shots of the Civil War were fired in Fort Sumter, South Carolina. Note that even though more American lives were lost in the Civil War than in any other war, not one person died on that first day. The war began because eleven Southern states seceded from the Union and tried to start their own government, The Confederate States of America.

Why did the states secede? The issue of slavery was a primary cause of the Civil War. The eleven southern states relied heavily on their slaves to foster their farming and plantation lifestyles. The northern states, many of whom had already abolished slavery, did not feel that the southern states should have slaves. The north wanted to free all the slaves and President Lincoln's goal was to both end slavery and preserve the Union. He had Congress declare war on the Confederacy on April 14, 1862. For four long, blood soaked years, the North and South fought.

From 1861 to mid 1863, it seemed as if the South would win this war. However, on July 1, 1863, an epic three day battle was waged on a field in Gettysburg, Pennsylvania. Gettysburg is remembered for being the bloodiest battle in American history. At the end of the three days, the North turned the tide of the war in their favor. The North then went on to dominate the South for the remainder of the war. Most well remembered might be General Sherman's "March to The Sea," where he famously led the Union Army through Georgia and the Carolinas, burning and destroying everything in their path.
In 1865, the Union army invaded and captured the Confederate capital of Richmond Virginia. Robert E. Lee, leader of the Confederacy surrendered to General Ulysses S. Grant, leader of the Union forces, on April 9, 1865. The Civil War was over and the Union was preserved.

13. What does secede mean?

a. To break away from
b. To accomplish
c. To join
d. To lose

14. Which of the following statements summarizes a FACT from the passage?

   a. Congress declared war and then the Battle of Fort Sumter began.
   b. Congress declared war after shots were fired at Fort Sumter.
   c. President Lincoln was pro slavery
   d. President Lincoln was at Fort Sumter with Congress

15. Which event finally led the Confederacy to surrender?

   a. The battle of Gettysburg
   b. The battle of Bull Run
   c. The invasion of the confederate capital of Richmond
   d. Sherman's March to the Sea

16. What does the word abolish as used in this passage mean?

   a. To ban
   b. To polish
   c. To support
   d. To destroy

Answer Key

1. A
We know that an annex is like an attic because the text states the annex was above Otto Frank's building.

Choice B is incorrect because an office building doesn't have bedrooms. Choice C is incorrect because a basement would be below the office building. Choice D is incorrect because there would not be a kitchen in an office building.

2. B
The diary has been published in 55 languages so people all over the world can learn about Anne. That is why the passage says it has been continuously in print.

Choice A is incorrect because it is too vague. Choice C is incorrect because it was published after Anne died and she did not write in all three languages. Choice D is incorrect because the passage does not give us any information about what languages Otto Frank spoke.

3. C
Use the process of elimination to figure this out.

Choice A cannot be the correct answer because otherwise the passage would have simply said that Anne and Margot both died of starvation. Choices B and D cannot be correct because if the Germans had done something specifically to murder Anne, the passage would have stated that directly. By the process of elimination, choice C has to be the correct answer.

4. D
We can figure this out using context clues. The paragraph is talking about Anne's diary and so, outlet in this instance is a place where Anne can pour her feelings.

Choice A is incorrect answer. That is the literal meaning of the word outlet and the passage is using the figurative meaning. Choice B is incorrect because that is the secondary literal meaning of the word outlet, as in an outlet mall. Again, we are looking for figurative meaning. Choice C is incorrect because there are no clues in the text to support that answer.

5. B
When someone is avid about something that means they are highly interested in the subject. The context clues are dull and boring, because they define the opposite of avid.

6. A
The author is using a simile to compare the books to medicine. Medicine is what you take when you want to feel better. They are suggesting that if a person wants to feel good, they should read Dr. Seuss' books.

Choice B is incorrect because there is no mention of a doctor's office. Choice C is incorrect because it is using the literal meaning of medicine and the author is using medicine in a figurative way. Choice D is incorrect because it makes no sense. We know not to eat books.

7. D
The publisher is described as intelligent because he knew to get in touch with a famous author to develop a book that children would be interested in reading.

Choice A is incorrect because we can assume that all book publishers must know how to read. Choice B is incorrect because it says in the article that more than one publisher was concerned about whether or not children liked to read. Choice D is incorrect because there is no mention in the article about how well The Cat in the Hat sold when it was first published.

8. B
The passage describes in detail how Dr. Seuss had a great effect on the lives of children through his writing. It names several of his books, tells how he helped children become avid readers and explains his style of writing.
Choice A is incorrect because that is just one single fact about the passage.
Choice C is incorrect because that is just one single fact about the passage.
Choice D is incorrect because that is just one single fact about the passage.
Again, choice B is correct because it encompasses ALL the facts in the passage,

not just one single fact.

9. B
The general tone is informal.

10. B
The statement, "Fewer people have aquariums in their office than at home," cannot be inferred from this article.

11. B
Light is necessary for the fish and plants.

12. B
The following statement is an opinion, " Aquarium gravel improves the aesthetics of the aquarium."

13. A
Secede means to break away from because the 11 states wanted to leave the United States and form their own country.

Choice B is incorrect because the states were not accomplishing anything. Choice C is incorrect because the states were trying to leave the USA not join it. Choice D is incorrect because the states seceded before they lost the war.

14. B
Look at the dates in the passage. The shots were fired on April 12 and Congress declared war on April 14.

Choice C is incorrect because the passage states that Lincoln was against slavery. Choice D is incorrect because it never mentions who was or was not at Fort Sumter.

15. C
The passage states that Lee surrendered to Grant after the capture of the capital of the Confederacy, which is Richmond.

Choice A is incorrect because the war continued for 2 years after Gettysburg. Choice B is incorrect because that battle is not mentioned in the passage. Choice D is incorrect because the capture of the capital occurred after the march to the sea.

16. A
When the passage said that the North had *abolished* slavery, it implies that slaves were no longer allowed in the North. In essence slavery was banned.

Choice B makes no sense relative to the context of the passage. Choice C is incorrect because we know the North was fighting slavery, not for it. Choice D is incorrect because slavery is not a tangible thing that can be destroyed. It is a practice that had to be outlawed or banned.

Help with Reading Comprehension

At first sight, reading comprehension tests look challenging especially if you are given long essays to answer only two to three questions. While reading, you might notice your attention wandering, or you may feel sleepy. Do not be discouraged because there are various tactics and long-range strategies that make comprehending even long, boring essays easier.

Your friends before your foes. It is always best to start with passages with familiar subjects rather than those with unfamiliar ones. This approach applies the same logic as tackling easy questions before hard ones. Skip passages that do not interest you and leave them for later.

Don't use 'special' reading techniques. This is not the time for speed-reading or anything like that – just plain ordinary reading – not too slow and not too fast.

Read through the entire passage and the questions before you do anything. Many students try reading the questions first and then looking for answers in the passage thinking this approach is more efficient. What these students do not realize is that it is often hard to navigate in unfamiliar roads. If you do not familiarize yourself with the passage first, looking for answers become not only time-consuming but also dangerous because you might miss the context of the answer you are looking for. If you read the questions first you will only confuse yourself and lose valuable time.

Familiarize yourself with reading comprehension questions. If you are familiar with the common types of reading questions, you are able to take note of important parts of the passage, saving time. There are six major kinds of reading questions.

- **Main Idea** - Questions that ask for the central thought or significance of the passage.

- **Specific Details** - Questions that asks for explicitly stated ideas.

- **Drawing Inferences** - Questions that ask for a logical extension of statements.

- **Tone or Attitude** - Questions that test your ability to sense the emotional state of the author.

- **Context Meaning** – Questions that ask for the meaning of a word depending on the context.

- **Technique** – Questions that ask for the method of organization or the writing style of the author.

Read. Read. Read. The best preparation for reading comprehension tests is always to read, read and read. If you are not used to reading lengthy passages, you will probably lose concentration. Increase your attention span by making a habit out of reading. Read everyday and increase the time slowly each day.

Reading comprehension tests become less daunting when you have trained yourself to read and understand fast. Always remember that it is easier to understand passages you are interested in. Do not read through passages hastily. Make mental notes of ideas you may be asked.

Reading Strategy

When facing the reading comprehension section of a standardized test, you need a strategy to be successful. You want to keep several steps in mind:

- **First, make a note of the time and the number of sections.** Time your work accordingly. Typically, four to five minutes per section is sufficient. Second, read the directions for each selection thoroughly before beginning (and listen carefully to any additional verbal instructions, as they will often clarify obscure or confusing written guidelines). You must know exactly how to do what you're about to do!

- **Now you're ready to begin reading the selection.** Read the passage carefully, noting significant characters or events on scrap paper or underlining on the test sheet. Many students find making a basic list in the margins helpful. Quickly jot down or underline one-word summaries of characters, notable happenings, numbers, or key ideas. This will help retain information and focus wandering thoughts. Remember, however, that your goal is to find the information that answers the questions. Even if you find the passage interesting, stay on track.

- **Now read the question and all the choices.** Now you have read the passage, have a general idea of the main ideas, and have marked the important points. Read the question and All the choices. Never choose an answer without reading them all! Questions are often designed to confuse – stay focussed and clear. Usually the answer choices will focus on one or two facts or inferences from the passage. Keep these clear in your mind.

- **Search for the answer.** With a very general idea of what the different choices are, go back to the passage and scan for the relevant information. Watch for big words, unusual or unique words. These make your job easier as you can scan the text for the particular word.

- **Mark the Answer.** Now you have the key information the question is looking for. Go back to the question, quickly scan the choices and mark the correct one.

Typically, there will be several questions dealing with facts from the selection, a couple more inference questions dealing with logical consequences of those facts, and periodically an application-oriented question surfaces to force you to make connections with what you already know. Some students prefer to answer the questions as listed, and feel classifying the question and then ordering is wasting precious time. Other students prefer to answer the different types of questions in order of how easy or difficult they are. The choice is yours and do whatever works for you. If you want to try answering in order of difficulty, here is a recommended order, answer fact questions first; they're easily found within the passage. Tackle inference problems next, after re-reading the question(s) as many times as you need to. Application or 'best guess' questions usually take the longest, so, save them for last.

Use the practice tests to try out both ways of answering and see what works for you.

For more help with reading comprehension, see Multiple Choice Secrets.

Main Idea and Supporting Details

Identifying the main idea, topic and supporting details in a passage can feel like an overwhelming task. The passages used for standardized tests can be boring and seem difficult - Test writers don't use interesting passages or ones that talk about things most people are familiar with. Despite these obstacles, all passages and paragraphs will have the information you need to answer the questions.

The topic of a passage or paragraph is its subject. It's the general idea and can be summed up in a word or short phrase. Sometimes, there is a short description of the passage if it's taken from a longer work. Make sure you read the description as it might state the topic of the passage. If not, read the passage and ask yourself, "Who or what is this about?" For example:

> Over the years, school uniforms have been hotly debated. Arguments are made that students have the right to show individuality and express themselves by choosing their own clothes. However, this brings up social and academic issues. Some kids cannot afford to wear the clothes they like and might be bullied by the "better dressed" students. With attention drawn to clothes and the individual, students will lose focus on class work and the reason they are in school. School uniforms should be mandatory.

Ask: What is this paragraph about?

Topic: school uniforms

Once you have the topic, it's easier to find the main idea. The main idea is a specific statement telling what the writer wants you to know. Writers usually state the main idea in the form of a thesis statement. If you're looking for the main idea of a single paragraph, the main idea is called the topic sentence and will probably be the first or last sentence. If you're looking for the main idea of an entire passage, look for the thesis statement in either the first or last paragraph. The main idea is usually restated in the conclusion. To find the main idea of a passage or paragraph, follow these steps:

1. Find the topic.

2. Ask yourself, "What point is the author trying to make about the topic?"

3. Create your own sentence summarizing the author's point.

4. Look in the text for the sentence closest in meaning to yours.

Look at the example paragraph again. It's already established that the topic of the paragraph is school uniforms. What is the main idea/topic sentence?

Ask: "What point is the author trying to make about school uniforms?"

Summary: Students should wear school uniforms.

Topic sentence: School uniforms should be mandatory.

Main Idea: School uniforms should be mandatory.

Each paragraph offers supporting details to explain the main idea. The details could be facts or reasons, but they will always answer a question about the main idea. What? Where? Why? When? How? How much/many? Look at the example paragraph again. You'll notice that more than one sentence answers a question about the main idea. These are the supporting details.

Main Idea: School uniforms should be mandatory.

Ask: Why? Some kids cannot afford to wear clothes they like and could be bullied by the "better dressed" kids. Supporting Detail

With attention drawn to clothes and the individual, Students will lose focus on class work and the reason they are in school. Supporting Detail

What if the author doesn't state the main idea in a topic sentence? The passage will have an implied main idea. It's not as difficult to find as it might seem. Paragraphs are always organized around ideas. To find an implied main idea, you need to know the topic and then find the relationship between the supporting details. Ask yourself, "What is the point the author is making about the relationship between the details?."

> Cocoa is what makes chocolate good for you. Chocolate comes in many varieties. These delectable flavors include milk chocolate, dark chocolate, semi-sweet, and white chocolate.

Ask: What is this paragraph about?

Topic: Chocolate

Ask: What? Where? Why? When? How? How much/many?

Supporting details: Chocolate is good for you because it is made of cocoa, Chocolate is delicious, Chocolate comes in different delicious flavors

Ask: What is the relationship between the details and what is the author's point?

Main Idea: Chocolate is good because it is healthy and it tastes good.

Testing Tips for Main Idea Questions

1. Skim the questions – not the answer choices - before reading the passage.

2. Questions about main idea might use the words "theme," "generalization," or "purpose."

3. Save questions about the main idea for last. On standardized tests like the TACHS, the answers to the rest of the questions can be found in order in the passage.

3. Underline topic sentences in the passage. Most tests allow you to write in your test booklet.

4. Answer the question in your own words before looking at the answer choices. Then match your answer with an answer choice.

5. Cross out incorrect answer choices immediately to prevent confusion.

6. If two of the answer choices mean the same thing but use different words, they are BOTH incorrect.

7. If a question asks about the whole passage, cross out the answer choices that apply to only part of it.

8. If only part of the information is correct, that answer choice is incorrect.

9. An answer choice that is too broad is incorrect. All information needs to be backed up by the passage.

10. Answer choices with extreme wording are usually incorrect.

Drawing Inferences And Conclusions

Drawing inferences and making conclusions happens all the time. In fact, you probably do it every time you read—sometimes without even realizing it! For example, remember the first time you saw the movie "The Lion King." When you meet Scar for the first time, he is trapping a helpless mouse with his sharp claws preparing to eat it. When you see this action you guess that Scar is going to be a bad character in the movie. Nothing appeared to tell you this. No caption came across the bottom of the screen that said "Bad Guy." No red arrow pointed to Scar and said "Evil Lion." No, you made an inference about his character based on the context clue you were given. You do the same thing when you read!

When you draw an inference or make a conclusion you are doing the same thing, you are making an educated guess based on the hints the author gives you. We call these hints "context clues." Scar trapping the innocent mouse is the context clue about Scar's character.

Usually you are making inferences and drawing conclusions the entire time that you are reading. Whether you realize it or not, you are constantly making educated guesses based on context clues. Think about a time you were reading a book and something happened that you were expecting to happen. You're not psychic! Actually, you were picking up on the context clues and making inferences about what was going to happen next!

Let's try an easy example. Read the following sentences and answer the questions at the end of the passage.

Shelly really likes to help people. She loves her job because she gets to help people every single day. However, Shelly has to work long hours and she can get called in the middle of the night for emergencies. She wears a white lab coat at work and most of the time she carries a stethoscope.

What is most likely Shelly's job?

   a. Musician
   b. Lawyer
   c. Doctor
   d. Teacher

This probably seemed easy. Drawing inferences isn't always this simple, but it is the same basic principle. How did you know Shelly was a doctor? She helps people, she works long hours, she wears a white lab coat, and she gets called in for emergencies at night. Context Clues! Nowhere in the paragraph did it say Shelly was a doctor, but you were able to draw that conclusion based on the information provided in the paragraph. This is how it's done!

There is a catch, though. Remember that when you draw inferences based on reading, you should only use the information given to you by the author. Sometimes it is easy for us to make conclusions based on knowledge that is already in our mind—but that can lead you to drawing an incorrect inference. For example, let's pretend there is a bully at your school named Brent. Now let's say you read a story and the main character's name is Brent. You could NOT infer that the character in the story is a bully just because his name is Brent. You should only use the information given to you by the author to avoid drawing the wrong conclusion.

Let's try another example. Read the passage below and answer the question.

Social media is an extremely popular new form of connecting and communicating over the internet. Since Facebook's original launch in 2004, millions of people have joined in the social media craze. In fact, it is estimated that almost 75% of all internet users aged 18 and older use some form of social media. Facebook started at Harvard University as a way to get students connected. However, it quickly grew into a worldwide phenomenon and today, the founder of Facebook, Mark Zuckerberg has an estimated net worth of 28.5 billion dollars.

Facebook is not the only social media platform, though. Other sites such as Twitter, Instagram, and Snapchat have since been invented and are quickly becoming just as popular! Many social media users actually use more than one type of social media. Furthermore, most social media sites have created mobile apps that allow people to connect via social media virtually anywhere in the world!

What is the most likely reason that other social media sites like Twitter and Instagram were created?

    a. Professors at Harvard University made it a class project.

    b. Facebook was extremely popular and other people thought they could also be successful by designing social media sites.

    c. Facebook was not connecting enough people.

    d. Mark Zuckerberg paid people to invent new social media sites because he wanted lots of competition.

Here, the correct answer is B. Facebook was extremely popular and other people thought they could also be successful by designing social media sites. How do we know this? What are the context clues? Take a look at the first paragraph. What do we know based on this paragraph? Well, one sentence refers to Facebook's original launch. This suggests that Facebook was one of the first social media sites. In addition, we know that the founder of Facebook has been extremely successful and is worth billions of dollars. From this we can infer that other people wanted to imitate Facebook's idea and become just as successful as Mark Zuckerberg.

Let's go through the other answers. If you chose A, it might be because Facebook started at Harvard University, so you drew the conclusion that all other social media sites were also started at Harvard University. However, there is no mention of class projects, professors, or students designing social media. So there doesn't seem to be enough support for choice A.

If you chose C, you might have been drawing your own conclusions based on outside information. Maybe none of your friends are on Facebook, so you made an inference that Facebook didn't connect enough people, so more sites were invented. Or maybe you think the people who connect on Facebook are too old, so you don't think Facebook connects enough people your age. This might be true, but remember inferences should be drawn from the information the author gives you!

If you chose D, you might be using the information that Mark Zuckerberg is worth over 28 billion dollars. It would be easy for him to pay others to design new sites, but remember, you need to use context clues! He is very wealthy, but that statement was giving you information about how successful Facebook was—not suggesting that he paid others to design more sites!

So remember, drawing inferences and conclusions is simply about using the information you are given to make an educated guess. You do this every single day so don't let this concept scare you. Look for the context clues, make sure they support your claim, and you'll be able to make accurate inferences and conclusions!

Point Of View And Purpose

You may not think so, but everything you read was written for a purpose. Now, it might not be the most exciting purpose, but regardless of whether it's a website, a magazine article, a book, or even a Facebook status—everything is written for a particular purpose. By understanding that purpose and the author's point of view, we can better comprehend what we read!

To determine the purpose of a written piece, you are asking yourself a very easy question. Why was this written? Usually the answer will be one of these three choices:

1. To inform

2. To persuade

3. To entertain.

First, you should ask yourself if the piece is fiction or non-fiction. Fiction is a type of writing that is not true. It is imaginary, made-up, or theoretical. For example, Harry Potter is fiction. While reading, it may seem like this world of wizards exists, but in reality, there is no Hogwarts or Diagon Alley. It is imaginary. Can you guess which purpose fiction has? Correct, choice 3—to entertain! So if you can tell if a piece is fiction or non-fiction, you can begin to narrow down the author's purpose!

Now, if a piece is non-fiction you are left with choice 1 or 2. To inform or to persuade. Here's another trick. If the piece is simply giving you INFORMation, the author's purpose is most likely to inform you! Think of an example of an informational piece you've read recently. Textbooks, most newspaper articles, how-to blogs, the instruction manual for your new cell phone, all these are great examples where the author's purpose was to inform you.

Some nonfiction pieces, though, are written to persuade you—meaning they are trying to convince you to do something or believe something. Can you think of a few examples where the author's purpose was to persuade?

When an author's purpose is to persuade you, they will have a point of view. What side is the author on? What are they trying to convince you to believe or do? Understanding a point of view will help you better understand the author's purpose.

Let's try a few examples. Determine what the author's purpose is for each of the following:

1. A packet that explains how to use an Xbox One

2. A story where a student plays Xbox One every day and becomes the youngest person to invent an Xbox One game.

3. An article that discusses the dangers of Xbox One and says nobody should ever play.

All three of these examples have similar information—Xbox One. However, the author has a different purpose in each.

Number 1 is simply to inform. It is giving you INFORMation. Number 2 is to entertain. It is a fiction story based on imagination, not facts. Number 3 is to persuade—the author is trying to convince readers that Xbox One is bad and people should stop playing.

Now that we have a better understanding of purpose, let's dive into point of view a little deeper. Read the passage below and answer the questions.

Mac computers are better than PC Computers. Mac computers are more expensive, but they are worth every penny. They are made better than PC computers and typically last longer. They have better software programs and almost never get viruses or break down. PC computers have to get fixed or replaced all the time and it ends up being more expensive than just buying a Mac computer in the first place! Plus, Mac computers are more user friendly and they will sync with your Ipad and Iphone! I highly suggest getting a Mac if you are looking to buy a new computer.

What was the author's purpose when they wrote this paragraph?

    a. Inform
    b. Persuade
    c. Entertain

Right, you should have chosen B, to persuade. The author has an opinion, which suggests they are persuading you to do something.

What is the author's point of view?

    a. PC Computers are the best computers to buy
    b. Both Mac's and PC's are great computers if you take care of them
    c. Mac Computers are better than PC Computers
    d. Everybody should own tablets rather than computers

The correct answer is C. The author clearly thinks that Mac computers are better than PC's. This is their point of view, or what side of the argument they are on! By understanding the author's purpose and point of view, you can better understand what you read. Just remember, everything was written for a purpose! Once you understand that purpose, you can better comprehend what point the author is trying to make!

Language

This section contains an English language self-assessment and tutorials. The Tutorials are designed to familiarize students with general principles and the self-assessment contains general questions similar to the English language questions likely to be on the TACHS exam, but are not intended to be identical to the exam questions. The tutorials are not designed to be a complete English course, and it is assumed that students have some familiarity with English. If you do not understand parts of the tutorial, or find the tutorial difficult, it is recommended that you seek out additional instruction.

Note that these questions are for skill practice only.

Tour of the TACHS English Content

The TACHS language section has two parts. The first part (40 questions, 23 minutes) covers spelling, capitalization, punctuation and English usage, and the second part covers paragraphs (10 questions, 7 minutes). Below is a detailed list of the topics likely to appear on the TACHS.

- English Grammar

- Meaning in Context (Vocabulary)

- Spelling

- Punctuation

- Capitalization

- Sentence Structure

- Paragraph organization, conciseness and clarity

The questions below are not the same as you will find on the TACHS - that would be too easy! And nobody knows what the questions will be and they change all the time. Mostly, the changes consist of substituting new questions for old, but the changes also can be new question formats or styles, changes to the number of questions in each section, changes to the time limits for each section, and combining sections. So, while the format and exact wording of the questions may differ slightly, and change from year to year, if you can answer the questions below, you will have no problem with the language section of the TACHS.

Language Self-Assessment

The purpose of the self-assessment is:

- Identify your strengths and weaknesses.
- Develop your personalized study plan (above)
- Get accustomed to the TACHS format
- Extra practice – the self-assessment is a 3rd test!
- Provide a baseline score for preparing your study schedule.

Since this is a self-assessment, and depending on how confident you are with English, timing yourself is optional. The TACHS language section has 30 questions which must be answered in 40 minutes. The self-assessment has 38 questions, so allow 50 minutes to complete this assessment.

Once complete, use the table below to assess your understanding of the content and prepare your study schedule described in chapter 1.

80% - 100%	Excellent – you have mastered the content!
60 – 79%	Good. You have a working knowledge. Even though you can just pass this section, you may want to review the Tutorials and do some extra practice to see if you can improve your mark.
40% - 59%	Below Average. You do not understand the content. Review the tutorials, and retake this quiz again in a few days, before proceeding to the Practice Test Questions.
Less than 40%	Poor. You have a very limited understanding. Please review the Tutorials, and retake this quiz again in a few days, before proceeding to the Practice Test Questions.

English Self-Assessment Answer Sheet

	A	B	C	D	E		A	B	C	D	E
1	○	○	○	○	○	21	○	○	○	○	○
2	○	○	○	○	○	22	○	○	○	○	○
3	○	○	○	○	○	23	○	○	○	○	○
4	○	○	○	○	○	24	○	○	○	○	○
5	○	○	○	○	○	25	○	○	○	○	○
6	○	○	○	○	○	26	○	○	○	○	○
7	○	○	○	○	○	27	○	○	○	○	○
8	○	○	○	○	○	28	○	○	○	○	○
9	○	○	○	○	○	29	○	○	○	○	○
10	○	○	○	○	○	30	○	○	○	○	○
11	○	○	○	○	○	31	○	○	○	○	○
12	○	○	○	○	○	32	○	○	○	○	○
13	○	○	○	○	○	33	○	○	○	○	○
14	○	○	○	○	○	34	○	○	○	○	○
15	○	○	○	○	○	35	○	○	○	○	○
16	○	○	○	○	○	36	○	○	○	○	○
17	○	○	○	○	○	37	○	○	○	○	○
18	○	○	○	○	○	38	○	○	○	○	○
19	○	○	○	○	○						
20	○	○	○	○	○						

Part I - Spelling, Capitalization, Punctuation, and Usage

Select the word that best fits the given sentence.

1. He didn't realize how serious the crime was. It wasn't simply a misdemeanor, but rather a _____ .

    a. Felony
    b. Trespass
    c. Infraction
    d. None of the Above

2. Choose the correct sentence.

    a. Does the sun set in the East or West?
    b. Does the sun set in the east or the west?
    c. Does the Sun set in the east or west?
    d. None of the Above.

3. Their new house is like a castle. I have never seen such a _____ home.

    a. Palace
    b. Palatial
    c. Meagre
    d. Humble

4. Fill in the blank.

She never does anything like that, so I doubt that she will do it herself. I am sure she will get one of her _____ to do it.

    a. Superiors
    b. Acquaintances
    c. Underlings
    d. None of the Above

5. He went to the store after school.

What is the subject of this sentence?

  a. School
  b. Store
  c. He
  d. After

6. He was exhausted and very tired when he finally finished the exam.

What part of this sentence is redundant?

  a. finished the exam
  b. He was exhausted
  c. And very tired
  d. When he finally

7. Choose the sentence with the correct usage.

  a. The ceremony had an emotional effect on the groom, but the bride was not affected.
  b. The ceremony had an emotional affect on the groom, but the bride was not affected.
  c. The ceremony had an emotional effect on the groom, but the bride was not effected.
  d. The ceremony had an emotional affect on the groom, but the bride was not affected.

8. I never want to speak to him again!

What type of sentence is this?

  a. Imperative
  b. Interrogative
  c. Exclamatory
  d. Declarative

9. Choose the correct sentence.

   a. Each boy and girl were given a toy.
   b. Each boy and girl was given a toy.
   c. A boy and girl is given a toy.
   d. None of the above.

10. He went to the store after school.

What is the simple predicate of the sentence?

   a. Went to the store
   b. After school
   c. He
   d. He went

11. Choose the sentence with the correct usage.

   a. Anna was taller then Luis, but then he grew four inches in three months.
   b. Anna was taller then Luis, but than he grew four inches in three months.
   c. Anna was taller than Luis, but than he grew four inches in three months.
   d. Anna was taller than Luis, but then he grew four inches in three months.

12. Sarah bought some <u>stationeries</u>.

Choose the correct word to replace the underlined word above.

   a. stationary
   b. stationarys
   c. stationaryes
   d. none of the above

13. I have two <u>son-in-laws</u>.

Choose the correct word to replace the underlined word above.

   a. sons-in-laws
   b. sons-on-law
   c. sons-in-law
   d. none of the above

14. Choose the sentence with the correct grammar.

    a. Mathematics were my best subject in school
    b. Mathematics are my best subject in school
    c. Mathematics was my best subject in school
    d. None of the above

Fill in the Blank.

15. All of the people at the school, including the teachers and _____ were glad when summer break came.

    a. students:
    b. students,
    c. students;
    d. students

16. My wife's brother is a good friend and my brother-in-law.

What part of this sentence is redundant?

    a. Is a good friend
    b. And my brother-in-law
    c. Good friend and my brother-in-law
    d. There is no redundancy in this sentence

17. Choose the sentence with the correct grammar.

    a. The tongs are now hot enough
    b. The tongs is now hot enough
    c. Both of the above
    d. None of the above

18. The Ford Motor Company was named for Henry Ford, _____.

    a. which had founded the company.
    b. who founded the company.
    c. whose had founded the company.
    d. whom had founded the company.

19. Choose the sentence with the correct grammar.

a. He would have postponed the camping trip, if he would have known about the forecast.

b. If he would have known about the forecast, he would have postponed the camping trip.

c. If he have known about the forecast, he would have postponed the camping trip.

d. If he had known about the forecast, he would have postponed the camping trip.

20. Choose the correct sentence.

a. Shakespeare wrote more than 37 Plays, including Much Ado about Nothing.

b. Shakespeare wrote more than 37 plays, including Much ado about nothing.

c. Shakespeare wrote more than 37 plays, including Much Ado about Nothing.

d. Shakespeare wrote more than 37 Plays, including Much Ado About Nothing.

21. Choose the correct spelling.

a. arguemint
b. arguement
c. argument
d. arguemant

22. Choose the correct spelling.

a. occurrence
b. ocurrence
c. occurence
d. ocurence

23. Choose the correct spelling.

a. desparate
b. desperete
c. desperate
d. despirate

24. Sit up straight _____

    a. ;
    b. ?
    c. .
    d. :

25. They asked what time the department store would open _____

    a. ?
    b. .
    c. ,
    d. ;

26. Who do you think will win the contest _____

    a. .
    b. !
    c. ?
    d. ,

27. The <u>lazy</u> brown fox jumper over the sleeping dog.
What part of speech is the underlined word?

    a. Noun
    b. Verb
    c. Adjective
    d. Adverb

28. The <u>tall</u> buildings blocked out the sun.
What part of speech is the underlined word?

    a. Noun
    b. Verb
    c. Adjective
    d. Adverb

29. Which of the following sentences contains a redundant phrase?

    a. I filled the tank to capacity.
    b. At the moment, she is getting ready.
    c. I won't be there for several minutes
    d. None of the above

30. Choose the correct sentence.

    a. They said it is going to rain on the radio.
    b. They said on the radio it is going to rain.
    c. They are going to say it is going to rain on the radio.
    d. None of the above.

Language Part II - Paragraphs

A Personal Satellite?

Many of us are already so loaded with technology, we don't have time to think about integrating even more! [1] In fact at this point it seems impossible to think about personal satellites now, just as we once thought about smart phones. [2] The reality of personal spacecraft is still in the realm of Star Trek and geeky space fantasies. [3]

However, the days when each of us will have our own personal satellite are not far away! [4] And what is even more exciting is they will be available for the cost of an iPhone! [5] At least, according to Zach Manchester, the inventor of the nano-satellite KickSat. [6] "I'd like to think of it as the people's satellite," says Manchester. [7] "We're pushing towards a personal satellite, where you can afford to put your own thing in space." [8]

The KickSat, a 30 cm. long hardware pack, is a space enthusiast's dream. [9] It contains the basics of a fully functional satellite. [10] Inside its compact design, the KickSat itself contains 200 more tinier satellites of cubic shape called "Sprites." [11] The Sprites are engineered and programmed so that they can be tracked and communicate via radio signals with a ground station on earth. [12] Each Sprite is available for purchase and is uniquely named after the sponsors who support Zach's project. [13] Anyone who has sponsored a Sprite will be able to track their personal satellite from a ground station installed in their balcony or roof! [14]

Language

31. Which sentence from the passage is an example of a sentence fragment?

    a. 4

    b. 7

    c. 6

    d. 10

32. Which of the following sentences should be edited to reduce redundancy?

    a. 5

    b. 4

    c. 10

    d. 16

33. Which of the following changes are needed to sentence 2?

    a. In fact at this point it seems impossible to think about personal satellites now - just as we once thought about smart phones.

    b. In fact, at this point, it seems impossible to think about personal satellites now, just as we once thought about smart phones.

    c. In fact, at this point, it seems impossible to think about personal satellites now - just as we once thought about smart phones.

    d. In fact at this point, it seems impossible to think about personal satellites now, just as we once thought about smart phones.

34. Which of the following changes are needed to sentence 11?

    a. Under its compact design, the KickSat itself contains 200 more tiny satellites of cubic shape called "Sprites."

    b. Under its compact design, the KickSat itself contains 200 more tiny satellites of cubic shapes called "Sprites."

    c. Inside its compact design, the KickSat itself contains 200 tinier satellites of cubic shapes called "Sprites."

    d. With its compact design, the KickSat contains 200 tiny cube-shaped satellites called "Sprites."

Alvin Lee's Guitar

Only a few of his contemporaries rocked the rock n' roll era with their guitars like Alvin Lee. [1] Even at the age of 67, just a year before his demise, he produced one of the finest albums of his five-decade long career with *Still on the Road to Freedom*. [2] Strikingly flamboyant with his guitar, Lee gained millions of admirers around the world with hits like "*I'd Love to Change the World*," "*On the Road to Freedom*" and "*Freedom for the Stallion*" which reflected popular worldviews at the time of their release. [3]

Alvin Lee began playing guitar at an early age, and was influenced by his parents' passion for music and inspired by the likes of Chuck Berry and Scotty Moore. [4] Lee started his career as the lead vocalist and guitarist in a band named the Jaybirds at the famous Marquee Club in London in 1962. [5] A few years later the band changed its name to *Ten Years After* and released its debut album under the new name. [6] Lee's lightning fast guitar playing at the Woodstock Festival gained him instant stardom and Lee was asked to tour the US. [7]

In the coming years, he worked with rock legends like Mylon LeFevre, George Harrison, Steve Winwood, Ronnie Wood and Mick Fleetwood and released the country rock masterpiece *On the Road to Freedom* which brought him overwhelming trans-Atlantic popularity. [8] In subsequent years, he continued addressing social and global issues in albums like *A Space in Time, Pump Iron!, Let It Rock* and *Rocket Fuel*. [9] With many of his songs, such as, "*I'd Love to Change the World*," Lee used the power of rock music to show his solidarity with ordinary people and their worldviews. [10] He also went on with inspiring the upcoming generations of rock stars by producing expressive and tasteful guitar performances in his 1980s albums *Free Fall, RX5* and *Detroit Diesel*. [11]

35. Which sentence in the second paragraph is the least relevant to the main idea of the second paragraph?

   a. 4
   b. 5
   c. 6
   d. 7

36. Which of the following changes is/are needed in sentence 6?

   a. A few years later, the band changed its name to *Ten Years After* and released its debut album under the new name.

   b. A few years later, the band changed its name to *Ten Years After*, and released its debut album under the new name.

   c. A few years later the band changed its name to *Ten Years After*, and released its debut album under the new name.

   d. A few years later, the band changed its name to *Ten Years After* and, released its debut album under the new name.

37. Which of the following sentences, if inserted before sentence 11, would best illustrate the main idea of the passage?

a. His charismatic personality earned him more fame and led him to perform even better for the sake of his admirers.

b. As he gained popularity because of his artistic creations he tried to implant political motives into his music.

c. At the same time, he thought of doing something for the future generations.

d. With the creative songs he composed, he established himself as an exemplary figure among fellow guitarists and the generations that followed.

38. Which of the following changes are needed to sentence 11?

a. He also went on inspiring the upcoming generations of rock stars by producing expressive and tasteful guitar performances in his 1980s albums *Free Fall, RX5* and *Detroit Diesel*.

b. He also went on to inspire the upcoming generations of rock stars by producing expressive and tasteful guitar performances in his 1980s albums *Free Fall, RX5* and *Detroit Diesel*.

c. He also went with inspiring the upcoming generations of rock stars by producing expressive and tasteful guitar performances in his 1980s albums *Free Fall, RX5* and *Detroit Diesel*. .

d. He also went on to inspiring the upcoming generations of rock stars by producing expressive and tasteful guitar performances in his 1980s albums *Free Fall, RX5* and *Detroit Diesel*.

Answer Key

1. A
Felony: A serious criminal offense, which, under federal law, is punishable by death or imprisonment for a term exceeding one year.

2. A
The cardinal directions, North, South East and West are capitalized. In general, the first letter is capitalized for well-defined regions, e.g. South America, Lower California, Tennessee Valley. This general rule also applies to zones of the Earth's surface (North Temperate Zone, the Equator). In other cases, do not capitalize the points of the compass (north China, south-east London) or other adjectives (western Arizona, central New Mexico, upper Yangtze, lower Rio Grande)

3. B
Palatial: Of or relating to a palace.

4. C
Underlings: A subordinate, or person of lesser rank or authority.

5. C
'He' is the subject of the sentence.

6. C
The phrase, 'and very tired' is redundant after saying he was exhausted.

7. A
"Affect" is a verb, while "effect" is a noun.

8. D
This is an exclamatory sentence.

9. B
Use the singular verb form when nouns are qualified with "every" or "each," even if they are joined by 'and.'

10. A
The simple predicate is the action being performed by the subject.

11. D
"Than" is used for comparison. "Then" is used to show a point in time.

12. A
"Stationary" is both the singular and plural forms.

13. C
The correct form is son-in-law in the singular and sons-in-law in the plural.

14. C
Always use the singular verb form for nouns like politics, wages, mathematics, innings, news, advice, summons, furniture, information, poetry, machinery, vacation, scenery etc.

15. B
The comma separates a phrase.

16. B
'And my brother-in-law' is redundant since we already know he is his wife's brother.

17. A
Use a plural verb for nouns like measles, tongs, trousers, riches, scissors etc.

18. B
The sentence refers to a person, so "who" is the only correct choice.

19. D
The third conditional is used for talking about an unreal situation (a situation that did not happen) in the past. For example, "If I had stud-

ied harder, [if clause] I would have passed the exam [main clause]. This has the same meaning as, "I failed the exam because I didn't study hard enough."

20. C
The names of plays are capitalized. All words except articles are capitalized.

21. C
Argument is the correct spelling.

22. A
Occurrence is the correct spelling.

23. C
Desperate is the correct spelling.

24. C
A period or an exclamation mark is used to end an imperative sentence, that is, at the end of a direction or a command.

25. B
A period is used to end an indirect question. An indirect question is always a part of a declarative sentence and it does not require an answer.

26. C
A question mark is used to end an interrogative sentence, that is, at the end of a direct question which requires an answer.

27. D
The underlined word, lazy, is an adverb. Adverbs are words or phrases that modify or qualify an adjective, verb, or other adverb or a phrase.

28. C
'Tall' in this sentence is an adjective. Adjectives are words or phrases naming an attribute, added to, or grammatically related to a noun to modify or describe it.

29. A
If the tank is filled, it is filled to capacity, so describing something as "filled to capacity" is redundant.

30. B
The correct sentence is, "They said on the radio it is going to rain." The first choice, "They said it is going to rain on the radio," means it is going to rain on the radio.

31. B
Sentence 6 is a fragment. "At least, according to Zach Manchester, the inventor of the nano-satellite KickSat."

This sentence fails to complete the thought, even though it is somewhat consistent with the previous sentence. Sentence 6 does not have a subject and thus does not form any main clause which is essential for constructing a complete thought. This fragment can be revised as "At least, this is according to Zach Manchester, the inventor of the nano-satellite KickSat."

32. B
Suggested changes to Sentence 4 to reduce redundancy, "However, the days when each of us will have our own personal spacecraft are truly not far away!"

The adjectives "own" and "personal" are used simultaneously. Either of them can be used, and the other must be eliminated. The correct form will be either one of the following:

- However, the days when each of us will have our own spacecraft are truly not far away!
- However, the days when each

of us will have our personal spacecraft are truly not far away!

33. C
The revised version of sentence 2 is, "In fact, at this point, it seems impossible to think about personal satellites now - just as we once thought about smart phones."

This choice uses the correct punctuation; two commas, one before and one after the subordinate conjunction "at this point" which bridges the adverbial clause after it with the adjective at the start of the sentence. Also the use of a hyphen to express extended thought is correct in choice C.

34. D
The only choice with correct grammar is choice D. It replaces "more tiny" with "tiny" as well as "cubic shaped" with "cube-shaped." Tinier is the correct comparative form of "tiny" and "cubic" is the adjective that must describe the singular noun "shape," not "shapes" or any of its verbal forms. Two word adjectives, such as "a 3-mile race" are hyphenated.

"Under its compact design" is incorrect. Replace with, "with its compact design … "

35. A
Sentence 4 is least relevant, "Alvin Lee began playing guitar at an early age, and was influenced by his parents' passion for music and inspired by the likes of Chuck Berry and Scotty Moore."

This sentence talks about Lee's source of motivation rather than his achievements, which is actually the main topic of the paragraph. Other sentences are related to a significant extent, but this sentence deviates from the main idea the most.

36. A
The edited version of sentence 6 is, "A few years later, the band changed its name to Ten Years After and released its debut album under the new name."

Choice A places a comma after the prepositional phrase "A few years later" that expresses time. No other punctuation is necessary for a coordinate conjunction "and" as proposed by choices B and C since the clause "released its debut album under the new name" is a subordinate rather than an independent one. Choice D offers an incorrect suggestion, placing a comma after "and."

37. D
The following sentence, if inserted after sentence 11, "With the songs he composed, he established himself as an exemplary figure among fellow guitarists and the immediate generation that followed" best illustrates the main idea of the passage.

This sentence best complements the other sentences and the main idea of the passage which concentrates on the impact Alvin Lee has made on his admirers and contemporaries with his skills and creations. The emphasis of the passage is on how he influenced them with his guitar work and that is complemented best if the sentence by choice D before sentence 11.

38. B
Suggested changes to sentence 11 are, "He also went on to inspire upcoming generations of rock stars by producing expressive and tasteful guitar performances in his 1980s albums. *Free Fall, RX5* and *Detroit Diesel.*"

The correction offered in choice B is the only appropriate one since the gerund form of "inspire" is not appropriate when starting the action. In this case, the author expresses initiation of the process of inspiring more than one generation. So, rather than continuing an already started process, this sentence refers to beginning of an additional process of inspiring as indicated by "also." The gerund form is used rather when the action represented by the verb is in a continuous process already in motion. Therefore, the to-infinitive must be used. As a result choice A can be eliminated. Choices C and D offer no valid gerund or infinitive.

English Grammar and Punctuation Tutorials

Capitalization

Although many of the rules for capitalization are pretty straight forward, there are several tricky points that are important to review.

Starting a Sentence

Everyone knows that you need to capitalize the first letter of the first word in a sentence, but is it really all that easy to figure out where one sentence starts and another stops? Take these three examples:

That was the moment it really sunk in: There would be no hockey this year.

It was April and that could mean only one thing: baseball.

We played for hours before heading home; everyone felt tired and happy.

In the first example, the first letter after the colon is capitalized while in the second example, it is not. That is because everything after the first example's colon is a complete sentence, while example two's colon there is only one word. In example three you have what could be a complete sentence ("everyone felt tired and happy"), but which is not because it follows a semicolon, making it just another clause instead.

Within a sentence you can have an additional complete sentence if the sentence follows a colon. However, if what could be a complete sentence follows a semicolon, it is a clause and does not get capitalized.

Remember that the same rules apply for quotation marks that apply for colons: A complete sentence inside quotation marks is capitalized, but a single word or phrase is not.

Proper Nouns

The first letter of all proper nouns needs to be capitalized. There are many categories of proper noun. The most common proper nouns are the specific names of people (such as Bill), places (such as Germany) or things (such as Honda Civic). However, there are several less obvious categories of words that should be capitalized as proper nouns.

Historical events such as World War II or the California Gold Rush need to be capitalized.

The names of celestial bodies such as Orion's Belt need to be capitalized.

The names of ethnicities such as African-American or Hispanic need to be capitalized.

Relationship words that replace a person's name such as Mom, Doctor and Mister need to be capitalized. However, this only happens when you use the word to replace the person's name. In the sentence, "My mom went to the store," you do not capitalize it, while in the sentence, "Hey Mom, did you get toothpaste at the store?" you do capitalize it.

Geographical locations are capitalized. This can be tricky because capitalized geographical locations and non-capitalized directions are easy to confuse. Saying, "We drove south for hours," is a direction, so the word "south" should not be capitalized. However, when saying, "While in the United States, we drove to the South to look at Civil War battle fields," you do capitalize the word "South." The difference is that in the first sentence "south" is just the direction you drove. In the second sentence "the South" is a specific region of the United States that formed itself into the Confederacy during the US Civil War.

Proper Adjectives

Proper adjectives are the adjective forms of proper nouns. People from Germany are German; people from Canada are Canadian. German and Canadian are proper adjectives because they are forms of proper nouns that are used to describe other nouns.

Titles of Works

Titles of works are generally capitalized following a specific pattern. Capitalize all the important words in a sentence. Do not capitalize unimportant words such as prepositions and articles.

For example: Alien Spaceship Spotted over Many of the World's Capitals

Notice that the prepositions "over" and "of," and the article "the" are the only non-capitalized words in the sentence.

Punctuation - Colons, Semicolons, Hyphens, Dashes, Parentheses and Apostrophes

Within a sentence there are several different types of punctuation marks that can denote a pause. Each of these punctuation marks has different rules when it comes to its structure and usage, so we will look at each one in turn.

Colon

The colon is used primarily to introduce information. It can start lists such as in the sentence, "There were several things Susan had to get at the store: bread, cereal, lettuce and tomatoes." Or a colon points out specific information, such as in the sentence, "It was only then that the group fully realized what had happened: The Martian invasion had begun."

Note that if the information after the colon is a complete sentence, you capitalize and punctuate it exactly like you would a sentence. If, however, it does not constitute a complete sentence, you don't have to capitalize anything. ("Peering out the window Meredith saw them: zombies.")

Semicolon

Semicolons are super commas. They denote a stronger stop than a comma does, but they are still weaker than a period, not capable of ending a sentence. Semicolons are primarily used to separate independent clauses that are not being separated by a coordinating conjunction. ("Chris went to the store; he bought chips and salsa.") Semicolons can only do this, however, when the ideas in each clause are related. For instance, the sentence, "It's raining outside; my sister went to the movies," is not a proper usage of the semicolon since those clauses have nothing to do with each other.

Semicolons can also be used in lists if one or more element in the list is itself made up of a smaller list. If you want to write a list of things you plan to bring to a picnic, and those things only include a Frisbee, a chair and some pasta salad, you would not need to use a semicolon. However, if you also wanted to bring plastic knives, forks and spoons, you would need to write your sentence like this: "For our picnic I am bringing a Frisbee; a chair; plastic knives, forks and spoons; and some pasta salad."

Using semicolons like this preserves the smaller list that you have in your larger list.

Hyphen

To join words together to show that they are linked you use hyphens. The most common use of hyphens is to link together words to show that they are working together in a sentence. ("The well-known actor was eating at the table behind us.") This shows explicitly that you are using "well-known" as a single concept and not as two descriptive words in a list.

Hyphens can also be used to split a word in half if you run out of space writing on one line of a page. This is often seen in newspapers and magazines when text is justified to both sides of a page or a column. For example:

The massive earthquake caused surpris-

ingly little damage in the affected areas.

However, you can only use a hyphen in this way if you split the word between syllables. Often students think that they can use hyphens to break up words wherever they want; this is wrong. For the word "surprisingly" you

could have a hyphen between "sur" and "prisingly," "surpris" and "ingly, and between "surprising" and "ly," but nowhere else.

Finally, hyphens can be used to add prefixes to words. This happens a lot in news reports with phrases such as "pro-government troops."

Dashes and Parentheses

Both dashes and parentheses are used to set aside information into parenthetical statements; statements that can be treated as an aside. They do not need to be there for the sentence to make sense, but the information they provide is interesting enough that you feel it should be included. Parentheses are considered stronger than dashes are. (Commas can also be used to separate nonessential information from a sentence, but they are considered to be the weakest of the three.)

As the previous sentence shows, parentheses can surround entire sentences, separating them from the paragraph. Dashes, on the other hand, can separate off the last statement in a sentence. ("Calvin came home and greeted his family for the first time in days—everyone smiled.") Obviously, that last sentence could also be written using a semicolon or as two sentences. The difference is in how you want it to sound to the reader. Should these thoughts be treated as two distinct pieces? Or should everyone smiling at Calvin be part of the main sentence, just separated a bit more strongly—with a slightly longer pause—than a comma could manage?

Apostrophe

There are two primary uses of the apostrophe in English: forming contractions and forming possessive nouns.

Contractions are formed by taking two words and combining them together with an apostrophe replacing the missing letters (do not becomes don't), or by shortening an existing word (cannot becomes can't). Apostrophes can

also make contractions by attaching verbs to nouns or pronouns. ("He's going to the store.")

When making singular nouns possessive the general rule is that you add an 's to the end of singular nouns. (This is Tim's bagel.) When dealing with plural nouns that do not end with the letter –s (such as children), the rule is that you also add an 's to the end of the word. (It was the children's favorite movie.) And when dealing with plural nouns that end with the letter –s, you simply add an apostrophe. (My sisters' favorite game is tag.)

However, and this is an important "however" given the controversy it can cause, when dealing with singular words that end with the letter –s (such as circus), there are two standards for how to make them possessive—each with its own grammar books to back it up.

One standard says that you still add an 's to the end of the word. (This is the circus's biggest tent.) The other says that, since the word ends with an –s, it can only get an apostrophe. (This is the circus' biggest tent.) Some style books, such as the Chicago Manual of Style will go so far as to say that the former choice is correct, but to avoid inflaming people's passions on the subject, using the latter is perfectly acceptable. The best thing to do is to find out which style the teacher or editor you are writing for at any given time prefers and conform to it for that person.

Comma

Commas are probably the most commonly used punctuation mark in English. Commas can break the flow of writing to give it a more natural sounding style, and they are the main punctuation mark used to separate ideas. Commas also separate lists, introductory adverbs, introductory prepositional phrases, dates and addresses.

The most rigid way that commas are used is when separating clauses. There are two primary types of clauses in a sentence, independent and subordinate (sometimes called dependent). Independent clauses are clauses that express a complete thought, such as, "Tim went to the store." Subordinate clauses, on the other hand, only express partial thoughts that expand on an independent clause, such as, "after the game ended," which you can see is clearly not a complete sentence. (You will learn more about clauses in different lessons.)

The rule for commas with clauses is that a comma must separate the clauses when a subordinate clause comes first in a sentence: "After the game ended, Tim went to the store." But there should not be a comma when a subordinate clause follows an independent clause: "Tim went to the store after the game ended." If you leave the comma out of the first example, you have a run-on sentence. If you add one into the second example, you have a comma-splice error. Also, when you have two independent clauses joined with a coordinating conjunction, you need to separate them with a comma. "Tim went to the store, and Beth went home."

There are some artistic exceptions to these rules, such as adding a pause for literary effect, but for the most part, they are set in stone.

Commas are also used to separate items in a list. This area of English is unfortunately less clear than it should be, with two separate rules depending on what standard you are following. To understand the two different rules, let's pretend you are having a party at your house, and you are making a list of refreshments your friends will want. You may decide to serve three things: 1) pizza 2) chips 3) drinks. There are two different rules governing how you should punctuate this. According to many grammar books, you would write this as, "At the store I will buy pizza, chips, and drinks." This variation puts a comma after each item in the list. It is the version that the style books used in most college English and history courses will prefer, so it is probably the one you should follow. However, the Associated Press style guide, which is used in college journalism classes and at newspapers and magazines, says the sentence should be written like this: "At the store I will buy pizza, chips and drinks." Here you only use a comma between the first two words, letting the word "and" act as the separator between the last two.

Another important place to use commas is when you have a modifier that describes an element of a sentence, but that does not directly follow the thing it describes. Look at the sentence: "Tim went over to visit Beth, watching the full moon along the way." In this sentence there is no confusion about who is "watching the full moon"; it is Tim, probably as he walks to Beth's house. If you remove the comma, however, you get this: "Tim went over to visit Beth watching the full moon along the way." Now it sounds as though Beth is watching the full moon, and we are forced to wonder what "way" the moon is traveling along.

Commas are also used when adding introductory prepositional phrases and introductory adverbs to sentences. A comma is always needed following an introductory adverb. ("Quickly, Jody ran to the car.") Commas are even necessary when you have an adverb introducing a clause within a sentence, even if the clause not the first clause of the sentence. ("Amanda wanted to go to the movie; however, she knew her homework was more important.")

With introductory prepositional phrases you only add a comma if the phrase (or if a group of introductory phrases) is five or more words long. Thus, the sentence you just read did not have a comma following its introductory

prepositional phrase ("With introductory prepositional phrases") because it was only four words. Compare that to this sentence with a five word introductory phrase: "After the ridiculously long class, the friends needed to relax."

The last main way that commas are used in sentences is to separate out information that does not need to be there. For instance, "My cousin Hector, who wore a blue hat at the party, thought you were funny." The fact that Hector wore a blue hat is interesting, but it is not vital to the sentence; it could be removed and not changed the sentence's meaning. Therefore it gets commas around it. Along these lines you should remember that any clause introduced by the word that is considered to provide essential information to the sentence and should not get commas around it. Conversely, any clause starting with the word which is considered nonessential and should not get commas around it.

Quotation Marks

Quotation marks are used in English in a variety of different ways. The most common use of quotation marks is to show quotations either as dialogue or when directly quoting a source in an essay or news article. Fortunately, both of these uses follow the same basic rules.

When you have a quote written as the second part of a sentence, you need to put a comma before the quotation marks and a period inside the quotation marks at the end. (Franklin said, "Let's go to the store.") Conversely, when you have quote as the first part of the sentence with information describing it second, a comma replaces the period at the end of the sentence inside the quotes. ("Let's go to the store," Franklin said.)

If the information in a quote is not a complete sentence, you do not need to capitalize it or put commas around it, if it is not dialogue. (No one thought the idea of "going to the store" sounded very fun.)

Note that when the last word in a sentence has both a quotation mark and a period attached to it, the period is always inside the quotes. This is the case when you have a complete sentence inside a quote ("Let's go to the store."), and when the last word in a sentence just happens to have quote marks around it (Kerri said I was "mean.") You also need to do the same thing with commas. (Kerri said I was "mean," and it made me feel bad.) However, other punctuation marks such as colons, semicolons and dashes do not follow this rule and should come outside the quotes. (Kerri said I was "mean"; it made me feel bad.)

When you want to use a quote inside a quote, you use the standard double-quotation marks for the outer quote and single-quotation marks for the inner quote. ("The sign on the door said 'no soliciting,' so we went to the next house.")

Quotation marks are also used around certain types of titles. To figure out which ones, it helps to look at which titles are not put in quotes as well.

Titles have two categories: large works and small works. Large works are things such as newspapers, magazines, CDs, books and television shows. The defining characteristic of a large work is that it is able to hold small works in it. Small works are the articles inside newspapers and magazines, the songs on a CD, the chapters in a book and the episodes of a television show. It is small works that get quotation marks around them. (Large works, meanwhile, are either underlined or italicized.)

Using quotation marks correctly in a title looks something like this: The two-page article entitled "San Francisco Giants Win World Series" appeared in yesterday's New York Times. The article title is in quotes, and the newspaper title is in italics.

How to Answer English Grammar Multiple Choice - Verb Tense

This tutorial is designed to help you answer English Grammar multiple choice questions as well as a very quick refresher on verb tenses. It is assumed that you have some familiarity with the verb tenses covered here. If you find these questions difficulty or do not understand the tense construction, we recommend you seek out additional instruction.

Tenses Covered

1. Past Progressive
2. Present Perfect
3. Present Perfect Progressive
4. Present Progressive
5. Simple Future
6. Simple Future – "Going to" Form
7. Past Perfect Progressive
8. Future Perfect Progressive
9. Future Perfect
10. Future Progressive
11. Past Perfect

1. The Past Progressive Tense

How to Recognize This Tense

He *was running* very fast when he fell.

They *were drinking* coffee when he arrived.

About the Past Progressive Tense

This tense is used to speak of an action that was in progress in the past when another event occurred.

The action was unfolding at a point in the past.

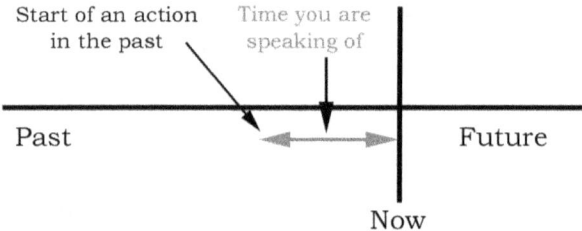

Past Progressive Tense Construction

This tense is formed by using the past tense of the verb "to be" plus the present participle of the main verb.

Sample Question

Bill _____ lunch when we arrived.

   a. will eat
   b. is eating
   c. eats
   d. was eating

How to Answer This Type of Question

1. First examine the question for clues about the time frame.

The sentence ends with "when we arrived," so we know the time frame is a point ("when") in the past (arrived).

The correct answer will refer to an ongoing action at a point of time in the past.

2. Examine the choices and eliminate any obviously incorrect answers.

Choice A is the future tense so we can eliminate.

Choice B is the present continuous so we can eliminate.

Choice C is present tense so we can eliminate.

Choice D refers to an action that takes place at a point of time in the past ("was eating").

2. The Present Perfect Tense

How to Recognize This Tense

I *have had* enough to eat.

We *have been* to Paris many times.

I *have known* him for five years.

I *have been* coming here since I was a child.

About the Present Perfect Tense

This tense expresses the idea that something happened (or didn't happen) at an unspecific time in the past up until the present. The action happened at an unspecified time in the past. (If there is a specific time mentioned, the simple past tense is used.) It can be used for repeated action, accomplishments, changes over time and uncompleted action.

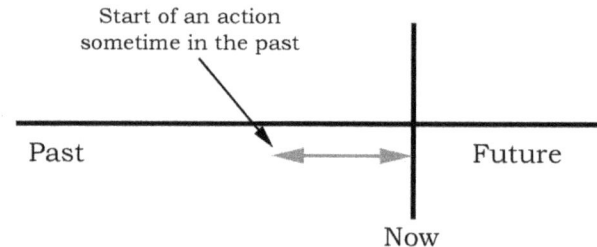

Present Perfect Tense Construction

It is also used with "for" and "since."

This tense is formed by using the present tense of the verb "to have" plus the past participle of the main verb.

Sample Question

I _____ these birds many times.

    a. am seeing
    b. will saw
    c. have seen
    d. have saw

How to Answer This Type of Question

1. First examine the question for clues about the time frame.

"Many times" tells us that the action is repeated and in the past.

2. Examine the choices and eliminate any obviously incorrect answers.

Choice A, "am seeing" is incorrect because it is a continuing action, i.e. in the present; it also doesn't use a form of 'have'.

Choice B is grammatically incorrect.

Choice C tells of something that has happened in the past and is now over. Best choice so far.

Choice D is grammatically incorrect.

3. The Present Perfect Progressive Tense

How to Recognize This Tense

We *have been seeing* a lot of rainy days.

I *have been reading* some very good books.

About the Present Perfect Progressive Tense

This tense expresses the idea that something happened (or didn't happen) in the relatively recent past, but <u>the action is not finished.</u> It is used to express the duration of the action.

NOTE: The present perfect speaks of an action that happened sometime in the past, but this action is finished. In the present perfect progressive tense, the action that started in the past is still going on.

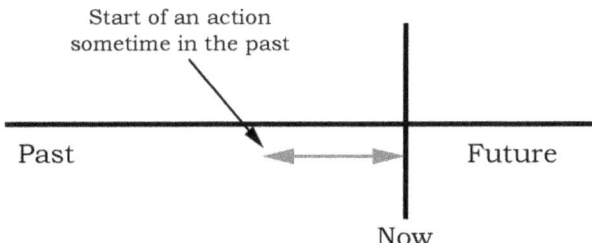

Present Perfect Progressive Tense Construction

This tense is formed by using the present tense of the verb "to have," plus "been," plus the present participle of the main verb.

Sample Question

Bill _____ there for two hours.

    a.   sits
    b.   sitting
    c. has been sitting
    d.   will sat

How to Answer This Type of Question

1. First examine the question for clues about the time frame.

"For two hours" tells us that the action, "sits," is continuous up to now, and may continue into the future.

Note this sentence could also be the simple past tense,

Bill sat there for two hours.

Or the future tense,

Bill will sit there for two hours.

However, these are not among the choices.

2. Examine the choices and eliminate any obviously incorrect answers.

Choice A is incorrect because it is the present tense.
Choice B is incorrect because it is the present continuous. Choice C is correct. "Has been sitting" expresses a continuous action in the past that isn't finished.
Choice D is grammatically incorrect.

4. The Present Progressive Tense

How to Recognize This Tense

We *are having* a delicious lunch.

They *are driving* much too fast.

About the Present Progressive Tense

This tense is used to express what the action is <u>right now</u>. The action started in the recent past, and is continuing into the future.

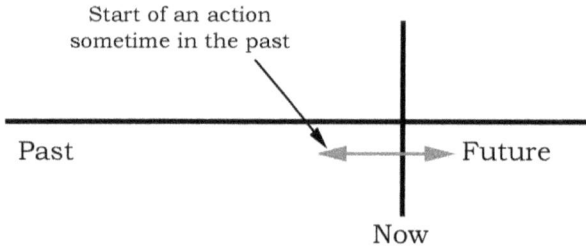

Present Perfect Tense Construction

The Present Progressive Tense is formed by using the present tense of "to be" plus the present participle of the main verb.

Sample Question

She _____ very hard these days.

    a. works

    b. is working

    c. will work

    d. worked

How to Answer This Type of Question

1. First examine the question for clues about the time frame.

The end of the sentence includes "these days" which tell us the action started in the past, continues into the present, and may continue into the future.

2. Examine the choices and eliminate any obviously incorrect answers.

Choice A, the simple present is incorrect.
Choice B, "is working" is correct.
Check the other two choices just to be sure. Choice C is future tense, and Choice D is past tense, so they can be eliminated.

The correct answer is Choice B.

5. The Simple Future Tense

How to Recognize This Tense

I *will see* you tomorrow.
We *will drive* the car.

About the Simple Future Tense

This tense shows that the action will happen some time in the future.

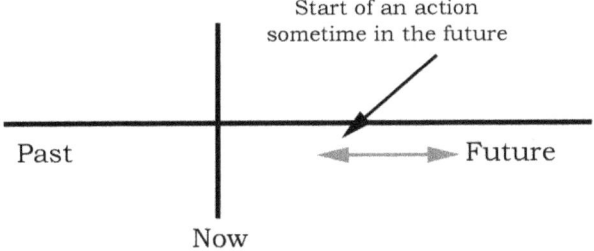

Simple Future Tense Construction

The tense is formed by using "will" plus the root form of the verb. (The root form of the verb is the infinitive without "to." Examples: read, swim.)

Sample Question

We _____ to Paris next year.

    a. went

    b. had been

    c. will go

    d. go

How to Answer This Type of Question

1. First examine the question for clues about the time frame.

The last two words of the sentence, "next year," clearly identify this sentence as referring to the future.

2. Examine the choices and eliminate any obviously incorrect answers.

Choice A is the past tense and can be eliminated.

Choice B is the past perfect tense and can be eliminated.

Choice D is the simple present and can be eliminated.

Choice C is the only one left and is the correct simple future tense.

6. The Simple Future Tense – The "Going to" Form

How to Recognize This Tense

I *am going to* see you tomorrow.

We *are going to* drive the car.

About the Simple Future Tense

This form of the future tense is used to show the intention of doing something in the future. (This is the strict grammatical meaning, but in daily speech, it is often used interchangeably with the simple future tense, the "will" form.)

The tense is formed by using the present conditional tense of "to go," plus the infinitive of the verb.

Language

Sample Question

I _____ shopping in an hour.

    a. go

    b. have gone

    c. am going to go

    d. went

How to Answer This Type of Question

1. First examine the question for clues about the time frame.

"In an hour" clearly identifies the action as taking place in the future.

2. Examine the choices and eliminate any obviously incorrect answers.

Choice A is the simple present tense and can be eliminated.

Choice B is the past perfect and can be eliminated.

Choice C is the correct answer.

Choice D is the past tense and can be eliminated.

7. The Past Perfect Progressive Tense

How to Recognize This Tense

I *had been sleeping* for an hour when you phoned.

We *had been eating* our dinner when they all came into the dining room.

About the Past Perfect Progressive Tense

This tense is used to show that the action had been going on for a period of time in the past when another action, also in the past, occurred.

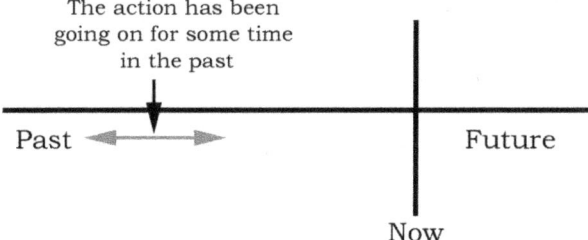

Past Perfect Tense Construction

The tense is formed by using the past perfect tense of the verb "to be" plus the present participle of the main verb.

Sample Question

How long _____ you _____ when I saw you?

    a. are _____ running
    b. had _____ running
    c.   had _____ been running
    d. was _____ running

How to Answer This Type of Question

1. First examine the question for clues about the time frame.

"When I saw" tells us the sentence happened at a point of time ("when") in the past ("saw").

2. Examine the choices and eliminate any obviously incorrect answers.

Choice A, "are running" is incorrect and can be eliminated.

Choice B, "Had ___ running" is grammatically incorrect and can be eliminated.

Choice C is correct.

Choice D is grammatically incorrect so the answer is Choice C.

8. Future Perfect Progressive Tense

How to Recognize This Tense

I *will have been working* here for two years in March.

I *will have been driving* for four hours when I get there, so I will be tired.

About the Future Perfect Progressive Tense

This tense is used to show that the action continues up to a point of time in the future.

Future Prefect Progressive Tense Construction

This tense is formed by using the future perfect tense of "to be" plus the present participle of the main verb.

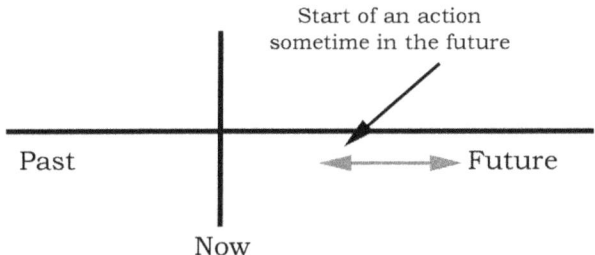

Sample Question

_____ you _____ all the time I am gone?

    a. have _____ been working
    b. will _____ have been working
    c. are _____ worked
    d. will _____ worked

How to Answer This Type of Question

1. First examine the question for clues about the time frame.

"All the time I am gone" refers to an action in the future ("time I am gone") and the action is progressive ("all the time"). The progressive action means the correct choice will be a verb tense that ends in "ing."

2. Examine the choices and eliminate any obviously incorrect answers.

Choice A, the past perfect, refers to a past continuous event and is also grammatically incorrect in the sentence, so Choice A can be eliminated.

Choice B looks correct because it refers to an action will be going on for a period of time in the future.

Examine Choices C and D just to be sure. Both choices are grammatically incorrect and can be eliminated.
Choice B is the correct answer.

9. The Future Perfect Tense

How to Recognize This Tense

By next November, I *will have received* my promotion.

By the time he gets home, she is going *to have cleaned* the entire house.

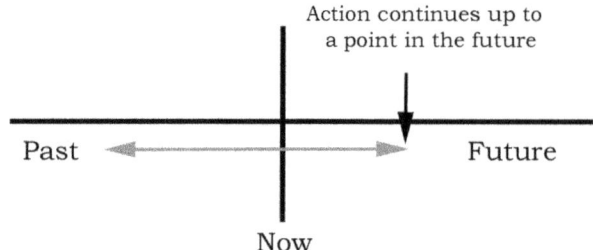

About the Future Perfect Tense

The future perfect tense expresses action in the future before another action in the future. This is the past in the future. For example:

He *will have prepared* dinner when she arrives.

Future Perfect Tense Construction

This tense is formed by "will + have + past participle."

Sample Question

They _____ their seats before the game begins.

    a. will have find
    b. will find
    c. will have found
    d. found

How to Answer This Type of Question

1. First examine the question for clues about the time frame.

This question could be several different tenses. The only clue about the time frame is "before the game begins," which refers to a specific point of time.

We know it isn't in the past, because "begins" is incorrect for the past tense. Similarly with the present. So the question is about something that happens in the future, before another event in the future.

2. Examine the choices and eliminate any obviously incorrect answers.

Choice A can be eliminated as incorrect.
Choice B looks good, so mark it and check the others before making a final decision.
Choice C is the past perfect and can be eliminated because the time frame is incorrect.
Choice D is the simple past tense and can be eliminated for the same reason.

10. Future Progressive Tense

How to Recognize This Tense

The teams *will be playing* soccer when we arrive.

At 3:45 the soccer fans *will be waiting* for the game to start at 4:00 o'clock

At 3:45 the soccer players *will be preparing* to play at 4:00 o'clock

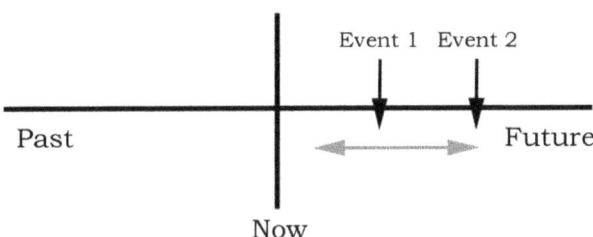

About the Future Progressive Tense

The future progressive tense talks about a continuing action in the future.

Future Progressive Tense Construction

will+ be + (root form) + ing = will be playing

Sample Question

Many excited fans _____ a bus to see the game at 4:00.

    a. catch
    b. catching
    c. have been catching
    d. will be catching

How to Answer This Type of Question

1. First examine the question for clues about the time frame.

"At 4:00," tells us the sentence is either in the past OR in the future.

2. Examine the choices and eliminate any obviously incorrect answers.

From the time frame of the sentence, the answer will be past or future tense.

Choice A is the present tense and can be eliminated.
Choice B is the present continuous tense and can be eliminated.
Choice C is the past perfect continuous and can be eliminated.
Choice D is the only one left. Quickly examining the tense, it is future progressive and is correct in the sentence.

11. The Past Perfect Tense

How to Recognize This Tense

The party *had* just *started* when the coach arrived.

We *had waited* for twenty minutes when the bus finally came.

About the Past Perfect

The past perfect tense talks about two events that happened in the past and establishes which event happened first.

Another example is, "We had eaten when he arrived."

The two events are "eat" and "he arrived." From the sentence above the past perfect tense tells us the first event, "eat" happened before the second event, "he arrived."

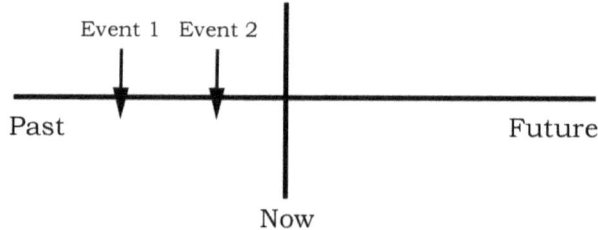

I had already eaten when my friends arrived.

Past Perfect Tense Construction

The past perfect is formed by "have" plus the past participle.

Sample Question

It was time to go home after they _____ the game.

    a. will win

    b. win

    c. had won

    d. wins

How to Answer This Type of Question

1. First examine the question for clues about the time frame.

"Was" tells us the sentence happened in the past. Also notice there are two events, "go home" and "after the game."

2. Examine the choices and eliminate any obviously incorrect answers.

Choice A is the future tense and can be eliminated. Choice B is the simple present and can be eliminated. Choice C is the past perfect and orders the two events in the past. Choice D is the present tense and incorrect and can be eliminated, so Choice C is the correct answer.

Common English Usage Mistakes - A Quick Review

Like some parts of English grammar, usage is definitely going to be on the exam and there isn't any tricky strategies or shortcuts to help you get through this section.

Here is a quick review of common usage mistakes.

1. May and Might

'May' can act as a principal verb, which can express permission or possibility.

Examples:

Lets wait, the meeting may have started.
May I begin now?

'May' can act as an auxiliary verb, which expresses a purpose or wish.

Examples:

May you find favour in the sight of your employer.

May your wishes come true.
People go to school so that they may be educated.

The past tense of may is might.

Examples:

I asked if I might begin

'Might' can be used to signify a weak or slim possibility or polite suggestion.

Examples:

You might find him in his office, but I doubt it.
You might offer to help if you want to.

2. Lie and Lay

The verb lay should always take an object. The three forms of the verb lay are: laid, lay and laid.

The verb lie (recline) should not take any object. The three forms of the verb lie are: lay, lie and lain.

Examples:

Lay on the bed.
The tables were laid by the students.
Let the little kid lie.
The patient lay on the table.

The dog has lain there for 30 minutes.

Note: The verb lie can also mean "to tell a falsehood." This verb can appear in three forms: lied, lie, and lied. This is different from the verb lie (recline) mentioned above.

Examples:

The accused is fond of telling lies.
Did she lie?

3. Would and should

The past tense of shall is 'should', and so "should" generally follows the same principles as "shall."
The past tense of will is "would," and so "would" generally follows the same

principles as "will."

The two verbs 'would and should' can be correctly used interchangeably to signify obligation. The two verbs also have some unique uses too. Should is used in three persons to signify obligation.

Examples:

I should go after work.
People should exercise everyday.
You should be generous.

"Would" is specially used in any of the three persons, to signify willingness, determination and habitual action.

Examples:

They would go for a test run every Saturday.
They would not ignore their duties.
She would try to be punctual.

4. Principle and Auxiliary Verbs

Two principal verbs can be used along with one auxiliary verb as long as the auxiliary verb form suits the two principal verbs.
Examples:

Several people have been employed and some promoted.

A new tree has been planted and the old has been cut down.
Again note the difference in the verb form.

5. Can and Could

A. Can is used to express capacity or ability.

Examples:

I can complete the assignment today
He can meet his target.
B. Can is also used to express permission.

Examples:

Yes, you can begin

In the sentence below, "can" was used to mean the same thing as "may."

However, the difference is that the word "can" is used for negative or interrogative sentences, while "may" is used in affirmative sentences to express possibility.

Examples:

They may be correct.   Positive sentence - use may.
Can this statement be correct? A question using "can."
It cannot be correct. Negative sentence using "can."

The past tense of can is could. It can serve as a principal verb when it is used to express its own meaning.
Examples:

Despite the difficulty of the test, he could still perform well.
"Could" here is used to express ability.

6. Ought

The verb ought should normally be followed by the word to.

Examples:

I *ought to* close shop now.

The verb 'ought' expresses:
A. Desirability

You ought to wash your hands before eating.   It is desirable to wash your hands.

B. Probability

She ought to be on her way back by now.   She is probably on her way.

C. Moral obligation or duty

The government ought to protect the oppressed.   It is the government's duty to protect the oppressed.

7. Raise and Rise

Rise
The verb rise means to go up, or to ascend.
The verb rise can appear in three forms, rose, rise, and risen. The verb should not take an object.

Examples:

The bird rose very slowly.
The trees rise above the house.
My aunt has risen in her career.

Raise

The verb raise means to increase, to lift up.
The verb raise can appear in three forms, raised, raise and raised.

Examples:

He raised his hand.
The workers requested a raise.
Do not raise that subject.

8. Past Tense and Past Participle

Pay attention to the proper use of these verbs: sing, show, ring, awake, fly, flow, begin, hang and sink.

Mistakes usually occur when using the past participle and past tense of these verbs as they are often mixed up.

Each of these verbs can appear in three forms:

Sing, Sang, Sung.
Show, Showed, Showed/Shown.
Ring, Rang, Rung.
Awake, awoke, awaken
Fly, Flew, Flown.
Flow, Flowed, Flowed.
Begin, Began, Begun.
Hang, Hanged, Hanged (a criminal)
Hang, Hung, Hung (a picture)
Sink, Sank, Sunk.

Examples:

The stranger rang the door bell. (simple past tense)
I have rung the door bell already. (past participle - an action completed in the past)

The stone sank in the river. (simple past tense)
The stone had already sunk. (past participle - an action completed in the past)

The meeting began at 4:00.
The meeting has begun.

9. Shall and Will

When speaking informally, the two can be used interchangeably. In formal writing, they must be used correctly.

"Will" is used in the second or third person, while "shall" is used in the first person. Both verbs are used to express a time or even in the future.

Examples:

I shall, We shall (First Person)
You will (Second Person)
They will (Third Person)

This principle however reverses when the verbs are to be used to express threats, determination, command, willingness, promise or compulsion. In these instances, will is now used in first person and shall in the second and third person.

Examples:

I will be there next week, no matter what.
This is a promise, so the first person "I" takes "will."

You shall ensure that the work is completed.
This is a command, so the second person "you" takes "shall."

I will try to make payments as promised.
This is a promise, so the first person "I" takes "will."

They shall have arrived by the end of the day.
This is a determination, so the third person "they" takes shall.

Note
A. The two verbs, shall and will should not occur twice in the same sentence when the same future is being referred to

Example:

I shall arrive early if my driver is here on time.

B. Will should not be used in the first person when questions are being asked

Examples:

Shall I go ?
Shall we go?

Subject Verb Agreement

Verbs in any sentence must agree with the subject of the sentence in person and number. Problems usually occur when the verb doesn't correspond with the right subject or the verb fails to match the noun close to it.

Unfortunately, there is no easy way around these principals - no tricky strategy or easy rule.   You just have to memorize them.

Here is a quick review:

The verb to be, present (past)

Person	Singular	Plural
First	I am (was)	we are (were)
Second	you are (were)	you are (were)
Third	he, she, it is (was)	they are (were)

The verb to have, present (past)

Person	Singular	Plural
First	I have (had)	we have (had)
Second	you have (had)	you have (had)
Third	he, she, it has (had)	they have (had)

Regular verbs, e.g. to walk, present (past)

Person	Singular	Plural
First	I walk (walked)	we walk (walked)
Second	you walk (walked)	you walk (walked)
Third	he, she, it walks (walked)	they work (walked)

1. Every and Each

When nouns are qualified by "every" or "each," they take a singular verb even if they are joined by 'and'

Examples:

Each mother and daughter *was* a given separate test.
Every teacher and student *was* properly welcomed.

2. Plural Nouns

Nouns like measles, tongs, trousers, riches, scissors etc. are all plural.
Examples:

The trousers *are* dirty.
My scissors *have* gone missing.
The tongs *are* on the table.

3. With and As Well

Two subjects linked by "with" or "as well" should have a verb that matches the first subject.

Examples:

The pencil, with the papers and equipment, *is* on the desk.
David as well as Louis is coming.

4. Plural Nouns

The following nouns take a singular verb:

politics, mathematics, innings, news, advice, summons, furniture, information, poetry, machinery, vacation, scenery

Examples:

The machinery *is* difficult to assemble
The furniture *has* been delivered
The scenery *was* beautiful

5. Single Entities

A proper noun in plural form that refers to a single entity requires a singular verb. This is a complicated way of saying; some things appear to be plural, but are really singular, or some nouns refer to a collection of things but the collection is really singular.

Examples:

The United Nations Organization *is* the decision maker in the matter.

Here the "United Nations Organization" is really only one "thing" or noun, but is made up of many "nations."

The book, "The Seven Virgins" *was* not available in the library.

Here there is only one book, although the title of the book is plural.

6. Specific Amounts are always singular

A plural noun that refers to a specific amount or quantity that is considered as a whole (dozen, hundred, score etc) requires a singular verb.

Examples:

60 minutes *is* quite a long time.
Here "60 minutes" is considered a whole, and therefore one item (singular noun).

The first million is the most difficult.

7. Either, Neither and Each are always singular

The verb is always singular when used with: either, each, neither, every one and many.

Examples:

Either of the boys *is* lying.
Each of the employees *has* been well compensated
Many a police officer *has* been found to be courageous
Every one of the teachers *is* responsible

8. Linking with Either, Or, and Neither match the second subject

Two subjects linked by "either," "or,""nor" or "neither" should have a verb that matches the second subject.

Examples:

Neither David nor Paul *will* be coming.
Either Mary or Tina *is* paying.
Note
If one of the subjects linked by "either," "or,""nor" or "neither" is in plural form, then the verb should also be in plural, and the verb should be close to the plural subject.

Examples:
Neither the mother *nor* her kids *have* eaten.
Either Mary *or* her *friends are* paying.

9. Collective Nouns are Plural

Some collective nouns such as poultry, gentry, cattle, vermin etc. are considered plural and require a plural verb.

Examples:

The *poultry are* sick.
The *cattle are* well fed.

Note
Collective nouns involving people can work with both plural and singular verbs.

Examples:

Nigerians are known to be hard working
Europeans live in Africa

10. Nouns that are Singular and Plural

Nouns like deer, sheep, swine, salmon etc. can be singular or plural and require the same verb form.

Examples:

The swine is feeding. (singular)
The swine are feeding. (plural)

The salmon is on the table. (singular)
The salmon are running upstream. (plural)

11. Collective Nouns are Singular

Collective nouns such as Army, Jury, Assembly, Committee, Team etc should carry a singular verb when they subscribe to one idea. If the ideas or views are more than one, then the verb used should be plural.

Examples:

The committee is in agreement in their decision.

The committee were in disagreement in their decision.
The jury has agreed on a verdict.
The jury were unable to agree on a verdict.

12. Subjects links by "and" are plural.

Two subjects linked by "and" always require a plural verb

Examples:

David and John are students.

Note
If the subjects linked by "and" are used as one phrase, or constitute one idea, then the verb must be singular

The color of his socks and shoe is black.
Here "socks and shoe" are two nouns, however the subject is "color" which is singular.

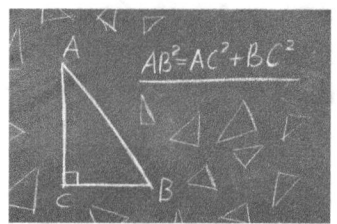

Mathematics

THIS CHAPTER CONTAINS A SELF-ASSESSMENT AND MATH TUTORIALS. The tutorials are designed to familiarize general principles and the self-assessment contains general questions similar to the mathematics questions likely to be on the TACHS exam, but are not intended to be identical to the exam questions. The tutorials are not designed to be a complete math course, and it is assumed that students have some familiarity with math. If you do not understand parts of the tutorial, or find the tutorials difficult, it is recommended that you seek out additional instruction.

Tour of the TACHS Mathematics Content

The TACHS mathematics section has 50 questions. Below is a detailed list of the mathematics topics likely to appear on the TACHS. Make sure that you understand these topics at the very minimum.

- Convert decimals, percent and fractions

- Basic arithmetic functions

- Probability and statistics

- Operations using fractions, percent and fractions

- Geometry

- Algebra

- Exponents

- Estimation

The questions in the self-assessment are not the same as you will find on the TACHS - that would be too easy! And nobody knows what the questions will be and they change all the time. Mostly, the changes consist of substituting new questions for old, but the changes also can be new question formats or styles, changes to the number of questions in each section, changes to the time limits for each section, and combining sections. So, while the format and exact wording of the questions may differ slightly, and changes from year to year, if you can answer the questions below, you will have no problem with the mathematics section of the TACHS.

Mathematics Self-Assessment

The purpose of the self-assessment is:

- Identify your strengths and weaknesses.
- Develop your personalized study plan (above)
- Get accustomed to the TACHS format
- Extra practice – the self-assessments are almost a full 3rd practice test!
- Provide a baseline score for preparing your study schedule.

Since this is a Self-assessment, and depending on how confident you are with Mathematics, timing yourself is optional. The TACHS has 50 questions, to be answered in 75 minutes. This self-assessment has 45 questions, so allow about 70 minutes to complete.

Once complete, use the table below to assess your understanding of the content, and prepare your study schedule described in chapter 1.

80% - 100%	Excellent – you have mastered the content
60 – 79%	Good. You have a working knowledge. Even though you can just pass this section, you may want to review the tutorials and do some extra practice to see if you can improve your mark.
40% - 59%	Below Average. You do not understand the content. Review the tutorials, and retake this quiz again in a few days, before proceeding to the practice test questions.
Less than 40%	Poor. You have a very limited understanding. Please review the tutorials, and retake this quiz again in a few days, before proceeding to the practice test questions.

Math Self-Assessment Answer Sheet

1. A B C D
2. A B C D
3. A B C D
4. A B C D
5. A B C D
6. A B C D
7. A B C D
8. A B C D
9. A B C D
10. A B C D
11. A B C D
12. A B C D
13. A B C D
14. A B C D
15. A B C D
16. A B C D
17. A B C D

18. A B C D
19. A B C D
20. A B C D
21. A B C D
22. A B C D
23. A B C D
24. A B C D
25. A B C D
26. A B C D
27. A B C D
28. A B C D
29. A B C D
30. A B C D
31. A B C D
32. A B C D
33. A B C D
34. A B C D

35. A B C D
36. A B C D
37. A B C D
38. A B C D
39. A B C D
40. A B C D
41. A B C D
42. A B C D
43. A B C D
44. A B C D
45. A B C D

Math Self-Assessment

1. A boy has 5 red balls, 3 white balls and 2 yellow balls. What percent of the balls are yellow?

    a. 2%
    b. 8%
    c. 20%
    d. 12%

2. The length a rectangle is twice its width and its area is equal to the area of a square of side 12 cm. What will be the perimeter of the rectangle near to the nearest whole number?

    a. 36 cm
    b. 46 cm
    c. 51 cm
    d. 56 cm

3. There are 15 yellow and 35 orange balls in a basket. How many more yellow balls must be added to make yellow balls 65%?

    a. 35
    b. 50
    c. 65
    d. 70

4. At the beginning of 2009, Marilyn invested $5,000 in a savings account. The account pays 4% interest per year. At the end of the year, after the interest was paid, how much did Marilyn have in the account?

    a. $5,200
    b. $5,020
    c. $5,110
    d. $7,000

5. The average weight of 13 students in a class of 15 (two were absent that day) is 42 kg. When the remaining 2 were weighed, the average became 42.7 kg. If one of the remaining students weighs 48, how much does the other weigh?

    a. 44.7 kg.
    b. 45.6 kg.
    c. 46.5 kg.
    d. 47.4 kg.

6. The total expense of building a fence around a square field is $2000 at a rate of $5 per meter. What is the length of one side?

    a. 40 meters
    b. 80 meters
    c. 100 meters
    d. 320 meters

7. Convert 23.67 to percent.

    a. 2.367%
    b 236.7%
    c. 23.67%
    d. 2367%

8. If 144 students need to go on a trip and the buses carry 36 students each, how many buses do they need?

    a. 6
    b. 5
    c. 4
    d. 3

9. A mother is making spaghetti for her son. The recipe calls for 500 grams of spaghetti, and 0.75 grams of salt. However, the mom just wants 125 grams of spaghetti. How much salt should she use?

   a. 0.38 grams
   b. 0.75 grams
   c. 0.19 grams
   d. 0.25 grams

10. A young student deposits $200 in a savings account hoping to buy a bicycle worth $245. If the bank offers a 15% interest rate, how long will the boy have to wait?

   a. 1½ years
   b. 2 ½ years
   c. 2 years
   d. 1 year

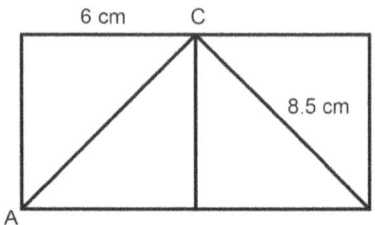

Note: figure not drawn to scale

11. Assuming the quadrangles are identical rectangles, what is the perimeter of △ABC in the above shape?

   a. 25.5 cm
   b. 27 cm
   c. 30 cm
   d. 29 cm

12. A pet store had total sales of $19,304.56 for the month of June. If the wholesale cost was $5,284.34, the employees were paid $8,384.76, and the rent was $2,920.00, how much profit did the store make in June?

   a. $5,635.46
   b. $2,714.47
   c. $14,020.22
   d. $10,019.80

13. Tony bought 15 dozen eggs for $80. 16 eggs were broken during loading and unloading. He sold the remainder for $0.54 each. What will be his percent profit? Provide answer in 2 significant digits.

   a. 11%
   b. 11.2%
   c. 11.5%
   d. 12%

14. The sale price of a car is $12,590, which is 20% off the original price. What is the original price?

   a. $14,310.40
   b. $14,990.90
   c. $15,108.00
   d. $15,737.50

15. Estimate 16 x 230.

   a. 31,000
   b. 301,000
   c. 3,100
   d. 3,000,000

16. In a small village there are 9 families with 3 children, 8 families with 2 children, and 4 families having 5 children. What is the average number of children in a family?

   a. 2.5
   b. 2.8
   c. 3
   d. 3.5

17. A goat eats 214 kg. of hay in 60 days, while a cow eats the same amount in 15 days. How long will it take to eat this hay together?

   a. 37.5
   b. 75
   c. 12
   d. 15

18. Sarah weighs 25 pounds more than Tony. If together they weigh 205 pounds, how much does Sarah weigh approximately in kilograms? Assume 1 pound = 0.4535 kilograms

   a. 41
   b. 48
   c. 50
   d. 52

19. Ann went from point A to point B. At the same time, Peter went from point B to point A. In 6 hours, they met, and in 3 more hours, Peter reached B. How many hours did it take Ann to travel from A to B?

   a. 18
   b. 9
   c. 15
   d. 12

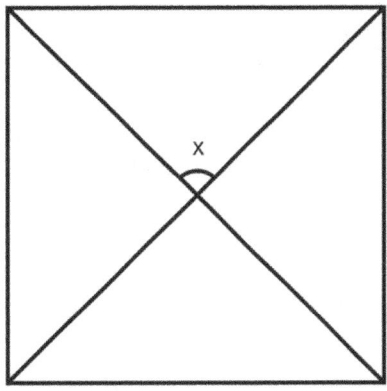

20. What is measurement of the indicated angle?

   a. 45°
   b. 90°
   c. 60°
   d. 30°

21. Mr. White wants to tile his rectangular backyard, which is 16 m × 11 m. The dimensions of each tile are 7 cm × 4 cm. If cost of each tile is $0.30 and 2.5% tiles break during handling, then what will be the total cost?

   a. $19234
   b. $20240
   c. $20895
   d. $21563

22. Translate the following into an equation: six times a number plus five.

   a. 6X + 5
   b. 6(X+5)
   c. 5X + 6
   d. (6 * 5) + 5

23. In the Euro cup football game, England won gold, Spain won silver and Holland won bronze medals. The three winners share the total prize money of $605,500 in the ratio of 4:2:1. How much money did Spain win?

  a. $86,500
  b. $173,000
  c. $201,830
  d. $346,000

24. Solve for b. 7 − 8b = 11 − 10b.

  a. 2
  b. 3
  c. 5
  d. 6

25. A building is 15 m long and 20 m wide and 10 m high. What is the volume of the building?

  a. 45 m³
  b. 3,000 m³
  c. 1500 m³
  d. 300 m³

26. Solve 3/4 + 2/4 + 1.2

  a. 1 1/7
  b. 2 3/4
  c. 2 9/20
  d. 3 1/4

27. 3 boys are asked to clean a surface that is 4 ft². If the portion is divided equally among the boys, what size will each of them clean?

  a. 1 ft 6 inches
  b. 14 inches
  c. 1 ft 2 inches
  d. 1 ft² 48 in²

28. Great Britain has a Value Added Tax of 15%. A shop sells a camera for $545. If the VAT is included in the price, what is the actual cost of the camera?

  a. $490.40
  b. $473.91
  c. $505.00
  d. $503.15

29. Simplify 0.12 + 1 2/5 − 1 3/5

  a. 1 1/25
  b. -2/25
  c. 1 2/5
  d. 2 3/5

30. A rectangular box measures 10 cm long and 8 cm wide and 10 cm high. What is the volume of the box?

  a. 28 cm³
  b. 2000 cm³
  c. 400 cm³
  d. 800 cm³

Mathematics

31. 5 men have to share a load weighing 10 kg 550 g equally among themselves. How much weight will each man have to carry?

   a. 900 g
   b. 1.5 kg
   c. 3 kg
   d. 2 kg 110 g

32. A worker's weekly salary was increased by 30%. If his new salary is $150, what was his old salary?

   a. $120.00
   b. $99.15
   c. $109.00
   d. $115.38

33. Estimate 46,227 + 101,032.

   a. 14,700
   b. 147,000
   c. 14,700,000
   d. 104,700

34. 2/15 ÷ 4/5 =

   a. 6/65
   b. 6/75
   c. 5/12
   d. 1/6

35. If Tim deposits $5,500 in a savings account that offers a 5% interest, what will be the total amount in his savings account after 3 years?

   a. $6,225
   b. $6,0325
   c. $325
   d. $6,325

36. The price of a product was increased by 45%. If the initial cost was $220, what is the new cost?

   a. $230
   b. $300
   c. $319
   d. $245

37. A map uses a scale of 1:2,000 How much distance on the ground is 5.2 inches on the map if the scale is in inches?

   a. 100,400
   b. 10, 500
   c. 10,400
   d. 10,400

38. Find 2 numbers that sum to 21 and the sum of the squares is 261.

   a. 14 and 7
   b. 15 and 6
   c. 16 and 5
   d. 17 and 4

39. Susan wants to buy a leather jacket that costs $545.00 and is on sale for 10% off. What is the approximate cost?

    a. $525
    b. $450
    c. $475
    d. $500

40. Translate the following into an equation: Five greater than 3 times a number.

    a. $3X + 5$
    b. $5X + 3$
    c. $(5 + 3)X$
    d. $5(3 + X)$

41. Richard gives 's' amount of salary to each of his 'n' employees weekly. If he has 'x' amount of money then how many days he can employ these 'n' employees.

    a. $sx/7n$
    b. $7x/nx$
    c. $nx/7s$
    d. $7x/ns$

42. A square box measures 20 cm long and 20 cm wide and 20 cm high. What is the volume of the box?

    a. 60 cm³
    b. 20,000 cm³
    c. 4,000 cm³
    d. 8,000 cm³

43. The owner of a pet store decided to increase the cost of all reptiles 45%. If the initial cost of a reptile was $200, what is the new cost?

    a. $230
    b. $300
    c. $290
    d. $245

44. A map uses a scale of 1:100,000. How much distance on the ground is 3 inches on the map if the scale is in inches?

    a. 13 inches
    b. 300,000 inches
    c. 30,000 inches
    d. 333.999 inches

45. What is 8 more than 2/5 of 20?

    a. 10
    b. 12
    c. 16
    d. 8

Answer Key

1. C
Total no. of balls = 10, number of yellow balls = 2, so, 2/10 X 100 = 20%

2. C
Area of the square = 12 × 12 = 144 cm². Let x be the width so 2x will be the length of rectangle. The area will be 2 x 2 and the perimeter will be 2(2x + x) = 6x. According to the condition 2 x 2 = 144 then x = 8.48 cm. The perimeter will be 6 × 8.48 = 50.88 = 51 cm.

3. B
There are 50 balls in the basket now. Let x be the yellow balls that are to be added to make it 65%. So the equation becomes X + 15 /X + 50 = 65/100. X = 50.

4. A
5000 X 4% = 200
5000 + 200 = $5200

5. C
Total weight of 13 students with average 42 will be = 42 * 13 = 546 kg.

The total weight of the remaining 2 will be found by subtracting the total weight of 13 students from the total weight of 15 students: 640.5 - 546 = 94.5 kg.

94.5 = the total weight of two students. One of these students weigh 48 kg, so;

The weight of the other will be = 94.5 – 48 = 46.5 kg

6. C
Total expense is $2000 and we are informed that $5 is spent per meter. Combining these two information, we know that the total length of the fence is 2000/5 = 400 meters.

The fence is built around a square-shaped field. If one side of the square is "a,' the perimeter of the square is "4a." Here, the perimeter is equal to 400 meters. So,

400 = 4a

100 = a -> this means that one side of the square is equal to 100 meters

7. D
To convert to percent, simply multiply the decimal by 100 or move the decimal point 2 places to the right. Therefore, 23.67 x 100 = 2367%

8. C
144 ÷ 36 = 4

9. C
125: 500 is the same as 25 : 100 or 1 : 4. So the amount of salt will be 0.75/4 = 0.1875, or about .19 grams.

10. A
$200 invested at 15% per year will yield $30 interest at the end of the first year. For the second year, the interest will be 34.50, so it will take about 1 1/2 years before he can buy the bike.

11. D
Perimeter of triangle ABC is asked.

Perimeter of a triangle = sum of three sides.

Here, Perimeter of ΔABC = |AC| + |CB| + |AB|.

Since the triangle is located in the middle of two adjacent and identical rectangles, we find the side lengths using these rectangles:

|AB| = 6 + 6 = 12 cm

|CB| = 8.5 cm

|AC| = |CB| = 8.5 cm

Perimeter = |AC| + |CB| + |AB| = 8.5 + 8.5 + 12 = 29 cm

12. A
19304.56 − 5284.34 − 8384.76 = 5635.46

13. A
Let us first mention the money Tony spent: $80

Now we need to find the money Tony earned:

He had 15 dozen eggs = 15 * 12 = 180 eggs. 16 eggs were broken. So,

Remaining number of eggs that Tony sold = 180 − 16 = 164.

Total amount he earned for selling 164 eggs = 164 * 0.54 = $88.56.

As a summary, he spent $80 and earned $88.56.

The profit is the difference: 88.56 - 80 = $8.56

Percentage profit is found by proportioning the profit to the money he spent:

8.56 * 100/80 = 10.7%

Checking the answers, we round 10.7 to the nearest whole number: 11%

14. D
Let the original price = x,
80/100 = 12590/X,
80X = 1259000,
X = 15737.50.

15. C
16 X 230 = 3680, or about 3100.

16. C
Let X = total number of families
Y= total number of children
Y = 9 x 3 + 8 x 2 + 4 x 5 = 63 and
X= 9 + 8 + 4 = 21
Average number of children in a family = Y/X = 63/21 = 3

17. C
Total hay = 214 kg,
The goat eats at a rate of 214/60 days = 3.6 kg per day.
The cow eats at a rate of 214/15 = 14.3 kg per day,
Together they eat 3.6 + 14.3 = 17.9 per day.
At a rate of 17.9 kg per day, they will consume 214 kg in 214/17.9 = 11.96 or 12 days approx.

18. D
Let us denote Sarah's weight by "x." Then, since she weighs 25 pounds more than Tony, Tony will be x-25. They together weigh 205 pounds which means that the sum of the two representations will be equal to 205:

Sarah : x

Tony : x - 25

x + (x - 25) = 205 ... by arranging this equation we have:

x + x - 25 = 205

2x - 25 = 205 ... we add 25 to each side to have x term alone:

2x - 25 + 25 = 205 + 25

2x = 230

x = 230/2

x = 115 pounds -> Sarah weighs 115 pounds. Since 1 pound is 0.4535 kilograms, we need to multiply 115 by 0.4535 to have her weight in kilograms:

x = 115 * 0.4535 = 52.1525 kilograms -> this is equal to 52 when rounded to the nearest whole number.

19. D
It took peter 3 hours to cover the distance Ann traveled in 6 hours (from point of meeting to point A, where Ann started). This means Peter is traveling at twice the speed of Ann. If it took peter 6 hours to reach the point of meeting, it will take Ann twice that long to get to Peter's point of origin = 6 x 2 = 12

20. A
The diagonals of a square intersect at right angles, so each angle measures 90° Half of that angle will be 45°

21. A
The area of each tile is 7 cm X 4 cm = 28 cm². The area of the yard is 16 m X 11 m = 176 m² = 1760000 cm². The number of tiles required is 1760000/28 = 62858. 2% of the tiles break during handling, so 1.02 X 62858 = 64115. Total cost will be 64115 X 0.3 = $19234.55.

22. B
Six times a number plus five is the same as saying six times (a number plus five). Or, 6 * (a number plus five). Let X be the number so, 6(X+5).

23. B
Spain won second prize so their ratio is 2/7
2/7 * 60550 = $173,000

24. A
7 – 8b = 11 – 10b. Bring same terms to same side of the equation by changing the negative or positive signs when they cross over, therefore -8b + 10b = 11 – 7, 2b = 4, b = 4/2 = 2

25. B
Formula for volume of a shape is L x W x H = 15 x 20 x 10 = 3,000 m³

26. C
3/4 + 2/4 + 1.2, first convert the decimal to fraction, = 3/4 + 2/4 + 1 1/5 = ¾ + 2/4 + 6/5 = (find common denominator) (15 + 10 + 24)/20 = 49/20 = 2 9/20

27. D
1 foot is equal to 12 inches. So 1 ft² = 12 * 12 in²
4 ft² = 4 * 12 * 12 in² = 576 in²

The total surface area is divided equally among 3 boys.

Each boy will clean 576/3 = 192 in²

192 in² = 144 in² + 48 in²; 144 in² = 1 ft²

So, each boy will clean 1 ft² and 48 in²

28. B
Actual cost = X, therefore, 545 = x + 0.15x, 545 = 1x + 0.15x, 545 = 1.15x, x = 545/1.15 = 473.91

29. B
0.12 + 2/5 + 3a/5, Convert decimal to fraction to get 3/25 + 2/5 + 3/5, = (3 + 10 + 15)/25, = 28/25 = 1 3/25

30. D
Formula for volume of a shape is L x W x H = 10 x 8 x 10 = 800 cm³

31. D
First convert the unit of measurements to be the same. Since 1000 g = 1 kg, 10 kg = 10 x 1000 = 10,000 + 550 g = 10,550 g. Divide 10,550 among 5 = 10550/5 = 2110 = 2 kg 110 g

32. D
Let old salary = X, therefore $150 = x + 0.30x, 150 = 1x + 0.30x, 150 = 1.30x, x = 150/1.30 = 115.38

33. B
46,227 + 101,032 is approximately 147,000. The actual total is 147,259.

34. D
To divide fractions, multiply the first fraction with the inverse of the second fraction. 2/15 x 5/4, (cancel out) = 1/3 x 1/2 = 1/6

35. D
P = $5,500, t = 3 years, r = 5%, I = ?
convert rate to decimal and 5% = 0.05
I = 5,500 x 0.05 x 3 = 825. Total amount in the account = principal + interest or 5,500 + 825 = $6,325

36. C
Initial cost was $220. new cost = 220 + 45% of 220, 45/100 x 220 = 99, therefore new price is 220 + 99 = $319.

37. C
1 inch on map = 2,000 inches on ground. So, 5.2 inches on map = 5.2 * 2,000 = 10,400 inches on ground.

38. B
The numbers are 15 and 6.
$x + 7 = 21 \Rightarrow x = 21 - 7$
$x^2 + y^2 = 261$

$(21 - 7)^2 + y^2 = 261$
$441 - 42y + y^2 + y^2 = 261$
$2y^2 - 42y + 180 = 0$
$y^2 - 21y + 90 = 0$
$y_{1,2} = 21 \pm \sqrt{441 - 360}/2$
$y_{1,2} = 21 \pm \sqrt{81}/2$
$y_{1,2} = 21 \pm 9/2$
$y_1 = 15$
$y_2 = 6$
$x_1 = 21 - y_1 = 21 - 15 = 6$
$x_2 = 21 - y_2 = 21 - 6 = 15$

39. D
The jacket costs $545.00 so we can round up to $550. 10% of $550 is 55. We can round down to $50, which is easier to work with.

$550 - $50 is $500. The jacket will cost about $500.

The actual cost will be 10% X 545 = $54.50

545 – 54.50 = $490.50

40. A
Five greater than 3 times a number.
5 + 3 times a number.
3X + 5

41. D
We understand that each of the n employees earn s amount of salary weekly. This means that one employee earns s salary weekly. So; Richard has ns amount of money to employ n employees for a week.

We are asked to find the number of days n employees can be employed with x amount of money. We can do simple direct proportion:

If Richard can employ n employees for 7 days with ns amount of money,

Richard can employ n employees for y days with x amount of money ... y is the number of days we need to find.

We can do cross multiplication:

y = (x * 7)/(ns)

y = 7x/ns

42. D
Formula for volume of a shape is L x W x H = 20 x 20 x 20 = 8,000 cm³

43. C. Initial cost was $200. New cost = 200 + 45% of 200, 45% of 200, 45/100 x 200 = 90, therefore new price is 200 + 90 = $290

44. B
1 inch on map = 100,000 inches on ground. So 3 inches on map = 3 x 100,000 = 300,000 inches on ground

45. C
2/5 of 20 = 8 + 8 = 16

How to Solve Word Problems

Most students find math word problems difficult. Solving word problems is much easier if you have a systematic approach which we outline below.

Here is the biggest tip for studying word problems.

Practice regularly and systematically. Sounds simple and easy right? Yes it is, and yes it really does work.

Word problems are a way of thinking and require you to translate a real world problem into mathematical terms.

Some math instructors go so far as to say that learning how to think mathematically is the main reason for teaching word problems.

So what do we mean by practice regularly and systematically? Studying word problems and math in general requires a logical and mathematical frame of mind. The only way you can get this is by practicing regularly, which means everyday.

It is critical that you practice word problems everyday for the 5 days before the exam as a bare minimum.

If you practice and miss a day, you have lost the mathematical frame of mind and the benefit of your previous practice is pretty much gone. Anyone who has done math will agree – you have to practice everyday.

Everything is important. The other critical point about word problems is that all the information given in the problem has some purpose. There is no unnecessary information! Word problems are typically around 50 words in 1 to 3 sentences. If the sometimes complicated relationships are to be explained in that short an explanation, every word has to count. Make sure that you use every piece of information.

Here are 9 simple steps to solving word problems.

Step 1 – Read through the problem at least three times. The first reading should be a quick scan, and the next two readings should be done slowly to find answers to these questions:

What does the problem ask? (Usually located towards the end of the problem)

What does the problem imply? (This is usually a point you were asked to remember).

Mark all information, and underline all important words or phrases.

Step 2 – Try to make a pictorial representation of the problem such as a circle and an arrow to indicate travel. This makes the problem a bit more real and sensible to you.

A favorite word problem is something like, 1 train leaves Station A traveling at

100 km/hr and another train leaves Station B traveling at 60 km/hr. ...

Draw a line, the two stations, and the two trains at either end. This will clarify the problem.

Step 3 – Use the information you have to make a table with a blank portion to indicate information you do not know.

Step 4 – Assign a single letter to represent each unknown data in your table. You can write down the unknown that each letter represents so that you do not make the error of assigning answers to the wrong unknown, because a word problem may have multiple unknowns and you will need to create equations for each unknown.

Step 5 – Translate the English terms in the word problem into a mathematical algebraic equation. Remember that the main problem with word problems is that they are not expressed in regular math equations. You ability to correctly identify the variables and translate the word problem into an equation determines your ability to solve the problem.

Step 6 – Check the equation to see if it looks like regular equations that you are used to seeing and whether it looks sensible. Does the equation appear to represent the information in the question? Take note that you may need to re-write some formulas needed to solve the word problem equation. For example, word distance problems may need you rewriting the distance formula, which is Distance = Time x Rate. If the word problem requires that you solve for time you will need to use Distance/Rate and Distance/Time to solve for Rate. If you understand the distance word problem you should be able to identify the variable you need to solve for.

Step 7 – Use algebra rules to solve the derived equation. Take note that the laws of equation demands that what is done on this side of the equation has to also be done on the other side. You have to solve the equation so that the unknown ends up alone on one side. Where there are multiple unknowns you will need to use elimination or substitution methods to resolve all the equations.

Step 8 – Check your final answers to see if they make sense with the information given in the problem. For example if the word problem involves a discount, the final price should be less or if a product was taxed then the final answer has to cost more.

Step 9 – Cross check your answers by placing the answer or answers in the first equation to replace the unknown or unknowns. If your answer is correct then both side of the equation must equate or equal. If your answer is not correct then you may have derived a wrong equation or solved the equation wrongly. Repeat the necessary steps to correct.

Types of Word Problems

Word problems can be classified into 12 types. Below are examples of each type with a complete solution. Some types of word problems can be solved quickly using multiple choice strategies and some cannot. Always look for ways to estimate the answer and then eliminate choices.

1. Age

A girl is 10 years older than her brother. By next year, she will be twice the age of her brother. What are their ages now?

    a. 25, 15
    b. 19, 9
    c. 21, 11
    d. 29, 19

Solution: B

We will assume that the girl's age is "a" and her brother's is "b." This means that based on the information in the first sentence,
$a = 10 + b$

Next year, she will be twice her brother's age, which gives
$a + 1 = 2(b + 1)$

We need to solve for one unknown factor and then use the answer to solve for the other. To do this we substitute the value of "a" from the first equation into the second equation. This gives

$10 + b + 1 = 2b + 2$
$11 + b = 2b + 2$
$11 - 2 = 2b - b$
$b = 9$

$9 = b$ this means that her brother is 9 years old. Solving for the girl's age in the first equation gives $a = 10 + 9$. $a = 19$ the girl is aged 19. So, the girl is aged 19 and the boy is 9

2. Distance or speed

Two boats travel down a river towards the same destination, starting at the same time. One of the boats is traveling at 52 km/hr, and the other boat at 43 km/hr. How far apart will they be after 40 minutes?

    a. 46.67 km
    b. 19.23 km
    c. 6.4 km
    d. 14.39 km

Solution: C

After 40 minutes, the first boat will have traveled = 52 km/hr x 40 minutes/60 minutes = 34.7 km
After 40 minutes, the second boat will have traveled = 43 km/hr x 40/60 minutes = 28.66 km
Difference between the two boats will be 34.7 km – 28.66 km = 6.04 km.

Multiple Choice Strategy

First estimate the answer. The first boat is traveling 9 km. faster than the second, for 40 minutes, which is 2/3 of an hour. 2/3 of 9 = 6, as a rough guess of the distance apart.

Choices A, B and D can be eliminated right away.

3. Ratio

The instructions in a cookbook states that 700 grams of flour must be mixed in 100 ml of water, and 0.90 grams of salt added. A cook however has just 325 grams of flour. What is the quantity of water and salt that he should use?

- a. 0.41 grams and 46.4 ml
- b. 0.45 grams and 49.3 ml
- c. 0.39 grams and 39.8 ml
- d. 0.25 grams and 40.1 ml

Solution: A

The Cookbook states 700 grams of flour, but the cook only has 325. The first step is to determine the percentage of flour he has 325/700 x 100 = 46.4%
That means that 46.4% of all other items must also be used.
46.4% of 100 = 46.4 ml of water
46.4% of 0.90 = 0.41 grams of salt.

Multiple Choice Strategy

The recipe calls for 700 grams of flour but the cook only has 325, which is just less than half, the amount of water and salt are going to be approximately half.

Choices C and D can be eliminated right away. Choice B is very close so be careful. Looking closely at Choice B, it is exactly half, and since 325 is slightly less than half of 700, it can't be correct.

Choice A is correct.

4. Percent

An agent received $6,685 as his commission for selling a property. If his commission was 13% of the selling price, how much was the property?

    a. $68,825

    b. $121,850

    c. $49,025

    d. $51,423

Solution: D

Let's assume that the property price is x
That means from the information given, 13% of x = 6,685
Solve for x,
x = 6685 x 100/13 = $51,423

Multiple Choice Strategy

The commission, 13%, is just over 10%, which is easier to work with. Round up $6685 to $6700, and multiple by 10 for an approximate answer. 10 X 6700 = $67,000. You can do this in your head. Choice B is much too big and can be eliminated. Choice C is too small and can be eliminated. Choices A and D are left and good possibilities.

Do the calculations to make the final choice.

5. Sales & Profit

A store owner buys merchandise for $21,045. He transports them for $3,905 and pays his staff $1,450 to stock the merchandise on his shelves. If he does not incur further costs, how much does he need to sell the items to make $5,000 profit?

    a. $32,500

    b. $29,350

    c. $32,400

    d. $31,400

Solution: D

Total cost of the items is $21,045 + $3,905 + $1,450 = $26,400
Total cost is now $26,400 + $5000 profit = $31,400

Multiple Choice Strategy

Round off and add the numbers up in your head quickly.
21,000 + 4,000 + 1500 = 26500. Add in 5000 profit for a total of 31500.

Choice B is too small and can be eliminated. Choices C and A are too large and can be eliminated.

6. Tax/Income

A woman earns $42,000 per month and pays 5% tax on her monthly income. If the Government increases her monthly taxes by $1,500, what is her income after tax?

    a. $38,400
    b. $36,050
    c. $40,500
    d. $39, 500

Solution: A

Initial tax on income was 5/100 x 42,000 = $2,100
$1,500 was added to the tax to give $2,100 + 1,500 = $3,600
Income after tax left is $42,000 - $3,600 = $38,400

7. Interest

A man invests $3000 in a 2-year term deposit that pays 3% interest per year. How much will he have at the end of the 2-year term?

    a. $5,200
    b. $3,020
    c. $3,182.7
    d. $3,000

Solution: C

This is a compound interest problem. The funds are invested for 2 years and interest is paid yearly, so in the second year, he will earn interest on the interest paid in the first year.

3% interest in the first year = 3/100 x 3,000 = $90
At end of first year, total amount = 3,000 + 90 = $3,090
Second year = 3/100 x 3,090 = 92.7.
At end of second year, total amount = $3090 + $92.7 = $3,182.7

8. Averaging

The average weight of 10 books is 54 grams. 2 more books were added and the average weight became 55.4. If one of the 2 new books added weighed 62.8 g, what is the weight of the other?

    a. 44.7 g b. 67.4 g
    c. 62 g
    d. 52 g

Solution: C

Total weight of 10 books with average 54 grams will be = 10 × 54 = 540 g
Total weight of 12 books with average 55.4 will be = 55.4 × 12 = 664.8 g
So total weight of the remaining 2 will be= 664.8 − 540 = 124.8 g
If one weighs 62.8, the weight of the other will be= 124.8 g − 62.8 g = 62 g

Multiple Choice Strategy

Averaging problems can be estimated by looking at which direction the average goes. If additional items are added and the average goes up, the new items much be greater than the average. If the average goes down after new items are added, the new items must be less than the average.

In this case, the average is 54 grams and 2 books are added which increases the average to 55.4, so the new books must weight more than 54 grams.

Choices A and D can be eliminated right away.

9. Probability

A bag contains 15 marbles of various colors. If 3 marbles are white, 5 are red and the rest are black, what is the probability of randomly picking out a black marble from the bag?

    a. 7/15
    b. 3/15
    c. 1/5
    d. 4/15

Solution: A

Total marbles = 15
Number of black marbles = 15 − (3 + 5) = 7
Probability of picking out a black marble = 7/15

10. Two Variables

A company paid a total of $2850 to book for 6 single rooms and 4 double rooms in a hotel for one night. Another company paid $3185 to book for 13 single rooms for one night in the same hotel. What is the cost for single and double rooms in that hotel?

    a. single= $250 and double = $345
    b. single= $254 and double = $350
    c. single = $245 and double = $305
    d. single = $245 and double = $345

Solution: D

We can determine the price of single rooms from the information given of the second company. 13 single rooms = 3185.

One single room = 3185 / 13 = 245
The first company paid for 6 single rooms at $245. 245 x 6 = $1470
Total amount paid for 4 double rooms by first company = $2850 - $1470 = $1380
Cost per double room = 1380 / 4 = $345

11. Geometry

The length of a rectangle is 5 in. more than its width. The perimeter of the rectangle is 26 in. What is the width and length of the rectangle?

- a. width = 6 inches, Length = 9 inches
- b. width = 4 inches, Length = 9 inches
- c. width =4 inches, Length = 5 inches
- d. width = 6 inches, Length = 11 inches

Solution: B

Formula for perimeter of a rectangle is 2(L + W)
p=26, so 2(L+W) = p
The length is 5 inches more than the width, so
2(w+5) + 2w = 26
2w + 10 + 2w = 26
2w + 2w = 26 - 10
4w = 16

W = 16/4 = 4 inches

L is 5 inches more than w, so L = 5 + 4 = 9 inches.

12. Totals and fractions

A basket contains 125 oranges, mangos and apples. If 3/5 of the fruits in the basket are mangos and only 2/5 of the mangos are ripe, how many ripe mangos are there in the basket?

- a. 30
- b. 68
- c. 55
- d. 47

Solution: A
Number of mangos in the basket is 3/5 x 125 = 75
Number of ripe mangos = 2/5 x 75 = 30

Fraction Tips, Tricks and Shortcuts

When you are writing an exam, time is precious, and anything you can do to answer questions faster, is a real advantage. Here are some ideas, shortcuts, tips and tricks that can speed up answering fraction problems.

Remember that a fraction is just a number which names a portion of something. For instance, instead of having a whole pie, a fraction says you have a part of a pie--such as a half of one or a fourth of one.

Two digits make up a fraction. The digit on top is known as the numerator. The digit on the bottom is known as the denominator. To remember which is which, just remember that "denominator" and "down" both start with a "d." And the "downstairs" number is the denominator. So for instance, in ½, the numerator is the 1 and the denominator (or "downstairs") number is the 2.

- It's easy to add two fractions if they have the same denominator. Just add the digits on top and leave the bottom one the same: 1/10 + 6/10 = 7/10.

- It's the same with subtracting fractions with the same denominator: 7/10 - 6/10 = 1/10.

- Adding and subtracting fractions with different denominators is a little more complicated. First, you have to get the problem so that they do have the same denominators. One of the easiest ways to do this is to multiply the denominators: For 2/5 + 1/2 multiply 5 by 2. Now you have a denominator of 10. But now you have to change the top numbers too. Since you multiplied the 5 in 2/5 by 2, you also multiply the 2 by 2, to get 4. So the first number is now 4/10. Since you multiplied the second number times 5, you also multiply its top number by 5, to get a final fraction of 5/10. Now you can add 5 and 4 together to get a final sum of 9/10.

- Sometimes you'll be asked to reduce a fraction to its simplest form. This means getting it to where the only common factor of the numerator and denominator is 1. Think of it this way: Numerators and denominators are brothers that must be treated the same. If you do something to one, you must do it to the other, or it's just not fair. For instance, if you divide your numerator by 2, then you should also divide the denominator by the same. Let's take an example: The fraction 2/10. This is not reduced to its simplest terms because there is a number that will divide evenly into both: the number 2. We want to make it so that the only number that will divide evenly into both is 1. What can we divide into 2 to get 1? The number 2, of course! Now to be "fair," we have to do the same thing to the denominator: Divide 2 into 10 and you get 5. So our new, reduced fraction is 1/5.

- In some ways, multiplying fractions is the easiest of all: Just multiply the two top numbers and then multiply the two bottom numbers. For instance, with this problem:

2/5 X 2/3 you multiply 2 by 2 and get a top number of 4; then multiply 5 by 3 and get a bottom number of 15. Your answer is 4/15.

- ☐ Dividing fractions is a bit more involved, but still not too hard. You once again multiply, but only AFTER you have turned the second fraction upside-down. To divide ⅞ by ½, turn the ½ into 2/1, then multiply the top numbers and multiply the bottom numbers: ⅞ X 2/1 gives us 14 on top and 8 on the bottom.

Converting Fractions to Decimals

There are a couple of ways to become good at converting fractions to decimals. One -- the one that will make you the fastest in basic math skills -- is to learn some basic fraction facts. It's a good idea, if you're good at memory, to memorize the following:

1/100 is "one hundredth," expressed as a decimal, it's .01.

1/50 is "two hundredths," expressed as a decimal, it's .02.

1/25 is "one twenty-fifths" or "four hundredths," expressed as a decimal, it's .04.

1/20 is "one twentieth" or ""five hundredths," expressed as a decimal, it's .05.

1/10 is "one tenth," expressed as a decimal, it's .1.

1/8 is "one eighth," or "one hundred twenty-five thousandths," expressed as a decimal, it's .125.

1/5 is "one fifth," or "two tenths," expressed as a decimal, it's .2.

1/4 is "one fourth" or "twenty-five hundredths," expressed as a decimal, it's .25.

1/3 is "one third" or "thirty-three hundredths," expressed as a decimal, it's .33.

1/2 is "one half" or "five tenths," expressed as a decimal, it's .5.

3/4 is "three fourths," or "seventy-five hundredths," expressed as a decimal, it's .75.

Of course, if you're no good at memorization, another good technique for converting a fraction to a decimal is to manipulate it so that the fraction's denominator is 10, 10, 1000, or some other power of 10. Here's an example: We'll start with ¾. What is the first number in the 4 "times table" that you can multiply and get a multiple of 10? Can you multiply 4 by something to get 10? No. Can you multiply it by something to get 100? Yes! 4 X 25 is 100. So let's take that 25 and multiply it by the numerator in our fraction ¾. The numerator is 3, and 3 X 25 is 75. We'll move the decimal in 75 all the way to the left, and we find that ¾ is .75.

We'll do another one: 1/5. Again, we want to find a power of 10 that 5 goes into evenly. Will 5 go into 10? Yes! It goes 2 times. So we'll take that 2 and multiply it by our numerator, 1, and we get 2. We move the decimal in 2 all the way to the left and find that 1/5 is equal to .2.

Converting Fractions to Percent

Working with either fractions or percents can be intimidating enough. But converting from one to the other? That's a genuine nightmare for those who are not math wizards. But really, it doesn't have to be that way. Here are two ways to make it easier and faster to convert a fraction to a percent.

- First, you might remember that a fraction is nothing more than a division problem: you're dividing the bottom number into the top number. So for instance, if we start with a fraction 1/10, we are making a division problem with the 10 on the outside of the bracket and the 1 on the inside. As you remember from your lessons on dividing by decimals, since 10 won't go into 1, you add a decimal and make it 10 into 1.0. 10 into 10 goes 1 time, and since it's behind the decimal, it's .1. And how do we say .1? We say "one tenth," which is exactly what we started with: 1/10. So we have a number we can work with now: .1. When we're dealing with percents, though, we're dealing strictly with hundredths (not tenths). You remember from studying decimals that adding a zero to the right of the number on the right side of the decimal does not change the value. Therefore, we can change .1 into .10 and have the same number--except now it's expressed as hundredths. We have 10 hundredths. That's ten out of 100--which is just another way of saying ten percent (ten per hundred or ten out of 100). In other words .1 = .10 = 10 percent. Remember, if you're changing from a decimal to a percent, get rid of the decimal on the left and replace it with a percent mark on the right: 10%. Let's review those steps again: Divide 10 into 1. Since 10 doesn't go into 1, turn 1 into 1.0. Now divide 10 into 1.0. Since 10 goes into 10 1 time, put it there and add your decimal to make it .1. Since a percent is always "hundredths," let's change .1 into .10. Then remove the decimal on the left and replace with a percent sign on the right. The answer is 10%.

- If you're doing these conversions on a multiple-choice test, here's an idea that might be even easier and faster. Let's say you have a fraction of 1/8 and you're asked what the percent is. Since we know that "percent" means hundredths, ask yourself what number we can multiply 8 by to get 100. Since there is no number, ask what number gets us close to 100. That number is 12: 8 X 12 = 96. So it gets us a little less than 100. Now, whatever you do to the denominator, you have to do to the numerator. Let's multiply 1 X 12 and we get 12. However, since 96 is a little less than 100, we know that our answer will be a percent a little MORE than 12%. So if your possible answers on the multiple-choice test are these:

a) 8.5%   b) 19%   c) 12.5%   d) 25%

then we know the answer is c) 12.5%, because it's a little MORE than the 12 we got in our math problem above.

Another way to look at this, using multiple choice strategy is you know the answer will be "about" 12. Looking at the other choices, they are all either too large or too small and can be eliminated right away.

This was an easy example to demonstrate, so don't be fooled! You probably won't get such an easy question on your exam, but the principle holds just the same. By estimating your answer quickly, you can eliminate choices immediately and save precious exam time.

Decimal Tips, Tricks and Shortcuts

Converting Decimals to Fractions

One of the most important tricks for correctly converting a decimal to a fraction doesn't involve math at all. It's simply to learn to say the decimal correctly. If you say "point one" or "point 25" for .1 and .25, you'll have more trouble getting the conversion correct. But if you know that it's called "one tenth" and "twenty-five hundredths," you're on the way to a correct conversion. That's because, if you know your fractions, you know that "one tenth" looks like this: 1/10. And "twenty-five hundredths" looks like this: 25/100.

Even if you have digits before the decimal, such as 3.4, learning how to say the word will help you with the conversion into a fraction. It's not "three point four," it's "three and four tenths." Knowing this, you know that the fraction which looks like "three and four tenths" is 3 4/10.

Of course, your conversion is not complete until you reduce the fraction to its lowest terms: It's not 25/100, but 1/4.

Converting Decimals to Percent

Changing a decimal to a percent is easy if you remember one math formula: multiply by 100. For instance, if you start with .45, you change it to a percent by simply multiplying it by 100. You then wind up with 45. Add the % sign to the end and you get 45%.

That seems easy enough, right? In this case think of it this way: You just take out the decimal and stick in a percent sign on the opposite sign. In other words, the decimal on the left is replaced by the % on the right.

It doesn't work quite that easily if the decimal is in the middle of the number. Let's use 3.7 as an example. In this case, take out the decimal in the middle and replace it with a 0 % at the end. So 3.7 converted to decimal is 370%.

Percent Tips, Tricks and Shortcuts

Percent problems are not nearly as scary as they appear, if you remember this neat trick:

Draw a cross as in:

Portion	Percent
Whole	100

In the upper left, write PORTION. In the bottom left write WHOLE. In the top right, write PERCENT and in the bottom right, write 100. Whatever your problem is, you will leave blank the unknown, and fill in the other four parts. For example, let's suppose your problem is: Find 10% of 50. Since we know the 10% part, we put 10 in the percent corner. Since the whole number in our problem is 50, we put that in the corner marked whole. You always put 100 underneath the percent, so we leave it as is, which leaves only the top left corner blank. This is where we'll put our answer. Now simply multiply the two corner numbers that are NOT 100. In this case, it's 10 X 50. That gives us 500. Now divide this by the remaining corner, or 100, to get a final answer of 5. 5 is the number that goes in the upper-left corner, and is your final solution.

Another hint to remember: Percents are the same thing as hundredths in decimals. So .45 is the same as 45 hundredths or 45 percent.

Converting Percents to Decimals

Percents are just a type of decimal, so it should be no surprise that converting between the two is actually fairly simple. Here are a few tricks and shortcuts to keep in mind:

- ☐ Remember that percent literally means "per 100" or "for every 100." So when you speak of 30% you're saying 30 for every 100 or the fraction 30/100. In basic math, you learned that fractions that have 10 or 100

as the denominator can easily be turned to a decimal. 30/100 is thirty hundredths, or expressed as a decimal, .30.
- Another way to look at it: To convert a percent to a decimal, simply divide the number by 100. So for instance, if the percent is 47%, divide 47 by 100. The result will be .47. Get rid of the % mark and you're done.
- Remember that the easiest way of dividing by 100 is by moving your decimal two spots to the left.

Converting Percents to Fractions

Converting percents to fractions is easy. After all, a percent is just a type of fraction; it tells you what part of 100 that you're talking about. Here are some simple ideas for making the conversion from a percent to a fraction:

- If the percent is a whole number -- say 34% -- then simply write a fraction with 100 as the denominator (the bottom number). Then put the percentage itself on top. So 34% becomes 34/100.
- Now reduce as you would reduce any percent. In this case, by dividing 2 into 34 and 2 into 100, you get 17/50.
- If your percent is not a whole number -- say 3.4% --then convert it to a decimal expressed as hundredths. 3.4 is the same as 3.40 (or 3 and forty hundredths). Now ask yourself how you would express "three and forty hundredths" as a fraction. It would, of course, be 3 40/100. Reduce this and it becomes 3 2/5.

How to Answer Basic Math Multiple Choice

Math is the one section where you need to make sure that you understand the processes before you ever tackle it. That's because the time allowed on the math portion is typically so short that there's not much room for error. You have to be fast and accurate. It's imperative that before the test day arrives, you've learned all of the main formulas that will be used, and then to create your own problems (and solve them).

On the actual test day, use the "Plug-Check-Check" strategy. Here's how it goes.

Read the problem, but not the answers. You'll want to work the problem first and come up with your own answers. If you did the work right, you should find your answer among the choices given.

If you need help with the problem, plug actual numbers into the variables

given. You'll find it easier to work with numbers than it is to work with letters. For instance, if the question asks, "If Y - 4 is 2 more than Z, then Y +

5 is how much more than Z?" try selecting a value for Y. Let's take 6. Your question now becomes, "If 6 - 4 is 2 more than Z, then 6 plus 5 is how much more than Z?" Now your answer should be easier to work with.

Check the answer choices to see if your answer matches one of those. If so, select it.

If no answer matches the one you got, re-check your math, but this time, use a different method. In math, it's common for there to be more than one way to solve a problem. As a simple example, if you multiplied 12 X 13 and did not get an answer that matches one of the answer choices, you might try adding 13 together 12 different times and see if you get a good answer.

Math Multiple Choice Strategy

The two strategies for working with basic math multiple choice are Estimation and Elimination.

Math Strategy 1 - Estimation.

Just like it sounds, try to estimate an approximate answer first. Then look at the choices.

Math Strategy 2 - Elimination.

For every question, no matter what type, eliminating obviously incorrect answers narrows the possible choices. Elimination is probably the most powerful strategy for answering multiple choice.

Here are a few basic math examples of how this works.

Solve 2/3 + 5/12

    a. 9/17

    b. 3/11

    c. 7/12

    d. 1 1/12

First estimate the answer. 2/3 is more than half and 5/12 is about half, so the answer is going to be very close to 1.

Next, Eliminate. Choice A is about 1/2 and can be eliminated, Choice B is very small, less than 1/2 and can be eliminated. Choice C is close to 1/2 and can be eliminated. Leaving only Choice D, which is just over 1.

Work through the solution, a common denominator is needed, a number which both 3 and 12 will divide into.
2/3 = 8/12. So, 8+5/12 = 13/12 = 1 1/12

Choice D is correct.

Solve 4/5 – 2/3

    a. 2/2

    b. 2/13

    c. 1

    d. 2/15

You can eliminate Choice A, because it is 1 and since both numbers are close to one, the difference is going to be very small. You can eliminate Choice C for the same reason.

Next, look at the denominators. Since 5 and 3 don't go into 13, you can eliminate Choice B as well.

That leaves Choice D.

Checking the answer, the common denominator will be 15. So 12-10/15 = 2/15. Choice D is correct.

Fractions shortcut - Cancelling out.

In any operation with fractions, if the numerator of one fractions has a common multiple with the denominator of the other, you can cancel out. This saves time, and simplifies the problem quickly, making it easier to manage.

Solve 2/15 ÷ 4/5

    a. 6/65

    b. 6/75

    c. 5/12

    d. 1/6

To divide fractions, we multiply the first fraction with the inverse of the second fraction. Therefore we have
2/15 x 5/4. The numerator of the first fraction, 2, shares a multiple with the denominator of the second fraction, 4, which is 2. These cancel out, which gives, 1/3 x 1/2 = 1/6

Cancelling Out solved the questions very quickly, but we can still use multiple choice strategies to answer.

Choice B can be eliminated because 75 is too large a denominator. Choice C can be eliminated because 5 and 15 don't go into 12.

Choice D is correct.

Decimal Multiple Choice Strategy and Shortcuts.

Multiplying decimals gives a very quick way to estimate and eliminate choices. Anytime that you multiply decimals, it is going to give a answer with the same number of decimal places as the combined operands.

So for example,

2.38 X 1.2 will produce a number with three places of decimal, which is 2.856.

Here are a few examples with step-by-step explanation:

Solve 2.06 x 1.2

    a. 24.82

    b. 2.482

    c. 24.72

    d. 2.472

This is a simple question, but even before you start calculating, you can eliminate several choices. When multiplying decimals, there will always be as many numbers behind the decimal place in the answer as the sum of the ones in the initial problem, so Choices A and C can be eliminate.

The correct answer is D: 2.06 x 1.2 = 2.472

Solve 20.0 ÷ 2.5

    a. 12.05

    b. 9.25

    c. 8.3

    d. 8

First estimate the answer to be around 10, and eliminate Choice A. And since it'd also be an even number, you can eliminate Choice B and C., leaving only choice D.

The correct Answer is D: 20.0 ÷ 2.5 = 8

Cartesian Plane, Coordinate Plane and Coordinate Grid

To locate dots and draw lines and curves, we use the coordinate plane. It also called Cartesian coordinate plane. It is a two-dimensional surface with a coordinate grid in it, which helps us to count the units. For the counting of those units, we use x-axis (horizontal scale) and y-axis (vertical scale).

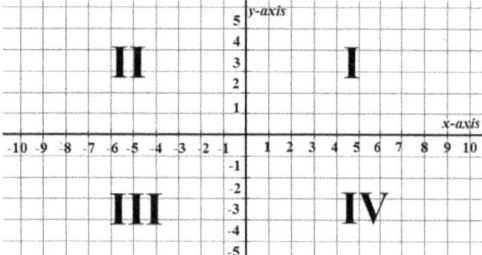

The whole system is called a coordinate system which is divided into 4 parts, called quadrants. The quadrant where all numbers are positive is the 1st quadrant (I), and if we go counterclockwise, we mark all 4 quadrants.

The location of a dot in the coordinate system is represented by coordinates. Coordinates are represented as a pair of numbers, where the 1st number is located on the x-axis and the 2nd number is located on the y-axis. So, if a dot A has coordinates a and b, then we write:

A=(a,b)   or   A(a,b)

The point where x-axis and y-axis intersect is called an origin. The origin is the point from which we measure the distance along the x and y axes.

In the Cartesian coordinate system we can calculate the distance between 2 given points. If we have dots with coordinates:
A=(a,b)
B=(c,d)

Then the distance d between A and B can be calculated by the following formula:

$$d = \sqrt{(c-a)^2 + (d-b)^2}$$

Cartesian coordinate system is used for the drawing of 2-dimentional shapes, and is also commonly used for functions.

Example:

Draw the function   y = (1 - x)/2

To draw a linear function, we need at least 2 points.
If we put that x=0 then value for y would be:

$$y = \frac{1-x}{2} = \frac{1-0}{2} = \frac{1}{2}$$

We found the 1st point, let's name it A, with following coordinates:

A = (0,1/2)

To find the 2nd point, we can put that x=1. In this case, the value for y would be:

$$y = \frac{1-x}{2} = \frac{1-1}{2} = \frac{0}{2} = 0$$

If we denote the 2nd point with B, then the coordinates for this point are:

B=(1,0)

Since we have 2 points necessary for the function, we find them in the coordinate system and we connect them with a line that represents the function,

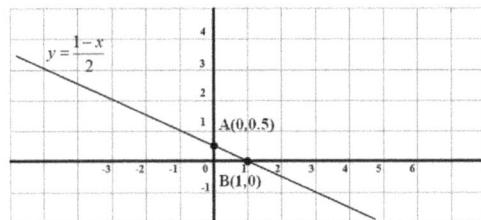

Perimeter Area and Volume

Perimeter and Area (2-dimentional shapes)

Perimeter of a shape determines the length around that shape, while the area includes the space inside the shape.

Rectangle:

P = 2a + 2b
A = ab

Square

P = 4a
$A = a^2$

Parallelogram

$P = 2a + 2b$
$A = ah_a = bh_b$

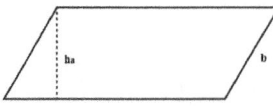

Rhombus

$P = 4a$
$A = ah = \dfrac{d_1 d_2}{2}$

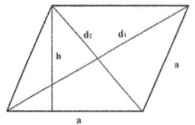

Triangle

$P = a + b + c$
$A = \dfrac{ah_a}{2} = \dfrac{bh_b}{2} = \dfrac{ch_c}{2}$

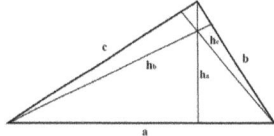

Equilateral Triangle

$P = 3a$
$A = \dfrac{a^2 \sqrt{3}}{4}$

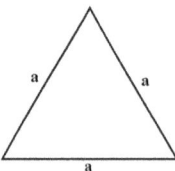

Trapezoid

$P = a + b + c + d$
$A = \dfrac{a+b}{2} h$

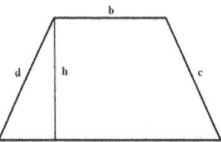

Circle

$P = 2r\pi$
$A = r^2 \pi$

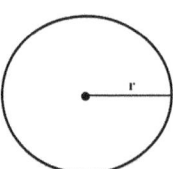

Area and Volume (3-dimentional shapes)

To calculate the area of a 3-dimentional shape, we calculate the areas of all sides and then we add them all.

To find the volume of a 3-dimentional shape, we multiply the area of the base (B) and the height (H) of the 3-dimentional shape.

$$V = BH$$

For a pyramid and a cone, the volume would be divided by 3.

$$V = BH/3$$

Here are some of the 3-dimentional shapes with formulas for their area and volume:

Cuboids

$A = 2(ab + bc + ac)$
$V = abc$

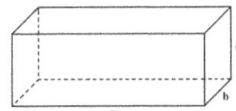

Cube

$A = 6a^2$
$V = a^3$

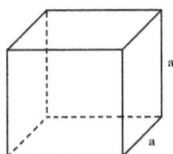

Pyramid

$A = ab + ah_a + bh_b$
$V = \dfrac{abH}{3}$

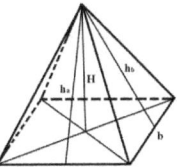

Cylinder

$A = 2r^2\pi + 2r\pi H$
$V = r^2\pi H$

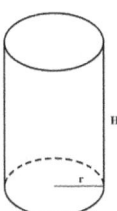

Cone

$A = (r+s)r\pi$
$V = \dfrac{r^2\pi H}{3}$

Pythagorean Geometry

If we have a right triangle ABC, where its sides (legs) are a and b and c is a hypotenuse (the side opposite the right angle), then we can establish a relationship between these sides using the following formula:

$c^2 = a^2 + b^2$

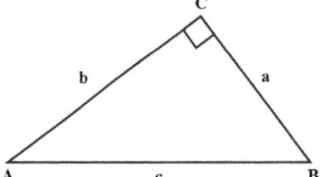

This formula is proven in the Pythagorean Theorem. There are many proofs of this theorem, but we'll look at just one geometrical proof:

If we draw squares on the right triangle's sides, then the area of the square upon the hypotenuse is equal to the sum of the areas of the squares that are upon other two sides of the triangle. Since the areas of these squares are a², b² and c², that is how we got the formula above.

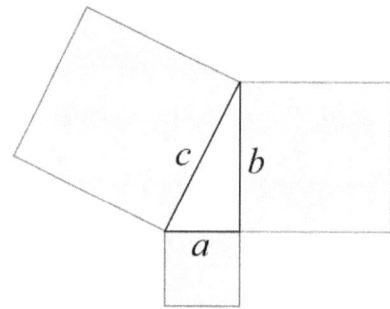

One of the famous right triangles is one with sides 3, 4 and 5. And we can see here that:

$3^2 + 4^2 = 5^2$
$9 + 16 = 25$
$25 = 25$

Example Problem:

The isosceles triangle ABC has a perimeter of 18 centimeters, and the difference between its base and legs is 3 centimeters. Find the height of this triangle.

We write the information we have about triangle ABC and we draw a picture

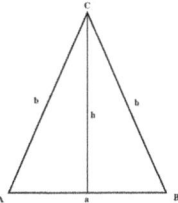

of it for better understanding of the relation between its elements:

P=18 cm
a - b = 3 cm
h=?

We use the formula for the perimeter of the isosceles triangle, since that is what is given to us:

P=a+2b=18 cm

Notice that we have 2 equations with 2 variables, so we can solve it as a system of equations:

a + 2b = 18
a − b = 3 / a + 2b = 18
2a - 2b = 6 / a + 2b + 2a - 2b = 18 + 6
3a = 24
a = 24/3 = 8 cm

Now we go back to find b:
a - b = 3
8 - b = 3
b = 8 - 3
b = 5 cm

Using Pythagorean Theorem, we can find the height using a and b, because the height falls on the side a at the right angle. Notice that height cuts side a exactly in half, and that's why we use in the formula a/2. In this case, b is our hypotenuse, so we have:

$b^2 = (a/2)^2 + h^2$
$h^2 = b^2 - (a/2)^2$
$h^2 = 5^2 - (8/2)^2$
$h^2 = 5^2 - (8/2)^2$
$h^2 = 25 - 4^2$
$h^2 = 26 - 16$
$h^2 = 9$
h = 3 cm.

Scale drawings

To draw some object accurately, but we can't draw it in its real size because it's either too small or too big, we use then scale drawing. It is called 'scale' because we use different scale – that is how much is the drawing of an object is bigger or smaller than its original size.

Scale drawing is written in the form of x:y, where x represents the drawn size of the object and y represents the actual size of the object, actually how many times the drawn object is smaller or bigger than the original one. If we have, for example, a scale drawing of 1:10, this means that the drawn object is 10 times smaller than the original one. Naturally, the bigger y is, the smaller the drawn object is. But, if we have a case of 10:1, this means that the drawn object is 10 times bigger than the original one.

If we are given sizes of a drawn and an original object, we can find the scale drawing (SD) if we divide drawn size (DS) by the actual size (AS):

SD = DS/AS

If we look at the smiley faces above, and we say that the left smiley is the original image and the right is the drawn one, then the scale drawing would be 1:2, where drawn smiley is 2 times smaller than the original one. If we say that the right smiley is the original smiley, in this case we would have a scale drawing of 2:1, where the drawn smiley is 2 times bigger than the original one.

Example Problem:

On a map that has a scale drawing of 1:250,000, the distance between 2 cities is 2 centimeters.

What is:
    a. the actual distance
    b. distance on a map that has a scale drawing of 1:80,000?

a. We have the scale drawing and we can use x and y to make an equation:
1:250,000 = x : y

We are given the distance on map, that is the drawn size, so we put 2 centimeters instead x: 1:250,000 = 2 cm : y

Now we multiply the outside numbers, which is equal to the multiplication of the inside numbers:

1 : 250,000 = 2 cm : y

1 * y = 250,000 * 2 cm
y = 500,000 cm
y = 5,000 m
y = 5 km

b. Now that we have the actual distance, we can use it to find the drawn distance on a map with scale 1:80,000. Now we put 5 kilometers instead of y:

1 : 80,000 = x : 5 km

5 km = 80,000x   / we convert km into cm

500,000 cm = 80,000x
x = 500,000 cm : 80,000
x = 4 cm

Quadrilaterals

Quadrilaterals are 2-dimentional geometrical shapes that have 4 sides and 4 angles. There are many types of quadrilaterals, depending on the length of its sides and if they are parallel and also depending on the size of its angles. All quadrilaterals have the following properties:

Sum of all interior angles is 360^0

Sum of all exterior angles is 360^0

A quadrilateral is a parallelogram is it fulfills at least one of the following conditions:

Angles on each side are supplementary
Opposite angles are equal
Opposite sides are equal
Diagonals intersect each other exactly in half

Here are some of the quadrilaterals:

Square

All sides are equal
All angles are right angles

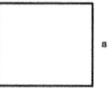

Rectangle

2 pairs of equal sides
All angles are right angles

Parallelogram

2 pairs of equal sides
Opposite angles are equal

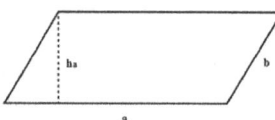

Rhombus

All sides are equal
Opposite angles are equal

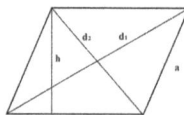

Trapezoid

One pair of parallel sides

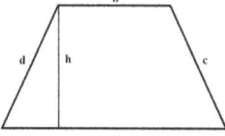

Example Problem

Find all angles of a parallelogram if one angle is greater than the other one by $40°$.

First, we draw an image of a parallelogram:

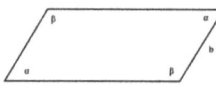

We denote angles by α and β, Since this is a parallelogram, the opposite angles are equal.

We are given that one angle is greater than the other one by $40°$, so we can write:

$\beta = \alpha + 40^0$

We solve this problem in two ways:
1) The sum of all internal angles of every quadrilateral is 360^0. There are 2 α and 2 β. So we have:
$2\alpha + 2\beta = 360^0$

Now, instead of β we write $\alpha + 40$:
$2\alpha + 2(\alpha + 40^0) = 360^0$
$2\alpha + 2\alpha + 80^0 = 360^0$
$4\alpha = 360^0 - 80^0$
$4\alpha = 280^0$
$\alpha = 280^0 / 4$
$\alpha = 70^0$
Now we can find β from α:
$\beta = \alpha + 40^0$
$\beta = 70^0 + 40^0$
$\beta = 110^0$

2) One of the conditions for parallelogram is " Angles on each side are supplementary" and we can use that to find these angles:
$\alpha + \beta = 180^0$
$\alpha + \alpha + 40^0 = 180^0$
$2\alpha = 180^0 - 40^0$
$2\alpha = 140^0$
$\alpha = 70^0$

Now we find β:
$\beta = \alpha + 40^0$
$\beta = 70^0 + 40^0$
$\beta = 110^0$

Exponents: Tips, Shortcuts & Tricks

Exponents seem like advanced math to most—like some mysterious code with a complicated meaning. In fact, though, an exponent is just short hand for saying that you're multiplying a number by itself two or more times. For instance, instead of saying that you're multiplying 5 x 5 x 5, you can show that you're multiplying 5 by itself 3 times if you just write 5^3. We usually say this as "five to the third power" or "five to the power of three." In this example, the raised 3 is an "exponent," while the 5 is the "base." You can even use exponents with fractions. For instance, $1/2^3$ means you're multiplying 1/2 x 1/2 x 1/2. (The answer is 1/8). Some other helpful hints for working with exponents:

- Here's how to do basic multiplication of exponents. If you have the same number with a different exponent (For instance $5^3 \times 5^2$) just add the exponents and multiply the bases as usual. The answer, then, is 25^5.
- This doesn't work, though, if the bases are different. For instance, in $5^3 \times 3^2$ we simply have to do the math the long way to figure out the final solution: 5 x 5 x 5, multiplying that result times the result for 3 X 2. (The answer is 750).
- Looking at it from the opposite side, to divide two exponents with the same base (or bottom number), subtract the smaller exponent from the larger one. If we were dividing the problem above, we would subtract the 2 from the 3 to get 1. 5 to the power of 1 is simply 5.
- One time when thinking of exponents as merely multiplication doesn't work is when the raised number is zero. Any number raised to the "zeroth" power is 1 (Not, as we tend to think, zero).

Number (x)	X^2	X^3
1	1	1
2	4	8
3	9	27
4	16	64
5	25	125
6	36	216
7	49	343
8	64	512
9	81	729
10	100	1000
11	121	1331
12	144	1728
13	169	2197
14	196	2744
15	225	3375
16	256	4096

Ability

This section contains an Ability self-assessment and tutorials. The Tutorials are designed to familiarize students with general principles and the self-assessment contains general questions similar to the Ability questions likely to be on the TACHS exam, but are not intended to be identical to the exam questions. The tutorials are not designed to be a complete course, and it is assumed that students have some familiarity with these types of questions. If you do not understand parts of the tutorial, or find the tutorial difficult, it is recommended that you seek out additional instruction.

Note that these questions are for skill practice only.

Tour of the TACHS Ability Content

The TACHS Ability section has three different types of questions. All the Ability questions are graphical. The first type of question presents a series of objects that are similar or linked, and asks you to choose from a series of four objects, one that is similar. The second type of questions presents two related shapes, and asks you to choose an object that has the same relationship as the first two. The third type of question presents a piece of paper and you are asked to select the diagram of how the paper would appear folded.

The questions below are not the same as you will find on the TACHS - that would be too easy! And nobody knows what the questions will be and they change all the time. Mostly, the changes consist of substituting new questions for old, but the changes also can be new question formats or styles, changes to the number of questions in each section, changes to the time limits for each section, and combining sections. So, while the format and exact wording of the questions may differ slightly, and change from year to year, if you can answer the questions below, you will have no problem with the Ability section of the TACHS.

Ability Self-Assessment

The purpose of the self-assessment is:

- Identify your strengths and weaknesses.
- Develop your personalized study plan (above)
- Get accustomed to the TACHS format
- Extra practice – the self-assessment is a 3rd test!

- Provide a baseline score for preparing your study schedule.

Once complete, use the table below to assess your understanding of the content and prepare your study schedule described in chapter 1.

80% - 100%	Excellent – you have mastered the content!
60 – 79%	Good. You have a working knowledge. Even though you can just pass this section, you may want to review the Tutorials and do some extra practice to see if you can improve your mark.
40% - 59%	Below Average. You do not understand the content. Review the tutorials, and retake this quiz again in a few days, before proceeding to the Practice Test Questions.
Less than 40%	Poor. You have a very limited understanding. Please review the Tutorials, and retake this quiz again in a few days, before proceeding to the Practice Test Questions.

Ability Self-Assessment Answer Sheet

1. A B C D   11. A B C D
2. A B C D   12. A B C D
3. A B C D   13. A B C D
4. A B C D   14. A B C D
5. A B C D   15. A B C D
6. A B C D
7. A B C D
8. A B C D
9. A B C D
10. A B C D

Directions: Questions 1 - 4:
The first 3 figures are related. Choose the figure that has the same relationship.

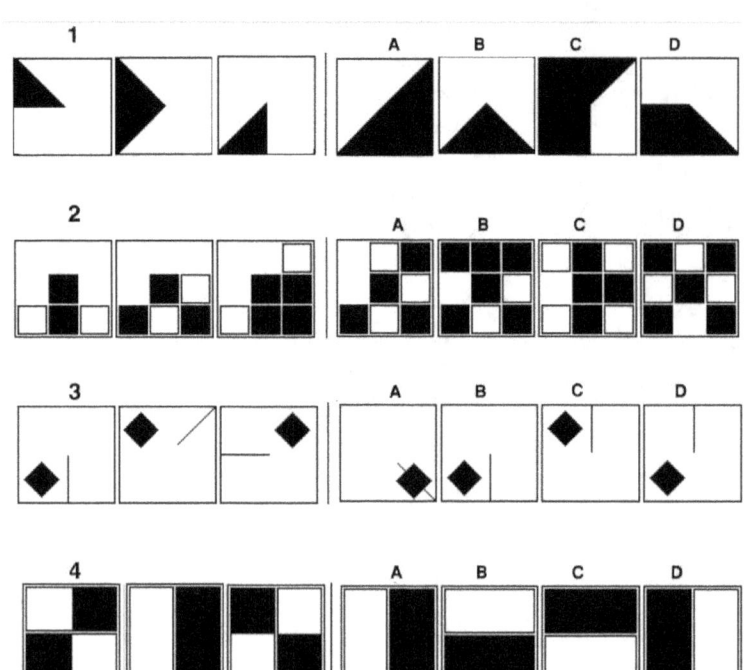

Directions Questions 5 - 10:
Select the figure with the same relationship.

5.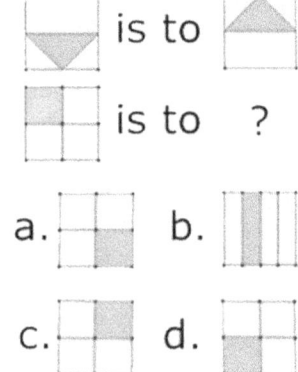

6.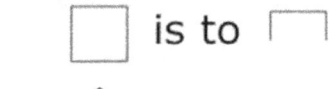
   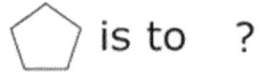

7.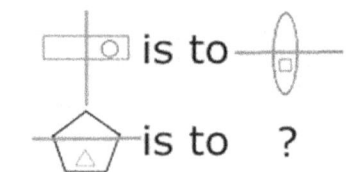

   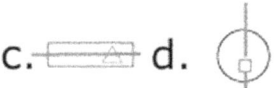

8.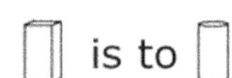

9.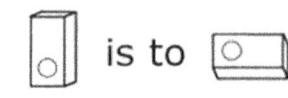
   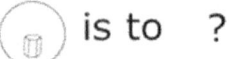

10.

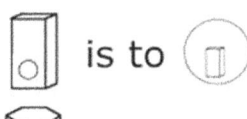

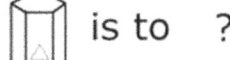

a. b. c. d.

11. When the two longest sides touch what will the shape be?

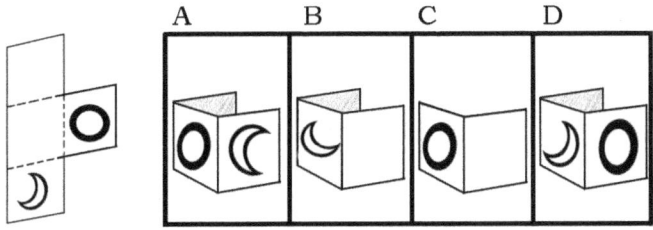

12. When folded, what pattern is possible?

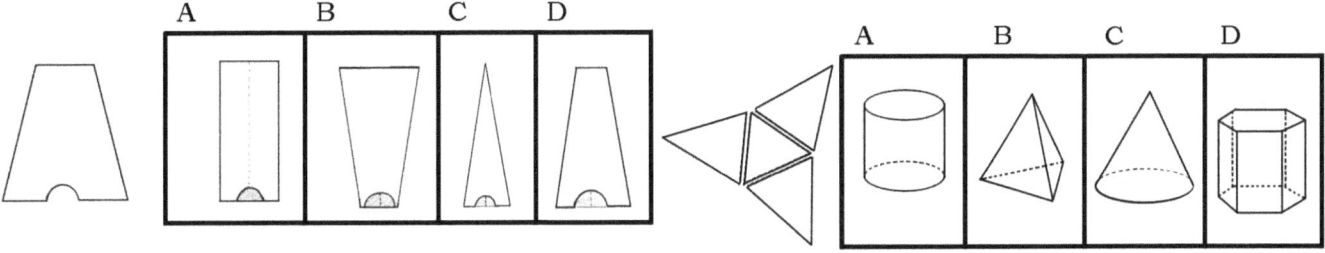

13. When folded into a loop, what will the strip of paper look like?

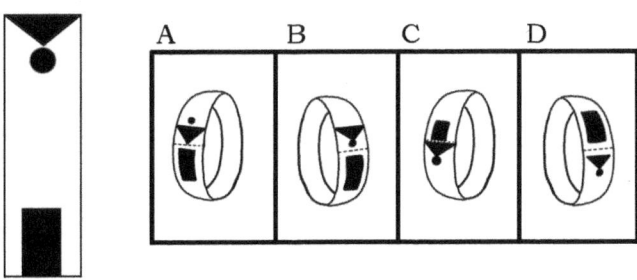

14. Which of the choices below is the same pattern at a different angle?

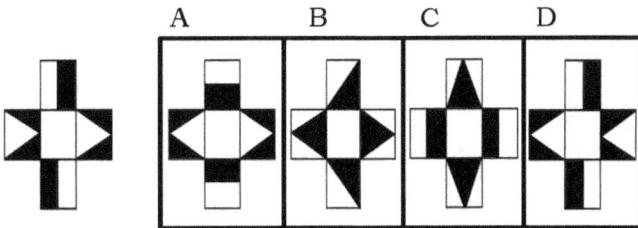

15. When put together, what 3-dimensional shape will you get?

Answer Key

1. B
Each figure is created by adding the mirror image of the previous figure.

2. B
Each square has 2 blank squares.

3. A
The inner square is rotated clockwise on the corner of the outside square.

4. C
The bottom box is rotated counter-clockwise.

5. D
The relationship is the same figure flipped vertically. In the top figures the shaded shape is flipped up, and in the bottom set, the shaded figure is flipped down.

6. C
The relation is the same figure with the bottom half removed.

7. D
The first pair is a rectangle with a circle inside and then an oval with a square inside. The given figures in the second pair has a triangle inside, so the match will be the circle with a square inside.

8. B
The relation is two upright figures in the first set, and 2 horizontal figures in the second set.

9. C
The first pair contains a box with a circle inside, and the same figure on its side.

10. C
The inside and larger shapes are reversed.

11. D
12. A
13. C
14. D
15. B

Practice Test Questions Set 1

THE QUESTIONS BELOW ARE NOT THE SAME AS YOU WILL FIND ON THE TACHS - THAT WOULD BE TOO EASY! And nobody knows what the questions will be and they change all the time. Below are general questions that cover the same subject areas as the TACHS. So, while the format and exact wording of the questions may differ slightly, and change from year to year, if you can answer the questions below, you will have no problem with the TACHS.

For the best results, take these practice test questions as if it were the real exam. Set aside time when you will not be disturbed, and a location that is quiet and free of distractions. Read the instructions carefully, read each question carefully, and answer to the best of your ability.

Use the bubble answer sheets provided. When you have completed the practice questions, check your answer against the Answer Key and read the explanation provided.

Do not attempt more than one set of practice test questions in one day. After completing the first practice test, wait two or three days before attempting the second set of questions.

Section I – Reading
Questions: 50
Time: 45 minutes

Section II - Language
Questions: 50
Time: 30 minutes

Section III – Mathematics
Questions: 50
Time: 40 Minutes

Section IV - Ability
Questions: 40
Time: 30 Minutes

Reading Answer Sheet

	A	B	C	D	E		A	B	C	D	E
1	○	○	○	○	○	26	○	○	○	○	○
2	○	○	○	○	○	27	○	○	○	○	○
3	○	○	○	○	○	28	○	○	○	○	○
4	○	○	○	○	○	29	○	○	○	○	○
5	○	○	○	○	○	30	○	○	○	○	○
6	○	○	○	○	○	31	○	○	○	○	○
7	○	○	○	○	○	32	○	○	○	○	○
8	○	○	○	○	○	33	○	○	○	○	○
9	○	○	○	○	○	34	○	○	○	○	○
10	○	○	○	○	○	35	○	○	○	○	○
11	○	○	○	○	○	36	○	○	○	○	○
12	○	○	○	○	○	37	○	○	○	○	○
13	○	○	○	○	○	38	○	○	○	○	○
14	○	○	○	○	○	39	○	○	○	○	○
15	○	○	○	○	○	40	○	○	○	○	○
16	○	○	○	○	○	41	○	○	○	○	○
17	○	○	○	○	○	42	○	○	○	○	○
18	○	○	○	○	○	43	○	○	○	○	○
19	○	○	○	○	○	44	○	○	○	○	○
20	○	○	○	○	○	45	○	○	○	○	○
21	○	○	○	○	○	46	○	○	○	○	○
22	○	○	○	○	○	47	○	○	○	○	○
23	○	○	○	○	○	48	○	○	○	○	○
24	○	○	○	○	○	49	○	○	○	○	○
25	○	○	○	○	○	50	○	○	○	○	○

Language Answer Sheet

	A B C D E		A B C D E
1	○ ○ ○ ○ ○	26	○ ○ ○ ○ ○
2	○ ○ ○ ○ ○	27	○ ○ ○ ○ ○
3	○ ○ ○ ○ ○	28	○ ○ ○ ○ ○
4	○ ○ ○ ○ ○	29	○ ○ ○ ○ ○
5	○ ○ ○ ○ ○	30	○ ○ ○ ○ ○
6	○ ○ ○ ○ ○	31	○ ○ ○ ○ ○
7	○ ○ ○ ○ ○	32	○ ○ ○ ○ ○
8	○ ○ ○ ○ ○	33	○ ○ ○ ○ ○
9	○ ○ ○ ○ ○	34	○ ○ ○ ○ ○
10	○ ○ ○ ○ ○	35	○ ○ ○ ○ ○
11	○ ○ ○ ○ ○	36	○ ○ ○ ○ ○
12	○ ○ ○ ○ ○	37	○ ○ ○ ○ ○
13	○ ○ ○ ○ ○	38	○ ○ ○ ○ ○
14	○ ○ ○ ○ ○	39	○ ○ ○ ○ ○
15	○ ○ ○ ○ ○	40	○ ○ ○ ○ ○
16	○ ○ ○ ○ ○	41	○ ○ ○ ○ ○
17	○ ○ ○ ○ ○	42	○ ○ ○ ○ ○
18	○ ○ ○ ○ ○	43	○ ○ ○ ○ ○
19	○ ○ ○ ○ ○	44	○ ○ ○ ○ ○
20	○ ○ ○ ○ ○	45	○ ○ ○ ○ ○
21	○ ○ ○ ○ ○	46	○ ○ ○ ○ ○
22	○ ○ ○ ○ ○	47	○ ○ ○ ○ ○
23	○ ○ ○ ○ ○	48	○ ○ ○ ○ ○
24	○ ○ ○ ○ ○	49	○ ○ ○ ○ ○
25	○ ○ ○ ○ ○	50	○ ○ ○ ○ ○

Mathematics Answer Sheet

Ability Answer Sheet

	A	B	C	D	E		A	B	C	D	E
1	○	○	○	○	○	26	○	○	○	○	○
2	○	○	○	○	○	27	○	○	○	○	○
3	○	○	○	○	○	28	○	○	○	○	○
4	○	○	○	○	○	29	○	○	○	○	○
5	○	○	○	○	○	30	○	○	○	○	○
6	○	○	○	○	○	31	○	○	○	○	○
7	○	○	○	○	○	32	○	○	○	○	○
8	○	○	○	○	○	33	○	○	○	○	○
9	○	○	○	○	○	34	○	○	○	○	○
10	○	○	○	○	○	35	○	○	○	○	○
11	○	○	○	○	○	36	○	○	○	○	○
12	○	○	○	○	○	37	○	○	○	○	○
13	○	○	○	○	○	38	○	○	○	○	○
14	○	○	○	○	○	39	○	○	○	○	○
15	○	○	○	○	○	40	○	○	○	○	○
16	○	○	○	○	○						
17	○	○	○	○	○						
18	○	○	○	○	○						
19	○	○	○	○	○						
20	○	○	○	○	○						
21	○	○	○	○	○						
22	○	○	○	○	○						
23	○	○	○	○	○						
24	○	○	○	○	○						
25	○	○	○	○	○						

Section I - Reading

Part I - Vocabulary

Directions: Choose the word that is closest in meaning to the underlined word.

1. The cut on her knee is bleeding.

    a. Slice
    b. Chop
    c. Gash
    d. Bone

2. Smoking can cause cancer. It is hazardous to one's health.

    a. Safe
    b. Beneficial
    c. Important
    d. Dangerous

3. The house has no lights on. It looks dark.

    a. Shadowy
    b. Sad
    c. Bright
    d. Scary

4. The judges will determine the winner of the contest.

    a. Award
    b. Choose
    c. Congratulate
    d. Explain

5. Please give us a definite answer to the question.

    a. Unclear
    b. Wrong
    c. Clear
    d. Different

6. I can't wait to try some of the delectable dishes served in the new restaurant.

    a. Unique
    b. Expensive
    c. New
    d. Delicious

7. Can you describe the character of Juliet in the play?

    a. Report
    b. Portray
    c. Explain
    d. Draw

8. The soldiers will destroy the camps of the rebels.

    a. Ruin
    b. End
    c. Fix
    d. Conquer

9. There is a big difference in the grades of Esther with that of Pete.

    a. Complication
    b. Dissimilarity
    c. Minus
    d. Increase

10. I can attain my goals in life if I study hard.

a. Finish
b. Forget
c. Effect
d. Achieve

11. The lecture was so boring everybody was starting to get sleepy.

a. Uninteresting
b. Sensible
c. Fast
d. Exciting

12. The eager crowd yelled and cheered for their favorite team during the basketball tournament.

a. Bored
b. Uninterested
c. Angry
d. Enthusiastic

13. The government is planning to end famine through mass food production.

a. Close
b. Avoid
c. Stop
d. Start

14. Children enjoy playing in the park with their playmates.

a. Dislike
b. Delight in
c. Spend
d. Uninterested

15. Can you elaborate on the reason behind your tardiness in class?

a. Define
b. Correct
c. Explain
d. Interpret

16. An evident or clear obvious truth.

a. Truism
b. Catharsis
c. Libertine
d. Tractable

17. Choose the best definition for: virago

a. A loud domineering woman
b. A quiet woman
c. A load domineering Man
d. A quiet man

18. When Joe broke his _____ in a skiing accident, his entire leg was in a cast.

a. Ankle
b. Humerus
c. Wrist
d. Femur

19. Select another word for the underlined word in the sentence below.

At first I thought she was very rude and boorish, but when I talked to her again she was very <u>genteel</u>.

   a. Chivalrous
   b. Hilarious
   c. Civilized
   d. Governance

20. Choose an adjective that means corrupted, impure.

   a. Adulterate
   b. Harbor
   c. Infuriate
   d. Inculcate

Part II - Reading Comprehension

Directions: Read each passage below carefully and then answer the questions that follow. Be careful to choose the best answer, given the four choices and only base your answer on the information given in the passage.

Questions 21 – 24 refer to the following passage.

Passage 1 - The Life of Helen Keller

Many people have heard of Helen Keller. She is famous because she was unable to see or hear, but learned to speak and read and went onto attend college and earn a degree. Her life is a very interesting story, one that she developed into an autobiography, which was then adapted into both a stage play and a movie. How did Helen Keller overcome her disabilities to become a famous woman? Read onto find out.

Helen Keller was not born blind and deaf. When she was a small baby, she had a very high fever for several days. As a result of her sudden illness, baby Helen lost her eyesight and her hearing. Because she was so young when she went deaf and blind, Helen Keller never had any recollection of being able to see or hear. Since she could not hear, she could not learn to talk. Since she could not see, it was difficult for her to move around. For the first six years of her life, her world was very still and dark.

Imagine what Helen's childhood was like. She could not hear her mother's voice. She could not see the beauty of her parent's farm. She could not recognize who was giving her a hug, or a bath or even where her bedroom was each night. More sad, she could not communicate with her parents in any way. She could not express her feelings or tell them the things she wanted. It must have been a very sad childhood.

When Helen was six years old, her parents hired her a teacher named Anne Sullivan. Anne was a young woman who was almost blind. However, she could hear and she could read Braille, so she was a perfect teacher for young Helen. At first, Anne had a very hard time teaching Helen anything. She described her first impression of Helen as a "wild thing, not a child." Helen did not like Anne at first either. She bit and hit Anne when Anne tried to teach her. However, the two of them eventually came to have a great deal of love and respect.

Anne taught Helen to hear by putting her hands on people's throats. She could feel the sounds that people made. In time, Helen learned to feel what people said. Next, Anne taught Helen to read Braille, which is a way that books are written for the blind. Finally, Anne taught Helen to talk. Although Helen did learn to talk, it was hard for anyone but Anne to understand her.

As Helen grew older, more and more people were amazed by her story. She went to college and wrote books about her life. She gave talks to the public, with Anne at her side, translating her words. Today, both Anne Sullivan and Helen Keller are famous women who are respected for their lives' work.

21. Helen Keller could not see and hear and so, what was her biggest problem in childhood?

    a. Inability to communicate

    b. Inability to walk

    c. Inability to play

    d. Inability to eat

22. Helen learned to hear by feeling the vibrations people made when they spoke. What were these vibrations were felt through?

    a. Mouth

    b. Throat

    c. Ears

    d. Lips

23. From the passage, we can infer that Anne Sullivan was a patient teacher. We can infer this because

    a. Helen hit and bit her and Anne still remained her teacher.

    b. Anne taught Helen to read only.

    c. Anne was hard of hearing too.

    d. Anne wanted to be a teacher.

24. Helen Keller learned to speak but Anne translated her words when she spoke in public. The reason Helen needed a translator was because

    a. Helen spoke another language.

    b. Helen's words were hard for people to understand.

    c. Helen spoke very quietly.

    d. Helen did not speak but only used sign language.

Questions 25 – 27 refer to the following passage.

Passage 2 - Ways Characters Communicate in Theater

Playwrights give their characters voices in a way that gives depth and added meaning to what happens on stage during their play. There are different types of speech in scripts that allow characters to talk with themselves, with other characters, and even with the audience.

It is very unique to theater that characters may talk "to themselves." When characters do this, the speech they give is called a soliloquy. Soliloquies are usually poetic, introspective, moving, and can tell audience members about the feelings, motivations, or suspicions of an individual character without that character having to reveal them to other characters on stage. "To be or not to be" is a famous soliloquy given by Hamlet as he considers difficult but important themes, such as life and death.

The most common type of communication in plays is when one character is speaking to another or a group of other characters. This is generally called dialogue, but can also be called monologue if one character speaks without being interrupted for a long time. It is not necessarily the most important type of communication, but it is the most common because the plot of the play cannot really progress without it.

Lastly, and most unique to theater (although it has been used somewhat in film) is when a character speaks directly to the audience. This is called an aside, and scripts usually specifically direct actors to do this. Asides are usually comical, an inside joke between the character and the audience, and very short. The actor will usually face the audience when delivering them, even if it's for a moment, so the audience can recognize this move as an aside.

All three of these types of communication are important to the art of theater, and have been perfected by famous playwrights like Shakespeare. Understanding these types of communication can help an audience member grasp what is artful about the script and action of a play.

25. According to the passage, characters in plays communicate to

    a. move the plot forward
    b. show the private thoughts and feelings of one character
    c. make the audience laugh
    d. add beauty and artistry to the play

26. When Hamlet delivers "To be or not to be," he can most likely be described as

   a. solitary
   b. thoughtful
   c. dramatic
   d. hopeless

27. The author uses parentheses to punctuate "although it has been used somewhat in film,"

   a. to show that films are less important
   b. instead of using commas so that the sentence is not interrupted
   c. because parenthesis help separate details that are not as important
   d. to show that films are not as artistic

Questions 28 – 30 refer to the following passage.

Passage 3 - Low Blood Sugar

As the name suggest, low blood sugar is low sugar levels in the bloodstream. This can occur when you have not eaten properly and undertake strenuous activity, or, when you are very hungry. When Low blood sugar occurs regularly and is ongoing, it is a medical condition called hypoglycemia. This condition can occur in diabetics and in healthy adults.

Causes of low blood sugar can include excessive alcohol consumption, metabolic problems, stomach surgery, pancreas, liver or kidneys problems, as well as a side-effect of some medications.

Symptoms

There are different symptoms depending on the severity of the case.

Mild hypoglycemia can lead to feelings of nausea and hunger. The patient may also feel nervous, jittery and have fast heart beats. Sweaty skin, clammy and cold skin are likely symptoms.
Moderate hypoglycemia can result in a short temper, confusion, nervousness, fear and blurring of vision. The patient may feel weak and unsteady.

Severe cases of hypoglycemia can lead to seizures, coma, fainting spells, nightmares, headaches, excessive sweats and severe tiredness.

Diagnosis of low blood sugar

A doctor can diagnosis this medical condition by asking the patient questions and testing blood and urine samples. Home testing kits are available for patients to monitor blood sugar levels. It is important to see a qualified doctor though. The doctor can administer tests to ensure that will safely rule out other medical conditions that could affect blood sugar levels.

Treatment

Quick treatments include drinking or eating foods and drinks with high sugar contents. Good examples include soda, fruit juice, hard candy and raisins. Glucose energy tablets can also help. Doctors may also recommend medications and well as changes in diet and exercise routine to treat chronic low blood sugar.

28. Based on the article, which of the following is true?

    a. Low blood sugar can happen to anyone.

    b. Low blood sugar only happens to diabetics.

    c. Low blood sugar can occur even.

    d. None of the statements are true.

29. Which of the following are the author's opinion?

    a. Quick treatments include drinking or eating foods and drinks with high sugar contents.

    b. None of the statements are opinions.

    c. This condition can occur in diabetics and also in healthy adults.

    d. There are different symptoms depending on the severity of the case

30. What is the author's purpose?

    a. To inform

    b. To persuade

    c. To entertain

    d. To analyze

31. Which of the following is not a detail?

    a. A doctor can diagnosis this medical condition by asking the patient questions and testing.

    b. A doctor will test blood and urine samples.

    c. Glucose energy tablets can also help.

    d. Home test kits monitor blood sugar levels.

    d. None of the above.

Questions 32 – 35 refer to the following passage.

How To Get A Good Nights Sleep

Sleep is just as essential for healthy living as water, air and food. Sleep allows the body to rest and replenish depleted energy levels. Sometimes we may for various reasons experience difficulty sleeping which has a serious effect on our
health. Those who have prolonged sleeping problems are facing a serious medical condition and should see a qualified doctor when possible for help. Here is simple guide that can help you sleep better at night.

Try to create a natural pattern of waking up and sleeping around the same time everyday. This means avoiding going to bed too early and oversleeping past your usual wake up time. Going to bed and getting up at radically different times everyday confuses your body clock. Try to establish a natural rhythm as much as you can.

Exercises and a bit of physical activity can help you sleep better at night. If you are having problem sleeping, try to be as active as you can during the day. If you are tired from physical activity, falling asleep is a natural and easy process
for your body. If you remain inactive during the day, you will find it harder to sleep properly at night. Try walking, jogging, swimming or simple stretches as you get close to your bed time.

Afternoon naps are great to refresh you during the day, but they may also keep you awake at night. If you feel sleepy during the day, get up, take a walk and get busy to keep from sleeping. Stretching is a good way to increase blood flow to the brain and keep you alert so that you don't sleep during the day. This will help you sleep better night.

> A warm bath or a glass of milk in the evening can help your body relax and prepare for sleep. A cold bath will wake you up and keep you up for several hours. Also avoid eating too late before bed.

32. How would you describe this sentence?

    a. A recommendation
    b. An opinion
    c. A fact
    d. A diagnosis

33. Which of the following is an alternative title for this article?

　a. Exercise and a good night's sleep

　b. Benefits of a good night's sleep

　c. Tips for a good night's sleep

　d. Lack of sleep is a serious medical condition

34. Which of the following cannot be inferred from this article?

　a. Biking is helpful for getting a good night's sleep

　b. Mental activity is helpful for getting a good night's sleep

　c. Eating bedtime snacks is not recommended

　d. Getting up at the same time is helpful for a good night's sleep

35. What is a disadvantage of taking naps?

　a. They may keep you awake.

　b. There are no disadvantages

　c. They may help you sleep better

　d. They may affect your diet

Question 36 refers to the following Table of Contents.

Contents

　　Science Self-assessment 81
　　Answer Key 91
　　Science Tutorials 96
　　Scientific Method 96
　　Biology 99
　　Heredity: Genes and Mutation 104
　　Classification 108
　　Ecology 110
　　Chemistry 112
　　Energy: Kinetic and Mechanical 126
　　Energy: Work and Power 130
　　Force: Newton's Three Laws 132

36. Consider the table of contents above. What page would you find information about natural selection and adaptation?

    a. 81
    b. 90
    c. 110
    d. 132

Questions 37 – 39 refer to the following passage.

Passage 5 - Pearl Harbor

A Day That Will Live in Infamy! Attack on Pearl Harbor
In 1941, the world was at war. The United States was trying very hard to keep itself out of the conflict. In Europe, the countries of Germany and Italy had formed an alliance to expand their land and territory. Germany had already taken over Poland, Denmark, and parts of France. They were heading next toward England and due to all the fighting in Europe, there were battles taking place as far south as North Africa, where the German and Italian armies were fighting the British.

This got even worse when the Asian nation of Japan formed an alliance with Germany and Italy. Together, the three countries called themselves, the AXIS. Now, the war was in the Pacific as well as in Europe and Northern Africa. A great deal of Americans felt that perhaps now was the time for the United States to join with its ally, Great Britain and stop the Axis from taking over more regions of the world.

In 1941, Franklin Roosevelt was President of the United States. His fear at the time was that Japan would try to take over many countries in Asia. He did not want to see that happen, so he moved some of the United States warships that had been stationed in San Diego, to the military base at Pearl Harbor, in Honolulu, Hawaii.

Japan quietly plotted their attack. They waited until the early hours of the morning on Sunday, December 7, 1941. Then, 350 Japanese war plans began to drop bombs on the U.S. ships at Pearl Harbor. The first bombs fell at 7:48 am and a mere 90 minutes later, the attack was over. Pearl Harbor was decimated. 8 battleships were damaged. Eleven ships were sunk and 300 U.S. planes were destroyed. Most devastating was the loss of life 2,400 U.S. military members was killed in the attack and 1, 282 were injured.

President Roosevelt addressed the country via the radio and said "Today is a day that will live in infamy." He asked Congress to declare war on Japan. War was declared on Japan on December 8th and on Germany and Italy on December 11th. The United States had entered World War Two.

37. After reading the passage, what can we infer infamy means?

a. Famous
b. Remembered in a good way
c. Remembered in a bad way
d. Easily forgotten

38. What three countries formed the Axis?

a. Italy, England, Germany
b. United States, England, Italy
c. Germany, Japan, Italy
d. Germany, Japan, United States

39. What do you think was President Roosevelt's reason for moving warships to Pearl Harbor?

a. He feared Japan would bomb San Diego
b. He knew Japan was going to attack Pearl Harbor
c. He was planning to attack Japan
d. He wanted to try and protect Asian countries from Japanese takeover

40. Why do you think Japan chose a Sunday morning at 7:48 am for their attack?

a. They knew the military slept late
b. There is a law against bombing countries on a Sunday
c. They wanted the attack to catch people by surprise
d. That was the only free time they had to attack.

Questions 41 - 44 refer to the following recipe.

If You Have Allergies, You're Not Alone

People who experience allergies might joke that their immune systems have let them down or are seriously lacking. Truthfully though, people who experience allergic reactions or allergy symptoms during certain times of the year have heightened immune systems that are, "better" than those of people who have perfectly healthy but less militant immune systems.

Still, when a person has an allergic reaction, they are having an adverse reaction to a substance that is considered normal to most people. Mild allergic reactions usually have symptoms like itching, runny nose, red eyes, or bumps or discoloration of the skin. More serious allergic reactions, such as those to animal and insect poisons or certain foods, may result in the closing of the throat, swelling of the eyes, low blood pressure, inability to breath, and can even be fatal.

Different treatments help different allergies, and which one a person uses depends on the nature and severity of the allergy. It is recommended to patients with severe allergies to take extra precautions, such as carrying an EpiPen, which treats anaphylactic shock and may prevent death, always in order for the remedy to be readily available and more effective. When an allergy is not so severe, treatments may be used just relieve a person of uncomfortable symptoms. Over the counter allergy medicines treat milder symptoms, and can be bought at any grocery store and used in moderation to help people with allergies live normally.

There are many tests available to assess whether a person has allergies or what they may be allergic to, and advances in these tests and the medicine used to treat patients continues to improve. Despite this fact, allergies still affect many people throughout the year or even every day. Medicines used to treat allergies have side effects of their own, and it is difficult to bring the body into balance with the use of medicine. Regardless, many of those who live with allergies are grateful for what is available and find it useful in maintaining their lifestyles.

41. According to this passage, it can be understood that the word "militant" belongs in a group with the words:

    a. sickly, ailing, faint

    b. strength, power, vigor

    c. active, fighting, warring

    d. worn, tired, breaking down

42. The author says that "medicines used to treat allergies have side-effects of their own" to

    a. point out that doctors aren't very good at diagnosing and treating allergies

    b. argue that because of the large number of people with allergies, a cure will never be found

    c. explain that allergy medicines aren't cures and some compromise must be made

    d. argue that more wholesome remedies should be researched and medicines banned

43. It can be inferred that _____ recommend that some people with allergies carry medicine with them.

    a. the author

    b. doctors

    c. the makers of EpiPen

    d. people with allergies

44. The author has written this passage to

    a. inform readers on symptoms of allergies so people with allergies can get help

    b. persuade readers to be proud of having allergies

    c. inform readers on different remedies so people with allergies receive the right help

    d. describe different types of allergies, their symptoms, and their remedies

Questions 45 – 46 refer to the following email.

SUBJECT: MEDICAL STAFF CHANGES

To all staff:

This email is to advise you of a paper on recommended medical staff changes has been posted to the Human Resources website.

The contents are of primary interest to medical staff, other staff may be interested in reading it, particularly those in medical support roles.

The paper deals with several major issues:

    1. Improving our ability to attract top quality staff to the hospital, and retain our existing staff. These changes will make our position and departmental names internationally recognizable and comparable with North American and North Asian departments and positions.

    2. Improving our ability to attract top quality staff by introducing greater flexibility in the departmental structure.

    3. General comments on issues to be further discussed in relation to research staff.

The changes outlined in this paper are significant. I encourage you to read the document and send to me any comments you may have, so that it can be enhanced and improved.

Gordon Simms
Administrator,
Seven Oaks Regional Hospital

45. Are all hospital staff required to read the document posted to the Human Resources website?

   a. Yes all staff are required to read the document.
   b. No, reading the document is optional.
   c. Only medical staff are required to read the document.
   d. none of the above are correct.

46. Have the changes to medical staff been made?

   a. Yes, the changes have been made.
   b. No, the changes are only being discussed.
   c. Some of the changes have been made.
   d. None of the choices are correct.

Questions 47 – 50 refer to the following passage.

When a Poet Longs to Mourn, He Writes an Elegy

Poems are an expressive, especially emotional, form of writing. They have been present in literature virtually from the time civilizations invented the written word. Poets often portrayed as moody, secluded, and even troubled, but this is because poets are introspective and feel deeply about the current events and cultural norms they are surrounded with. Poets often produce the most telling literature, giving insight into the society and mind-set they come from. This can be done in many forms.

The oldest types of poems often include many stanzas, may or may not rhyme, and are more about telling a story than experimenting with language or words. The most common types of ancient poetry are epics, which are usually extremely long stories that follow a hero through his journey, or ellegies, which are often solemn in tone and used to mourn or lament something or someone. The Mesopotamians are often said to have invented the written word, and their literature is among the oldest in the world, including the epic poem titled "Epic of Gilgamesh." Similar in style and length to "Gilgamesh" is "Beowulf," an ellegy written in Old English and set in Scandinavia. These poems are often used by professors as the earliest examples of literature.

The importance of poetry was revived in the Renaissance. At this time, Europeans discovered the style and beauty of ancient Greek arts, and poetry was among those. Shakespeare is the most well-known poet of the time, and he used poetry not only to write poems but also to write plays for the theater. The most popular forms of poetry during the Renaissance included villanelles, (a nineteen-line poetic form) sonnets, as well as the epic. Poets during this time focused on style and form, and developed very specific rules and outlines for how an exceptional poem should be written.

As often happens in the arts, modern poets have rejected the constricting rules of Renaissance poets, and free form poems are much more popular. Some modern poems would read just like stories if they weren't arranged into lines and stanzas. It is difficult to tell which poems and poets will be the most important, because works of art often become more famous in hindsight, after the poet has died and society can look at itself without being in the moment. Modern poetry continues to develop, and will no doubt continue to change as values, thought, and writing continue to change.

Poems can be among the most enlightening and uplifting texts for a person to read if they are looking to connect with the past, connect with other people, or try to gain an understanding of what is happening in their time.

47. In summary, the author has written this passage

    a. as a foreword that will introduce a poem in a book or magazine

    b. because she loves poetry and wants more people to like it

    c. to give a brief history of poems

    d. to convince students to write poems

48. The author organizes the paragraphs mainly by

    a. moving chronologically, explaining which types of poetry were common in that time

    b. talking about new types of poems each paragraph and explaining them a little

    c. focusing on one poet or group of people and the poems they wrote

    d. explaining older types of poetry so she can talk about modern poetry

49. The author's claim that poetry has been around "virtually from the time civilizations invented the written word" is supported by the detail that

    a. Beowulf is written in Old English, which is not really in use any longer

    b. epic poems told stories about heroes

    c. the Renaissance poets tried to copy Greek poets

    d. the Mesopotamians are credited with both inventing the word and writing "Epic of Gilgamesh"

50. According to the passage, it can be understood that the word "telling" means

   a. speaking

   b. significant

   c. soothing

   d. wordy

Section II - Language

Part I - English

1. Choose the sentence with the correct grammar.

   a. Don would never have thought of that book, but you could have reminded him.

   b. Don would never of thought of that book, but you could have reminded him.

   c. Don would never have thought of that book, but you could of have reminded him.

   d. Don would never of thought of that book, but you could of reminded him.

2. Choose the correct sentence.

   a. The boy and girl are related.

   b. The boy and girl is related.

   c. The boy and girl was related.

   d. None of the above.

3. Choose the sentence with the correct grammar.

   a. There was scarcely no food in the pantry, because nobody ate at home.

   b. There was scarcely any food in the pantry, because nobody ate at home.

   c. There was scarcely any food in the pantry, because not nobody ate at home.

   d. There was scarcely no food in the pantry, because not nobody ate at home.

4. Choose the sentence with the correct grammar.

    a. Its important for you to know its official name; its called the Confederate Museum.

    b. It's important for you to know it's official name; it's called the Confederate Museum.

    c. It's important for you to know its official name; it's called the Confederate Museum.

    d. Its important for you to know it's official name; it's called the Confederate Museum.

5. Choose the sentence with the correct grammar.

    a. The man as well as his son has arrived.

    b. The man as well as his son have arrived.

    c. Both of the above.

    d. None of the above.

6. Thomas Edison _____ since he invented the light bulb, television, motion pictures, and phonograph.

    a. has always been known as the greatest inventor

    b. was always been known as the greatest inventor

    c. must have had been always known as the greatest inventor

    d. will had been known as the greatest inventor

7. The weatherman on Channel 6 said that this has been the

    a. most hotter summer on record.

    b. most hottest summer on record.

    c. hottest summer on record.

    d. hotter summer on record.

8. Although Joe is tall for his age, his brother Elliot is _____ of the two.

    a. the tallest

    b. more tallest

    c. the tall

    d. the taller

9. When KISS came to town, all of the tickets _____ before I could buy one.

    a. will be sold out
    b. had been sold out
    c. were being sold out
    d. was sold out

10. The rules of most sports _____ more complicated than we often realize.

    a. are
    b. is
    c. was
    d. has been

11. _____ won first place in the Western Division?

    a. Who
    b. Whom
    c. Which
    d. What

12. There are now several ways to listen to music, including radio, CDs, and Mp3 files _____ you can download onto an MP3 player.

    a. on which
    b. who
    c. whom
    d. which

13. Choose the sentence with the correct grammar.

    a. Each of them have to be given a ticket.
    b. Each of them is to be given a ticket.
    c. Each of them are to be given a ticket.
    d. None of the above.

14. Choose the correct spelling.

a. maintainance
b. maintenace
c. maintanance
d. maintenance

15. Choose the correct spelling.

a. humoros
b. humouros
c. humorous
d. humorus

16. Choose the correct spelling.

a. mathematics
b. mathmatics
c. matematics
d. mathamatics

17. Choose the sentence below with the correct punctuation.

a. Ted and Janice, who had been friends for years, went on vacation together every summer.
b. Ted and Janice, who had been friends for years, went on vacation together, every summer.
c. Ted, and Janice who had been friends for years, went on vacation together every summer.
d. Ted and Janice who had been friends for years went on vacation together every summer.

18. Choose the sentence with the correct capitalization.

a. The Sahara Desert is found in the northern part of Africa.
b. The Sahara Desert is found in the Northern part of Africa.
c. The Sahara desert is found in the northern part of Africa.
d. The Sahara desert is found in the Northern part of Africa.

19. She went with him to the dance.

What is the subject of this sentence?

    a. She
    b. Dance
    c. Him
    d. With

20. She studied long and hard and her marks showed it.

What is the predicate of this sentence?

    a. Studied long and hard
    b. Marks showed it
    c. Showed it
    d. None of the above

21. What is on the test?

What type of sentence is this?

    a. Imperative
    b. Interrogative
    c. Exclamatory
    d. Declarative

22. The aquarium featured brightly-colored tropical fish that came from the tropics.

What part of this sentence is redundant?

    a. Brightly-colored
    b. Tropical fish
    c. That came from the tropics
    d. Aquarium

23. Choose the correct sentence.

    a. Historians have been guessing the doctor was a woman for more than 100 years.
    b. Historians have been guessing for more than 100 years the doctor was a woman.
    c. Historians guessed the doctor was a woman for more than 100 years.
    d. None of the above.

24. Choose the correct sentence.

a. None of us want to go to the party not even, if there will be live music.
b. None of us want to go to the party, not even if there will be live music.
c. None of us want to go to the party not even if there will be live music.
d. None of us want to go to the party; not even if there will be live music.

25. Choose the correct sentence.

a. I own two dogs, a cat named Jeffrey, and Henry, the goldfish.
b. I own two dogs a cat, named Jeffrey, and Henry, the goldfish.
c. I own two dogs, a cat named Jeffrey; and Henry, the goldfish.
d. I own two dogs, a cat, named Jeffrey and Henry, the goldfish.

26. Choose the correct sentence.

a. During the years he was President, the country fought two wars.
b. During the years he was president, the country fought two wars.
c. During the years he was president, the Country fought two wars.
d. During the years he was President, the Country fought two wars.

27. Alice jumped when she saw the rabbit.

What part of speech is the underlined word?

a. Noun
b. Verb
c. Adjective
d. Adverb

28. Which of the following sentences contains a redundant phrase?

a. I will be leaving shortly.
b. I think the situation calls for a direct confrontation.
c. The fish swam upstream with great difficulty.
d. None of the above.

Directions: For each of the questions below, choose the word with the meaning best suited to the sentence based on the context.

29. Paul's rose bushes were being destroyed by Japanese beetles, so he invested in a good _____.

    a. Fungicide

    b. Fertilizer

    c. Sprinkler

    d. Pesticide

30. Because of a pituitary dysfunction, Karl lacked the necessary _____ to grow as tall as his father.

    a. Glands

    b. Hormones

    c. Vitamins

    d. Testosterone

Part II - Paragraphs

Curiosity's Mission

Mankind's thirst for knowledge about ourselves and the universe has always been insatiable, making curiosity a driving force for human advances through history. [1] Not only that, human curiosity and creativity have created countless works of fiction that speculate about future discoveries. [2]

Our neighboring planet Mars, for example, has long led scientists and writers to generate stories about living on the Red Planet. [3] Serious endeavors in science and technology are motivated by our never-ending questions. [4] So far, NASA has carried out several exploratory missions to Mars and the rover robot Curiosity is the latest and most sophisticated. [5]

Curiosity was launched in late November 2011 from Cape Canaveral Air Force Station in Florida. [6] It successfully landed on Mars on August 6, 2012 searching for evidence of life. [7] The car sized robot, weighing about a ton, is equipped with all the technical capacities to carry out its mission to explore our neighbor for biological, geological and geochemical traces of life. [8] It will also test the Martian soil and surface to collect data about its planetary evolution and surface radiation. [9]

Curiosity has been engineered with cutting-edge technologies worth over 2.5 billion US dollars. [10] The most incredible component of the rover is the on-board science lab. [11] Apart from that, it consists of a communications system that allows transmission of commands to the rover from the control centre at NASA, enabling direct control of the robot's activities on the surface of the Red Planet. [12] The Curiosity rover has a number of mounted cameras which assists navigation, as well as capturing images from the Martian surface and transmitting them back to Earth. [13]

1. How would you re-write sentence 1?

a. No changes

b. Mankind's thirst for knowledge has always been insatiable, making curiosity a driving factor for human advances through history.

c. Mankind's thirst for knowledge is insatiable, making curiosity a driving factor for human advances through history.

d. Humankind's thirst for knowledge is insatiable, making curiosity a driving force in advances throughout history.

2. Which sentence in the third paragraph is least relevant to the main idea of the third paragraph?

a. 6

b. 8

c. 9

d. 10

3. Which of the following changes would focus attention on the main idea of the last paragraph?

a. To achieve its goals, Curiosity has been engineered with cutting-edge technologies worth over 2.5 billion US dollars.

b. Because a lot of funding was available for this project, Curiosity has been engineered with cutting-edge technologies worth over 2.5 billion US dollars.

c. As there is no guarantee that it will succeed in its mission, Curiosity has been engineered with cutting-edge technologies worth over 2.5 billion US dollars.

d. NASA's scientific data is so reliable that, being assured of no risk of failure in the mission, Curiosity has been engineered with cutting-edge technologies worth over 2.5 billion US dollars.

4. Which of the following is/are needed in sentence 5?

a. So far, "NASA" has carried out several exploration missions to Mars and the rover robot Curiosity is the latest and most sophisticated of all.

b. So far, NASA has carried out several exploratory missions to Mars and the rover robot Curiosity is the latest and most sophisticated of all.

c. So far, NASA has carried out several exploration missions to Mars and the rover robot -Curiosity- is the latest and most sophisticated of all.

d. So far, NASA has carried out several exploratory missions to Mars and the rover robot "Curiosity" is the latest and most sophisticated of all.

Green Energy from Olive Oil

The debate over developing sustainable energy sources have been very active in the past two decades. [1] With continued concern over global climate change, environmentalists are urging governments for lowering their dependence on fossil fuels in order for ensuring reduced carbon emission into the atmosphere. [2] Consequently, governments worldwide are turning their attention to the search for non-emissive sources of energy. [3] Renewable substitutes under extensive research are solar power, wind, geothermal energy and harnessing energy from ocean waves. [4]

While the search for environment friendly energy sources is already under way, developing these alternatives at a reasonable cost is a major challenge. [5] No cost-effective replacement for fossil fuels has yet been found. [6] However, recent years have seen remarkable progress in the field of solar energy. [7] Ted Sargent, a Professor at University of Toronto, Canada, has discovered that olive oil has the capacity to capture solar radiation and emit electrons resulting in an electric current. [8] This is a major discovery in the solar power generation industry as it offers a cheap source of harnessing the Sun's energy. [9]

Oleic acid, the main ingredient of olive oil, absorbs infrared radiation is the major component of the Sun's radiation reaching the Earth. [10] The discovery is significant because so far, no attempt has been made to use the abundant infrared radiation we receive throughout the year. [11] Capturing this heat wave radiation, along with the photons that are present in sunlight, increases the efficiency of the solar cells that are already being manufactured commercially. [12] And to make it possible, Professor Sargent has developed a new kind of solar cell called "quantum dots," tiny cells made from gels of tin, bismuth, lead, sulphur and selenium mixed with extra pure olive oil. [13] The resulting ink-like crystal absorbs both photons and infrared radiation and has the capacity to transmit electrons and produce a current. [14]

This new method of capturing the Sun's energy is considered a breakthrough in the solar power industry as it offers cheaper alternatives to the existing use of silicon crystals which are costly to manufacture. [15] And although the invention is yet to prove its efficiency, a lot of funding has already been dedicated to further research. [16]

5. What sentence from the passage is an example of a sentence fragment?

    a. 6
    b. 10
    c. 11
    d. 13

6. Which of the following sentences should be deleted to reduce redundancy?

    a. 5
    b. 6
    c. 9
    d. 15

7. Which of the following changes are needed in sentence 10?

    a. Oleic acid, the main ingredient of olive oil, absorbs infrared radiation is the major component of the Sun's radiation reaching the Earth.
    b. Oleic acid, the main ingredient of olive oil, absorbs infrared radiation, which is the major component of the Sun's radiation reaching the Earth.
    c. Oleic acid, the main ingredient of olive oil absorbs infrared radiation that is the major component of the Sun's radiation reaching the Earth.
    d. Oleic acid, the main ingredient of olive oil, absorbs infrared radiation what is the major component of the Sun's radiation reaching the Earth.

8. Which of the following changes are needed in sentence 2?

    a. With continued concern over global climate change, environmentalists are urging governments to lowering their dependence on fossil fuels to ensuring reduced carbon emission into the atmosphere.
    b. With continued concern over global climate change, environmentalists are urging governments lower their dependence on fossil fuels in order for ensuring reduced carbon emission into the atmosphere.
    c. With continued concern over global climate change, environmentalists are urging governments to lower their dependence on fossil fuels in order for ensuring reduced carbon emission into the atmosphere.
    d. With continued concern over global climate change, environmentalists are urging governments to lower their dependence on fossil fuels to ensure reduced carbon emission into the atmosphere.

Hunting Lost Cities from Space

Satellite imaging has become widespread with improvements in telecommunication over the past two decades. [1] Communication satellites in orbit around the Earth have enabled large-scale mapping of the planet's surface which has become freely available thanks to technology giants like Google. [2] Satellite mapping has opened up new possibilities in diverse fields of science and technology. [3]

The key feature of the new tool, according to Professor Sarah Parcak, who discovered many cities, temples and pyramids covered under sands and sediment; is that it offers a wider perspective in size and scale of the location under study. [4] Along with the visual information that the satellite images provide, numerous details about the sites can be obtained from infrared (IR) and gravitational field images. [5] This information, coupled with conventional on-site procedures, are vital for archeology. [6]

IR data collected from satellite imaging provide clues about the activities of humans living in the contemporary times of their civilizations- including their agriculture, vegetation, structures, habitation roads and much more. [7] This type of information is derived from IR imagery which detects IR radiation present in sunlight as it is reflected by the Earth. [8] Different points in a civilization reflect IR radiation in different proportions, revealing the contrast between different areas and provide detailed insight about the causes of these differing heat signatures. [9]

9. Which of the following changes in sentence 6 would focus attention on the main idea of the second paragraph?

> a. These information, along with a supply of some heavy machinery, will help the excavation of every archeological site accomplished within a short period of time.
>
> b. This information, coupled with conventional on-site procedures, help archeologists plan their excavation carefully and efficiently.
>
> c. Such details are valuable records of ancient history and are essential assets of any civilization.
>
> d. Such details, unfortunately, are available to archeological firms who are willing to invest a lot of money on putting satellites into orbit.

10. Which of the following sentences should be modified to reduce redundancy?

> a. 7
> b. 8
> c. 9
> d. 10

Section III – Math

1. Simplify 2 1/3 ÷ 1 2/5

    a. 1 2/5
    b. 1 2/3
    c. 1 1/7
    d. 2 2/5

2. 2/3 x 1 4/7 x 5 1/4

    a. 3 1/4
    b. 5 1/2
    c. 6 2/3
    d. 4 2/5

3. Simplify 4 1/5 ÷ 2 1/3

    a. 1 4/5
    b. 2 1/4
    c. 1 3/7
    d. 2 1/4

4. 10/3 x 2 1/4 x 3 1/5

    a. 1 3/4
    b. 24
    c. 7 2/7
    d. 5 1/5

5. Simplify 3 1/9 ÷ 2 2/3

    a. 2 1/5
    b. 2 3/4
    c. 1 1/6
    d. 1 1/4

6. What is -9 + (+6) – (-2)

    a. -3
    b. -1
    c. 5
    d. -5

7. Smith and Simon are playing a card game. Smith will win if a card drawn from a deck of 52 is either a 7 or a diamond, and Simon will win if the drawn card is an even number. Which statement is more likely to be correct?

    a. Simon will win more games.
    b. Smith will win more games.
    c. They have same winning probability.
    d. A decision cannot be made from the provided data.

8. By practicing, a typist increases his typing speed by 2 words per minute daily. If his current typing speed is 18 words per minute and he practice 3 hours a day, then how many hours will he need to practice to attain 40 words per minute?

    a. 27
    b. 30
    c. 33
    d. 36

9. If the speed of a train is 72 kilometers per hour, what distance will it cover in 12 seconds?

    a. 200 m
    b. 220 m
    c. 240 m
    d. 260 m

10. In a class of 83 students, 72 are present. What percent of the students are absent? Provide answer up to two significant digits.

  a. 12
  b. 13
  c. 14
  d. 15

11. A driver traveled from city A to city B in 1 hour and 13 minutes. On the way, he had to stop at 5 traffic signals, with an average time of 80 seconds. If the distance between the cities is 65 kilometers then what was the average driving speed?

  a. 56.42
  b. 58.77
  c. 60.34
  d. 63.25

12. Mr. Micheal runs a factory. His total assets are $256,800 that consists of a building worth $80,500, machinery worth $125.000 and $51,300 cash. After one year what will be the value of his total assets if he has additional cash of $75,600 and the value of his building has increased by 10% per year, and his machinery depreciated by 20% per year?

  a. $24,3450
  b. $25,2450
  c. $26,4150
  d. $27,2350

13. Martin earns $25,000 as basic pay, $500 rent and $860 for medical insurance. He spends 40% of his total earning on food and clothing, 10% on children's education and pays $800 for utility bills. What percent of his earning he is saving?

  a. 54%
  b. 50%
  c. 47%
  d. 44%

14. Prize money of $1,050 is to be shared among top three contestants in ratio of 7:5:3 as 1st, 2nd and 3rd prizes respectively. How much more money will the 1st prize contestant receive than the 3rd prize contestant?

  a. $210
  b. $280
  c. $350
  d. $490

15. The manager of a weaving factory estimates that if 10 machines run on 100% efficiency for 8 hours, they will produce 1450 meters of cloth. Due to some technical problems, 4 machines run of 95% efficiency and the remaining 6 at 90% efficiency. How many meters of cloth can these machines will produce in 8 hours?

  a. 1479 meters
  b. 1310 meters
  c. 1334 meters
  d. 1285 meters

Practice Test Questions 1

16. A car covers a distance in 3.5 hours at an average speed of 60 km/hr. How much time in hours will a motorbike take to cover this distance at an average speed of 40km/hr?

   a. 4.5
   b. 4.75
   c. 5
   d. 5.25

17. A grandfather is 8 times older than his grandson is now. After 6 years, he will be 5 times older than his grandson will. How old is the grandfather now?

   a. 48
   b. 56
   c. 64
   d. 72

18. Solve for n. 5n + (19 – 2)) = 67.

   a. 21
   b. 10
   c. 15
   d. 7

19. A boy is given 2 apples while his sister is given 8 oranges. What is the ratio between his apples and her oranges?

   a. 1:2
   b. 2:4
   c. 1:4
   d. 2:1

20. A box contains 7 black pencils and 28 blue ones. What is the ratio between the black and blue pens?

   a. 1:4
   b. 2:7
   c. 1:8
   d. 1:9

21. If X + (32 + 356) = 920. What is x?

   a. 450
   b. 388
   c. 532
   d. 623

22. A boy buys 10 candies. The packet contains 3 green candies, 12 red and 9 blue candies. What is the ratio the green, red and blue sweets?

   a. 1:3:4
   b. 1:4:3
   c. 2:3:1
   d. 1:5:4

23. Solve for x. (12 x 12)/x = 12

   a. 12
   b. 13
   c. 8
   d. 14

24. Solve for A. A – (34 x 2) = 18.

   a. 86
   b. 78
   c. 50
   d. 73

25. Solve for X. X% of 120 = 30.

   a. 15
   b. 12
   c. 4
   d. 25

26. Solve for X. X * 25% of 100 = 76.

   a. 5
   b. 3
   c. 21
   d. 13

27. Solve for X. X% of 250 = 50.

   a. 30
   b. 35
   c. 25
   d. 20

28. What is the least common multiple of 4 and 3?

   a. 24
   b. 6
   c. 16
   d. 12

29. What is the ratio between 2 gold coins, 6 silver coins and 12 bronze coins?

   a. 2:3:4
   b. 1:2:4
   c. 1:3:6
   d. 2:3:4

30. What is the least common multiple of 8 and 12?

   a. 24
   b. 36
   c. 12
   d. 8

31. Solve for x. -7 + 3x = 20.

   a. 7
   b. 5
   c. 4
   d. 9

32. What is the least common multiple of 2 and 3?

   a. 2
   b. 4
   c. 6
   d. 3

33. Solve for c, when 124 = 12c - 20.

   a. 6
   b. 12
   c. 10
   d. 15

34. Simplify 3 8/9 + 5 5/6.

   a. 8 13/15
   b. 8 3/9
   c. 9 13/18
   d. 8 12/18

35. Simplify 7 4/5 + 2 2/5.

   a. 5 3/5
   b. 5 1/5
   c. 4 2/5
   d. 5 2/5

36. Translate the following into an equation: three plus a number times 7 equals 42.

   a. 7(3 + X) = 42
   b. 3(X + 7) = 42
   c. 3X + 7 = 42
   d. (3 + 7)X = 42

37. Estimate 5205 / 25

   a. 108
   b. 308
   c. 208
   d. 408

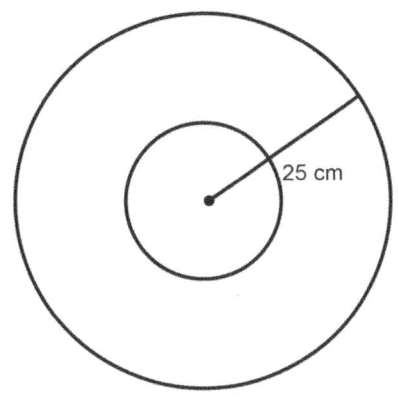

Note: figure not drawn to scale

39. What is the distance travelled by the wheel above, when it makes 175 revolutions?

   a. 87.5 π m
   b. 875 π m
   c. 8.75 π m
   d. 8750 π m

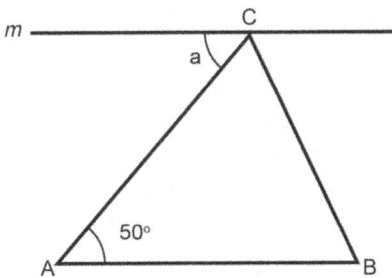

Note: figure not drawn to scale

38. If the line m is parallel to the side AB of △ABC, what is angle a?

   a. 130°
   b. 25°
   c. 65°
   d. 50°

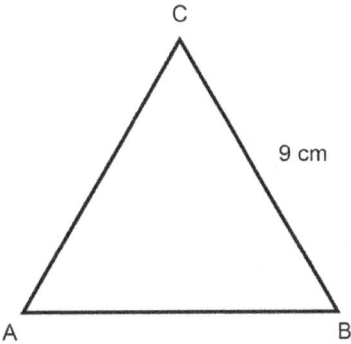

Note: figure not drawn to scale

40. What is the perimeter of the equilateral △ABC above?

   a. 18 cm
   b. 12 cm
   c. 27 cm
   d. 15 cm

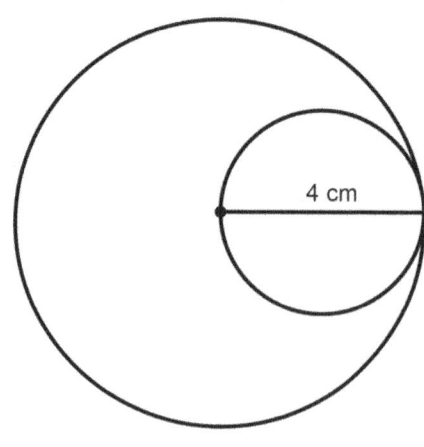

Note: figure not drawn to scale

41. Assuming the diameter of the small circle is the radius of the larger circle, what is (area of large circle) - (area of small circle) in the figure above?

   a. 8 π cm²
   b. 10 π cm²
   c. 12 π cm²
   d. 16 π cm²

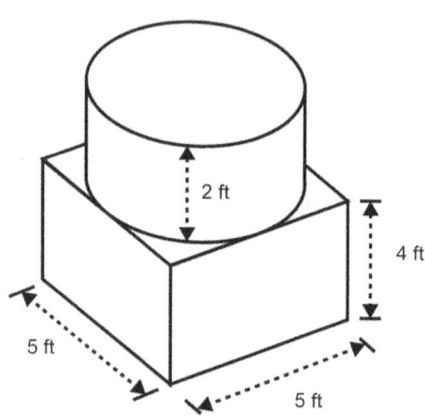

Note: figure not drawn to scale

42. What is the approximate total volume of the above solid?

   a. 120 ft³
   b. 100 ft³
   c. 140 ft³
   d. 160 ft³

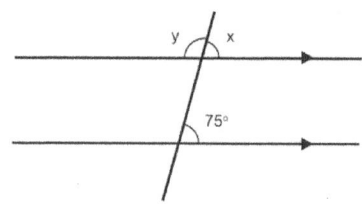

43. What is the value of the angle y?

   a. 25°
   b. 15°
   c. 30°
   d. 105°

44. In a local election at polling station A, 945 voters cast their vote out of 1270 registered voters. At polling station B, 860 cast their vote out of 1050 registered voters and at station C, 1210 cast their vote out of 1440 registered voters. What is the total turnout including all three polling stations?

   a. 70%
   b. 74%
   c. 76%
   d. 80%

45. 3a + 4b x d =? When A = 2, b = 4 and d = 8.

   a. 40
   b. 90
   c. 80

d. 65

46. $4^2 \times 4^7 =$

    a. 16^{-5}

    b. 4^9

    c. 16^{11}

    d. 4^{-5}

47. $10^{65} \div 10^{13}$

    a. 10^{52}

    b. 10^{78}

    c. 100^{62}

    d. 100^{78}

48. Consider the following population growth chart.

Country	Population 2000	Population 2005
Japan	122,251,000	128,057,000
China	1,145,195,000	1,341,335,000
United States	253,339,000	310,384,000
Indonesia	184,346,000	239,871,000

What country is growing the fastest?

    a. Japan

    b. China

    c. United States

    d. Indonesia

49. What is the smallest value?

    a. 0.4 portion of 200

    b. 50% of 100

    c. 0.06 portion of 2000

    d. 2% of 1000

50. What number multiplied by 5 is 10 less than 52?

    a. 8.4

    b. 10.24

    c. 20

    d. 22.5

Section IV - Ability

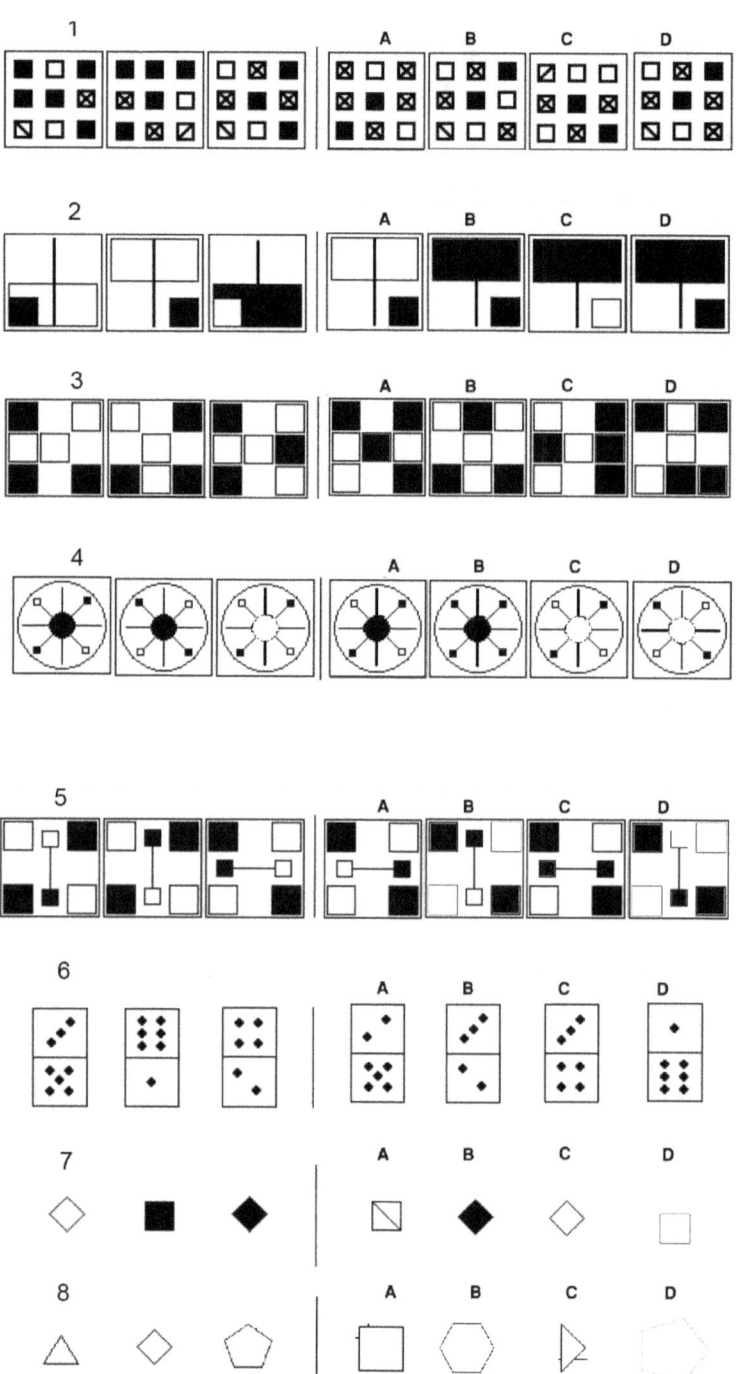

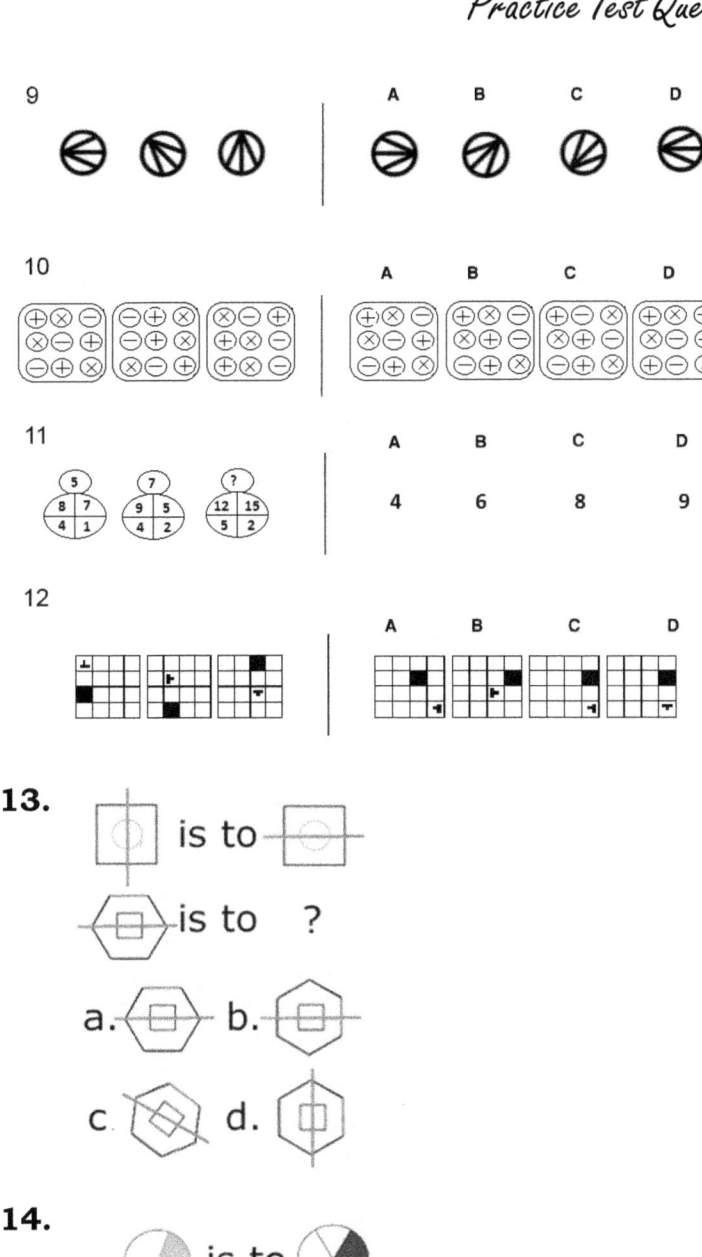

9

10

11 | A | B | C | D |
| 4 | 6 | 8 | 9 |

12

13.

14.

15.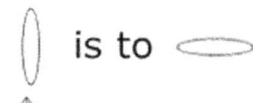

a. b.

c. d.

16. is to

is to ?

a. b.

c. d.

17. is to

is to ?

a. b.

c. d.

18.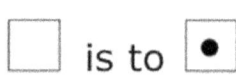

is to ?

a. b.

c. d.

19. is to

is to ?

a. b.

c. d.

20.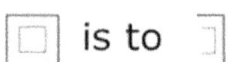

is to ?

a. b.

c. d.

21.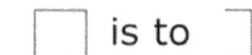

is to ?

a. b.

c. d.

22.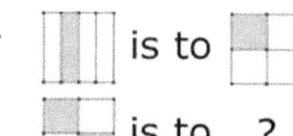

is to ?

a. b.

c. d.

23.

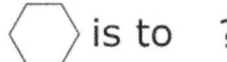 is to ?

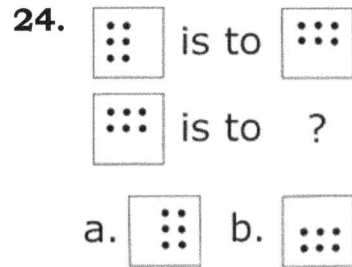

24.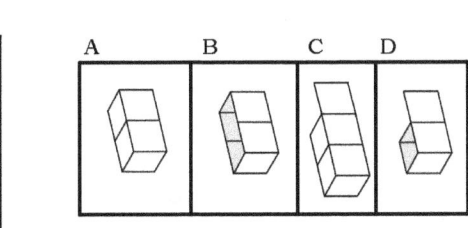

25. **When folded, which shape is possible?**

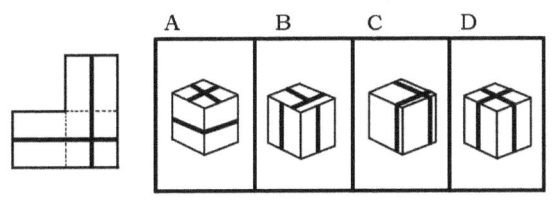

26. **When folded, what pattern is possible?**

27. **When folded into a loop, what will the strip of paper look like?**

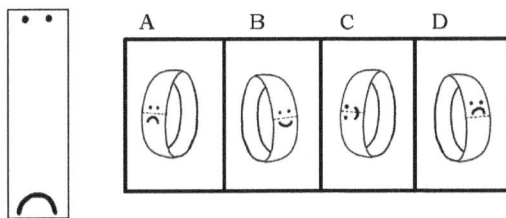

28. **Which of the choices is the same pattern at a different angle?**

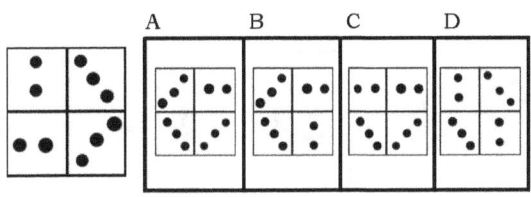

29. **When folded along the dotted lines, which shape will you get?**

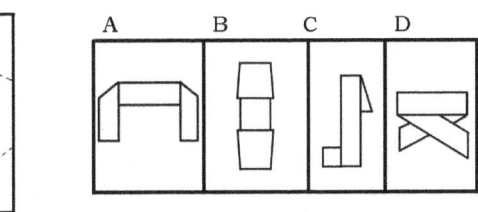

30. **When folded, what pattern is possible?**

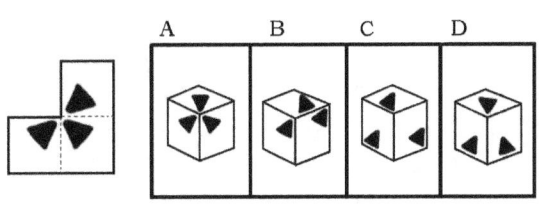

31. When folded into a loop, what will the strip of paper look like?

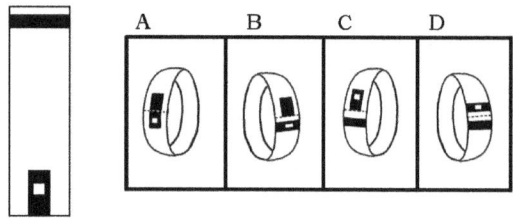

35. When folded, what pattern is possible?

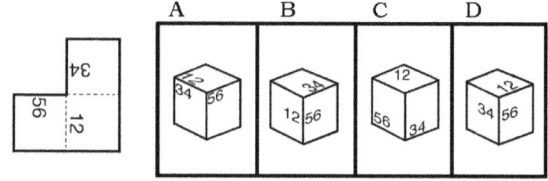

32. Which of the choices is the same pattern at a different angle?

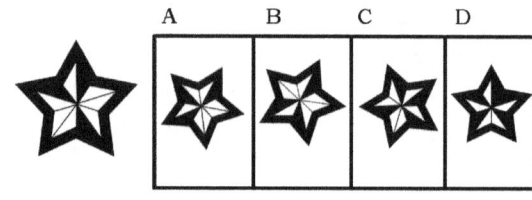

36. When folded into a loop, what will the strip of paper look like?

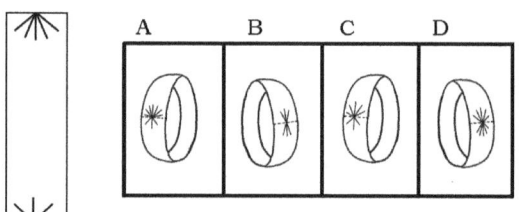

33. When folded along the dotted line, which shape will you get?

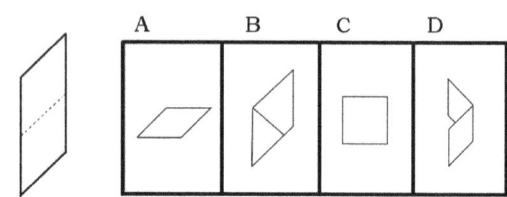

37. Which of the choices is the same pattern at a different angle?

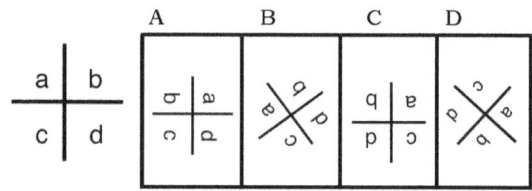

34. When folded, what pattern is possible?

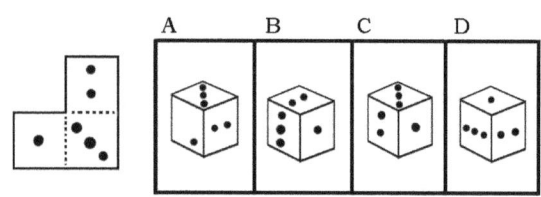

38. When folded, what pattern is possible?

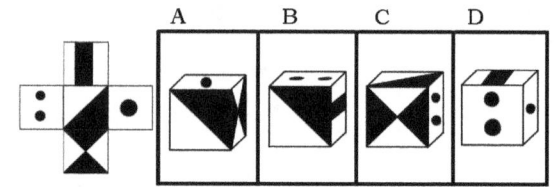

39. When folded into a loop, what will the strip of paper look like?

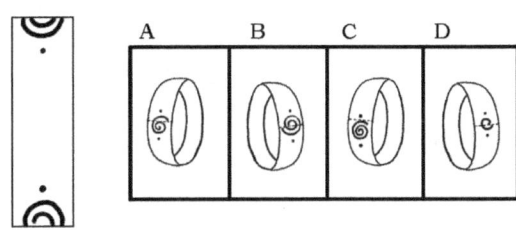

40. When folded, what pattern is possible?

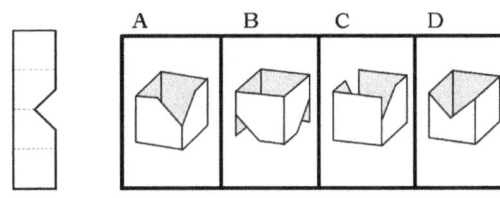

Answer Key

Reading - Part I - Vocabulary

1. C
Cut has the same meaning as gash.

2. D
Hazardous has the same meaning as dangerous.

3. A
Dark has the same meaning as shadowy.

4. B
Determine has the same meaning as choose.

5. C
Definite has the same meaning as clear.

6. D
Delectable has the same meaning as delicious.

7. B
Describe has the same meaning as portray.

8. A
Destroy has the same meaning as ruin.

9. B
Difference has the same meaning as dissimilarity.

10. D
Attain has the same meaning as achieve.

11. A
Boring has the same meaning as uninteresting.

12. D
Eager has the same meaning as enthusiastic.

13. C
End has the same meaning as stop.

14. B
Enjoy has the same meaning as delight in.

15. C
Elaborate has the same meaning as explain.

16. A
Truism: n. self evident or clear obvious truth.

17. A
Virago: Given to undue belligerence or ill manner at the slightest provocation; a shrew, a termagant.

18. D
Femur: n. The bone of the thigh or upper hind limb, articulating at the hip and the knee.

19. C
Genteel: Polite and well-mannered. Stylish or elegant. Aristocratic

20. A
Adulterate: v. To render (something) poorer in quality by adding another substance, typically an inferior one.

Part II - Reading Comprehension

21. B
The correct answer because that fact is stated directly in the passage. The passage explains that Anne taught Helen to hear by allowing her to feel the vibrations in her throat.

22. A
We can infer that Anne is a patient teacher because she did not leave or lose her temper when Helen bit or hit her; she just kept trying to teach Helen. Choice B is incorrect because Anne taught Helen to read and talk. Choice C is incorrect because Anne could hear. She was partially blind, not deaf. Choice D is incorrect because it does not have to do with patience.

23. B
The passage states that it was hard for anyone but Anne to understand Helen when she spoke. Choice A is incorrect because the passage does not mention Helen spoke a foreign language. Choice C is incorrect because there is no mention of how quiet or loud Helen's voice was. Choice D is incorrect because we know from reading the passage that Helen did learn to speak.

24. D
This question tests the reader's summarization skills. The other choices A, B, and C focus on portions of the second paragraph that are too narrow and do not relate to the specific portion of text in question. The complexity of the sentence may mislead students into selecting one of these answers, but rearranging or restating the sentence will lead the reader to the correct answer. In addition, choice A makes an assumption that may or may not be true about the intentions of the company, choice B focuses on one product rather than the idea of the products, and choice C makes an assumption about women that may or may not be true and is not supported by the text.

25. D
This question tests the reader's summarization skills. The question is asking very generally about the message of the passage, and the title, "Ways

Characters Communicate in Theater," is one indication of that. The other choices A, B, and C are all directly from the text, and therefore readers may be inclined to select one of them, but are too specific to encapsulate the entirety of the passage and its message.

26. B
The paragraph on soliloquies mentions "To be or not to be," and it is from the context of that paragraph that readers may understand that because "To be or not to be" is a soliloquy, Hamlet will be introspective, or thoughtful, while delivering it. It is true that actors deliver soliloquies alone, and may be "solitary" (choice A), but "thoughtful" (choice B) is more true to the overall idea of the paragraph. Readers may choose C because drama and theater can be used interchangeably and the passage mentions that soliloquies are unique to theater (and therefore drama), but this answer is not specific enough to the paragraph in question. Readers may pick up on the theme of life and death and Hamlet's true intentions and select that he is "hopeless" (choice D), but those themes are not discussed either by this paragraph or passage, as a close textual reading and analysis confirms.

27. C
This question tests the reader's grammatical skills. Choice B seems logical, but parenthesis are actually considered to be a stronger break in a sentence than commas are, and along this line of thinking, actually disrupt the sentence more.

Choices A and D make comparisons between theater and film that are simply not made in the passage, and may or may not be true. This detail does clarify the statement that asides are most unique to theater by adding that it is not completely unique to theater, which may have been why the author didn't chose not to delete it and instead used parentheses to designate the detail's importance (choice C).

28. A
Low blood sugar occurs both in diabetics and healthy adults.

29. B
None of the statements are the author's opinion.

30. A
The author's purpose is the inform.

31. A
The only statement that is not a detail is, "A doctor can diagnosis this medical condition by asking the patient questions and testing."

32. A
This sentence is a recommendation.

33. C
Tips for a good night's sleep is the best alternative title for this article.

34. B
Mental activity is helpful for a good night's sleep is cannot be inferred from this article.

35. A
From the passage, one disadvantage of taking naps is they may keep you awake at night.

36. A
Based on the partial table of contents, this book is most likely about how to answer multiple choice.

37. C
To be infamous means to be remembered for an evil or terrible action.

Therefore, the word infamy means to remember a bad or terrible thing. Choice A is incorrect because being famous is not the same as being infamous. Choice B is incorrect because the attack on Pearl Harbor was not good. Choice D is incorrect because Pearl Harbor was not forgotten.

38. C
Each answer choice except choice C contains the name of at least one country that was not part of the AXIS powers.

39. D
It is stated in the passage. Choice A is not correct because there was no indication that Japan would attack San Diego. Choice B is incorrect because the attack on Pearl Harbor was a surprise. Choice C is incorrect because Roosevelt was not planning to attack Japan.

40. C
The passage clearly states that Japan planned a surprise attack. They chose that early time to catch the U.S. military off guard. Choice A is incorrect because the military does not sleep late. Choice B is incorrect because there is no law against bombing countries. Choice D is incorrect because it makes no sense.

41. C
This question tests the reader's vocabulary skills. The uses of the negatives "but" and "less," especially right next to each other, may confuse readers into answering with choices A or D, which list words that are antonyms to "militant." Readers may also be confused by the comparison of healthy people with what is being described as an overly healthy person--both people are good, but the reader may look for which one is "worse" in the comparison, and therefore stray toward the antonym words. One key to understanding the meaning of "militant" if the reader is unfamiliar with it is to look at the root of the word; readers can then easily associate it with "military" and gain a sense of what the word signifies: defense (especially considered that the immune system defends the body). Choice C is correct over choice B because "militant" is an adjective, just as the words in choice C are, whereas the words in choice B are nouns.

42. C
This question tests the reader's understanding of function within writing. The other choices are details included surrounding the quoted text, and may therefore confuse the reader. A somewhat contradicts what is said earlier in the paragraph, which is that tests and treatments are improving, and probably doctors are along with them, but the paragraph doesn't actually mention doctors, and the subject of the question is the medicine. Choice B may seem correct to readers who aren't careful to understand that, while the author does mention the large number of people affected, the author is touching on the realities of living with allergies rather about the likelihood of curing all allergies. Similarly, while the author does mention the "balance" of the body, which is easily associated with "wholesome," the author is not really making an argument and especially is not making an extreme statement that allergy medicines should be outlawed. Again, because the article's tone is on living with allergies, choice C is an appropriate choice that fits with the title and content of the text.

43. B
This question tests the reader's inference skills. The text does not state who is doing the recommending, but the use of the "patients," as well as the general context of the passage, lends itself to the logical partner, "doctors," choice B. The author does mention the recommendation but doesn't present it as her own (i.e. "I recommend that"), so choice A may be eliminated. It may seem plausible that people with allergies (choice D) may recommend medicines or products to other people with allergies, but the text does not necessarily support this interaction taking place. Choice C may be selected because the EpiPen is specifically mentioned, but the use of the phrase "such as" when it is introduced is not limiting enough to assume the recommendation is coming from its creators.

44. D
This question tests the reader's global understanding of the text. Choice D includes the main topics of the three body paragraphs, and isn't too focused on a specific aspect or quote from the text, as the other questions are, giving a skewed summary of what the author intended. The reader may be drawn to choice B because of the title of the passage and the use of words like "better," but the message of the passage is larger and more general than this.

45. B
Reading the document posted to the Human Resources website is optional.

46. B
The document is recommended changes and have not be implemented yet.

47. C
This question tests the reader's summarization skills. The use of the word "actually" in describing what kind of people poets are, as well as other moments like this, may lead readers to selecting choices B or D, but the author is more information than trying to persuade readers. The author gives no indication that she loves poetry (choice B) or that people, students specifically (D), should write poems. Choice A is incorrect because the style and content of this paragraph do not match those of a foreword; forewords usually focus on the history or ideas of a specific poem to introduce it more fully and help it stand out against other poems. The author here focuses on several poems and gives broad statements. Instead, she tells a kind of story about poems, giving three very broad time periods in which to discuss them, thereby giving a brief history of poetry, as choice C states.

48. A
This question tests the reader's summarization skills. Key words in the topic sentences of each of the paragraphs ("oldest," "Renaissance," "modern") should give the reader an idea that the author is moving chronologically. The opening and closing sentence-paragraphs are broad and talk generally. B seems reasonable, but epic poems are mentioned in two paragraphs, eliminating the idea that only new types of poems are used in each paragraph. Choice C is also easily eliminated because the author clearly mentions several different poets, groups of people, and poems. Choice D also seems reasonable, considering that the author does move from older forms of poetry to newer forms, but use of "so (that)" makes this statement false, for the author gives no indication that she is rushing (the paragraphs are about the same size) or that she prefers modern poetry.

49. D
This question tests the reader's attention to detail. The key word is "invented"--it ties together the Mesopotamians, who invented the written word, and the fact that they, as the inventors, also invented and used poetry. The other selections focus on other details mentioned in the passage, such as that the Renaissance's admiration of the Greeks (choice C) and that Beowulf is in Old English (choice A). Choice B may seem like an attractive answer because it is unlike the others and because the idea of heroes seems rooted in ancient and early civilizations.

50. B
This question tests the reader's vocabulary and contextualization skills. "Telling" is not an unusual word, but it may be used here in a way that is not familiar to readers, as an adjective rather than a verb in gerund form. A may seem like the obvious answer to a reader looking for a verb to match the use they are familiar with. If the reader understands that the word is being used as an adjective and that choice A is a ploy, they may opt to select choice D, "wordy," but it does not make sense in context. Choice C can be easily eliminated, and doesn't have any connection to the paragraph or passage. "Significant" (choice B) makes sense contextually, especially relative to the phrase "give insight" used later in the sentence.

Section II - Language

Part I - Spelling, Usage, Capitalization and Punctuation

1. A
The third conditional is used for talking about an unreal situation (a situation that did not happen) in the past. For example, "If I had studied harder, [if clause] I would have passed the exam" [main clause]. This has the same meaning as, "I failed the exam, because I didn't study hard enough."

2. A
Use a plural verb form for two subjects linked by "and."

3. B
In double negative sentences, one negative is replaced with "any."

4. C
"It's" is a contraction for it is or it has. "Its" is a possessive pronoun.

5. A
When two subjects are linked by "with" or "as well," use the verb form that matches the first subject.

6. A
The sentence requires the past perfect "has always been known." This is the only grammatically correct choice.

7. C
The superlative, "hottest," is used when expressing a temperature greater than that of anything to which it is being compared.

8. D
When comparing two items, use "the taller." When comparing more than two items, use "the tallest."

9. B
The past perfect form is used to

describe an event that occurred in the past, and prior to another event. Here there are two things that happened, both of them in the past, and something the person wanted to do.

Event 1: Kiss came to town
Event 2: All the tickets sold out
What I wanted to do: Buy a ticket

The events are arranged:
When KISS came to town, all of the tickets **had been sold out** before I could buy one.

10. A
The subject is "rules" so the present tense plural form, "are," is used to agree with "realize."

11. A
"Who" is correct because the question uses an active construction. "To whom was first place given?" is a passive construction.

12. D
"Which" is correct, because the files are objects and not people.

13. B
Use a singular verb with either, each, neither, everyone and many.

14. D
Maintenance is the correct spelling.

15. C
Humorous is the correct spelling.

16. A
Mathematics is the correct spelling.

17. A
Use a comma to separate phrases.

18. A
The Sahara Desert is a proper name so capitalized. The names of countries, ie Africa are capitalized.

19. A
'She' is the simple subject of this sentence.

20. A
The simple predicate is 'studied long and hard.' The predicate of a sentence is the action performed by the subject.

21. B
This is an interrogative sentence.

22. C
It is not necessary to say the fish came from the topics, since we already know they are tropical.

23. B
The correct sentence is
Historians have been guessing for more than 100 years the doctor was a woman.

Here the phrase 'for more than 100 years' refers to how long historians have been guessing, and not to how long the doctor has been a woman.

24. B
Use a comma separates independent clauses. None of us wants to go to the party, not even if there will be live music.

25. A
This is an example where a comma appears before 'and,' but is disambiguating. Without the comma, the sentence would be "I own two dogs, a cat named Jeffrey and Henry, the goldfish." This means there is a cat named Jeffrey and Henry, and a goldfish with no name mentioned. The comma appears to show the distinction.
I own two dogs, a cat named Jeffrey, and Henry, the goldfish.

26. B
President is not capitalized unless used with a name as in, President Obama.

27. B
'Jumped' is a verb. Verbs describe an action, state, or occurrence.

28. B
A confrontation is a head-on conflict, so a direct confrontation is redundant.

29. D
Pesticide: NOUN a substance, usually synthetic although sometimes biological, used to kill or contain the activities of pests.

30. B
Hormones: NOUN any substance produced by one tissue and conveyed by the bloodstream to another to effect physiological activity.

Part II - Paragraphs

1. D
Suggested revision of sentence 1, "Humankind's thirst for knowledge is insatiable, making curiosity a driving force for advances throughout history."
Use the gender neutral "humankind. Replace the past perfect "has always been" with the present tense to make a simpler and more direct sentence. "Though history" is incorrect. Use "throughout" when referring to a time period. Replace the preposition "for" with "in."

2. A
Sentence 6 is the least relevant. "Curiosity was launched in late November 2011 from Cape Canaveral Air Force Station in Florida."
The third paragraph talks about the objectives of the rover. All sentences other than sentence 7 mention the objectives. This sentence, however, informs about when the spacecraft was launched.

3. A
Sentence 10 is least relevant to the main idea of the third paragraph. The following changes are suggested, "<u>To achieve its goals</u>, Curiosity has been engineered with cutting-edge technologies worth a budgetary expense exceeding 2.5 billion US dollars."

Clearly, the last paragraph talks about how Curiosity has been engineered to accomplish its objectives. The previous paragraph addressing the objectives of the rover, addition of the phrase "To achieve its goals," in choice A acts as a transition sentence between the paragraphs.

4. D
The changes needed to sentence 5 are, "So far, NASA has carried out several exploratory missions to Mars and the rover robot "Curiosity" is the latest and most sophisticated of all."

"Curiosity" is the name of a spacecraft that was assigned the particular name because of its association of its mission to satisfy our curiosity about the planet Mars. In this respect, the name bears a special meaning and emphasis, which must be reflected in representing it using the quotation mark.

Use of the adjective "exploratory" to describe the missions is correct.

Choice D offers these changes.

5. C
Sentence 11 is a fragment. "The dis-

covery is significant because so far, no attempt has been made to use the abundant infrared radiation we receive throughout the year."

The fragment contains a subordinate clause derived from the complete thought "The discovery is significant because so far no attempt has been made to make use of the infra-red radiation that we receive in an abundant supply all throughout the year." It also contains the subject of the main clause, "The discovery," but does not have any verbal phrase for the main clause. Since the main clause remains incomplete, the thought is expressed in part. Therefore, it is a sentence fragment.

6. C
Sentence 9 can be deleted to reduce redundancy. "This is a major discovery in the solar power generation industry as it offers a cheap source of harnessing the Sun's energy."

Sentence 9 contributes to double redundancy; that is, it repeats two separate ideas. Along with repeating the cost-effective characteristic of the new discovery, it also reiterates the fact that it is a major discovery, both of which are unnecessary. It also interferes in the paragraph transition which can be established between sentence 8 and 10 if it is removed.

7. B
Suggested corrections to sentence 10, "Oleic acid, the main ingredient of olive oil, absorbs infra-red radiation, which is the major component of the Sun's radiation reaching the Earth."

The sentence is missing the subordinate conjunction "which" or "that" necessary to construct the subordinate clause, with a comma before "which." Choices B and C suggest these changes, but since choice C contains a punctuation error, only B is has the valid answer.

8. D
Suggested changes to sentence 2, "With continued concern over global climate change, environmentalists are urging governments to lower their dependence on fossil fuels to ensure reduced carbon emission into the atmosphere."

This sentence contains inappropriate use of gerunds and infinitives. To-infinitives are preferred when the continuous form of a main verb is used right before or after them. In this case, "urging" should be followed by the to-infinitive of "lower." Further across the sentence, the linking phrase "to," has only one acceptable form; itself. Therefore, the verb which is linked to must contain the infinitive form. The gerund form must be discarded. The only valid choice is D.

9. B
Suggested changes to sentence 6 are, "This information, coupled with conventional on-site procedures, help archeologists plan their excavation carefully and efficiently."
The second paragraph points out the significance of satellite imaging for archeological studies. The original sentence only makes a general claim. Choice A contradicts excavation principles by adding "along with a supply of heavy machinery" which would destroy the site. Choice B, more appropriately, adds the aspects of archeological excavation that are going to be boosted by the technology. Choices C and D offer very little relevance to satellite imaging and the dimensions of excavation that are going to be affected.

10. C

Sentence 9 can be re-written, "Different points in a civilization reflect IR radiation differently, provide detailed insight about the causes of these differing heat signatures."

This is a much shorter and more concise sentence which eliminates some details.

Section III – Mathematics

1. B
First change all the terms to fractions, therefore, we get 7/3 / 7/5, to divide we need to invert the second fraction, 7/3 x 5/7, and then we cancel out to reduce to the lowest terms, 1/3 x 5/1 = 5/3, convert back to proper fraction to get 1 2/3

2. B
First, convert all the terms to fractions and then cancel out. Therefore, 2/3 x 11/7 x 21/4 = 2/3 x 11/1 x 3/4, 1/3 x 11/1 x 3/2, 1/1 x 11/1 x 1/2 = 11/2 = 5 1/2

3. A
First change all the terms to fractions, therefore, we get 21/5 / 7/3, to divide we need to invert the second fraction, 21/5 x 3/7, and then we cancel out to reduce to the lowest terms, 3/5 x 3/1 = 9/5, convert back to proper fraction to get 1 4/5

4. B
First, convert all the terms to fractions and then cancel out. Therefore, 10/3 x 9/4 x 16/5 = 10/1 x 3/4 x 16/5, 10/1 x 3/1 x 4/5, 2/1 x 3/1 x 4/1 = 24/1 = 24

5. C
First change all the terms to fractions, 28/9 / 8/3, to divide we need to invert the second fraction, 28/9 x 3/8, and then we cancel out to reduce to the lowest terms, 7/3 x 1/2 = 7/6, convert back to proper fraction to get 1 1/6

6. B
+(+) becomes a positive sign and -(-) equals +, therefore -9 + (+6) – (-2) = -9 + 6 + 2 = -3 + 2 = -1

7. B
There are 52 cards. Smith has 16 cards in which he can win. Therefore, his winning probability in a single game will be 16/52. Simon has 20 cards of wining so his probability of winning in single draw is 20/52. Simon will win more games.

8. C
This is an arithmetic series question where the 1st term is 18 and last term is 40. Expressing the question as a series, we have

18, 20, 22, 24, 26, 28, 30, 32, 34, 36, 38, 40
Therefore, after 11 days of practice he attains that 40 word per minute. As he practices 3 hours daily, the total number of hours required will be 33.

9. C
1 hour is equal to 3600 seconds and 1 kilometer is equal to 1000 meters. Therefore, a train covers 72000 meters in 36000 seconds.
Distance covered in 12 seconds = 12 × 72000/3600 = 240 meters.

10. B
Absent students = 83 – 72 = 11
Percent of absent students =   11/83 X 100 = 13.25
Reducing up to two significant digits will be 13.

Day	Absent	Present	% Attendance
Monday	5	40	88.88%
Tuesday	9	36	80.00%
Wednesday	4	41	91.11%

Thursday	10	35	77.77%
Friday	6	39	86.66%

11. B
Time taken to travel from A to B in seconds = 3600 + (13 X 60) = 3600 + 780 = 4380 seconds.
Total time spent at traffic signals = 80 X 5 = 400 seconds.
The remaining driving time = 4380 – 400 = 3980 seconds = 3980/3600 = 1.106 hours
The speed will be 65/1.106 = 58.77 km/hr

12. C
Cash assets = 75600
Building assets after one year = 80500 X 1.1 = $88550
Machinery assets after one year = 125000 X 0.8 = 100,000
Total value of assets = 264150

13. C
Total earnings = 25000 + 500 + 860 = $26360
Food and Clothing expenses = 0.4 X 26360 = 10544
Children's education expense = 26360 X 0.1 = $2636
Utility Bills = $800
Savings = 26360 – 10544 – 2636 – 800 = $12380
Percent savings = 100 X 12380/26360 = 47%

14. B
1st prize winner receives, 7 X 1050/15 = $490
3rd price winner receives, 3 X 1050/15 = $210
Difference = 490 – 210 = $280

15. C
At 100% efficiency 1 machine produces 1450/10 = 145 m of cloth.

At 95% efficiency, 4 machines produce 4 * 145 * 95/100 = 551 m of cloth.

At 90% efficiency, 6 machines produce 6 * 145 * 90/100 = 783 m of cloth.

Total cloth produced by all 10 machines = 551 + 783 = 1334 m

Since the information provided and the question are based on 8 hours, we did not need to use time to reach the answer.

16. D
Distance covered by the car = 60 X 3.5 = 210 km.
Time required by the motorbike = 210/40 = 5.25 hr.

17. C
Let the grandson's age be X and the grandfather's age be Y. According we have,
y = 8x
and
y + 6 = 5(x + 6)
Solving we get y = 64

18. B
5n + (19 – 2)) = 67, 5n + 17 = 67, 5n = 67 -17, 5n = 50, n = 50/5 = 10

19. C
The ratio between apples and oranges is 2 to 8 or 2:8. Bring to the lowest terms by dividing both sides by 2 gives 1:4.

20. A
The ratio between black and blue pens is 7 to 28 or 7:28. Bring to the lowest terms by dividing both sides by 7 gives 1:4.

21. C
X + 32 + 356 = 920. Therefore X + 388 = 920, X = 920 – 388 = 532

22. B
The ratio between green, red and blue candies is 3:12:9. Bring to the lowest

terms by dividing the sides by 3 gives 1:4:3.

23. A
12 x 12 = 144, so 144/x =12, X = 12

24. A
34 x 2 = 68, so A – 68 = 18, A = 68 + 18 = 86

25. D
X% of 120 = 30, so X = 30/120 x 100/1 = 300/12 = 25

This questions can be estimated quickly just by looking at the numbers. 30 and 120 are related by, as 4 X 30 = 120. 4 expressed as a percent is 25%. Check quickly, 25% of 120 = 30.

26. B
X * 25% x 100 = 75, therefore, X * 25 = 75, X = 75/25 = 3

27. D
X% of 250 = 50, so X = 50/250 x 100/1= 100/5 = 20

28. D
Multiples of 3 are 3, 6, 9, 12 and Multiples of 4 are 4, 8, 12, Therefore the least common multiple is 12.

This can be estimated quickly. 3 is a prime number so the only possible multiples of 3 and any other number, say X, will be 3X.

29. C
The ratio between gold, silver and bronze coins is 2:6:8. Bring to the lowest terms by dividing each element in the original ratio by 2 gives 1:3:6.

30. A
Multiples of 8 are 8, 16, 24 and multiples of 12 are 12, 24, 36, so the least common multiple is 24.

31. D
3x = 20 + 7 = 27, x = 27/3, x = 9.

32. C
Multiples of 2 are 2, 4, 6 and Multiples of 3 are 3, 6, so the least common is 6.

33. B
124 = 12c - 20, 124 + 20 = 12c, 144 = 12c, c = 144/12 = 12.

34. C
Add the whole numbers and then add the fractions, therefore 3 + 5 {8/9 + 5/6}, then find a common denominator for the fractions 8 {16/18 + 15/18} = 8 31/18, then simplify to 9 13/18

35. D
Subtract the whole numbers and then subtract the fractions, therefore 7 - 2 {4/5 - 2/5}, the fractions has a common denominator, so 5 (4-2/5) = 5 2/5.

36. A
Three plus a number times 7 equals 42. Let X be the number.
(3 + X) times 7 = 42
7(3 + X) = 42

37. C
5205 / 25 = 208.20 or, approximately 208.

38. D
Two parallel lines(m & side AB) intersected by side AC
a = 50° (interior angles)

39. A
The wheel travels 2πr distance when it makes one revolution. Here, r stands for the radius. The radius is given as 25 cm in the figure. So,

2πr = 2π * 25 = 50π cm is the distance travelled in one revolution.

In 175 revolutions: 175 * 50π = 8750π cm is travelled.

We are asked to find the distance in meter.

1 m = 100 cm So;

8750π cm = 8750π / 100 = 87.5π m

40. C
Equilateral triangle with 9 cm sides
Perimeter = 9+9+9
= 27 cm.

41. C
In the figure, we are given a large circle and a small circle inside it; with the diameter equal to the radius of the large one. The diameter of the small circle is 4 cm. This means that its radius is 2 cm. Since the diameter of the small circle is the radius of the large circle, the radius of the large circle is 4 cm. The area of a circle is calculated by: $πr^2$ where r is the radius.

Area of the small circle: π(2)2 = 4π

Area of the large circle: π(4)2 = 16π

The difference area is found by:

Area of the large circle - Area of the small circle = 16π - 4π = 12π

42. C
Volume of a cylinder is π x r^2 x h
Diameter = 5 ft. so radius is 2.5 ft.
Volume of the cylinder = π x 2.5^2 x 2
= π x 6.25 x 2 = 12.5 π
Approximate π to 3.142
Volume of the cylinder = 39.25

Volume of a rectangle = height X width X length.
= 5 X 5 X 4 = 100

Total volume = Volume of rectangular solid + volume of cylinder
Total volume = 100 + 39.25

Total volume = 139.25 ft^3 or approximately 140 ft^3

43. D
Two parallel lines intersected by a third line with angles of 75°
x = 75° (corresponding angles)
x + y = 180°(supplementary angles)
y = 180° - 75°
y = 105°

44. D
To find the total turnout in all three polling stations, we need to proportion the number of voters to the number of all registered voters.

Number of total voters = 945 + 860 + 1210 = 3015

Number of total registered voters = 1270 + 1050 + 1440 = 3760

Percentage turnout over all three polling stations = 3015 * 100/3760 = 80.19%

Checking the answers, we round 80.19 to the nearest whole number: 80%

45. C
Substitute the known terms, (3 x 2) + (4 x 4) x 8 =, 6 + 4 x 8=, 10 x 8 = 80

46. B
When multiplying exponent, add the exponents. Therefore $4^{2+7} = 4^9$

47. A
When dividing exponents, subtract the exponents. $10^{65-13} = 10^{52}$

48. D
Indonesia is growing the fastest at about 30%.

49. D
a. 0.4 portion of 200 = 80
b. 50% of 100 = 50
c. 0.06 portion of 2000 = 120

d. 2% of 1000 = 20
D is the smallest

50. A
5z = 52 − 10
Z = 10.4 − 2 (divide both sides by 5)
Z = 8.4

Section IV -Ability

1. D
Each figure has one more square with a cross inside.

2. C
Two large square boxes and one small square box are inverted.

3. B
Every box has three black square boxes inside.

4. D
The shape with empty inside circle has been rotated counter-clockwise.

5. A
The colors of the two square boxes are reversed.

6. B
The sum of inside dots decreases by one.

7. D
The box is rotated and the shading reversed.

8. B
The number of sides increases by one.

9. B
The shape rotates clockwise.

10. A
The top and bottom rows cycle forward and the middle row cycles backward.

11. D
The sum of the top two numbers is divided by subtracting the bottom two numbers.

12. C
The black box goes to the bottom and the t symbol rotates.

13. D
The relation is the same figure rotated.

14. D
The shaded area is divided in half in the second figure.

15. D
The relation is the same figure rotated to the right.

16. B
The relation is the number of dots is one-half the number of sides.

17. C
The pattern is the same figure with a dot inside.

18. A
The relation is the same figure smaller, plus another figure with one more side.

19. B
The relation is the bottom half of the figure.

20. C
The relation is the right half of the first object.

21. B
The relation is the right half of the first object.

22. B
The first two figures have one-quarter of the area shaded. The figure given

has one-half shaded which matches figure B.

23. D
Each figure has a smaller version if itself inside.

24. A
The figures are rotated 45 degrees.

25. B
26. D
27. B
28. B
29. A
30. A
31. C
32. B
33. D
34. C
35. D
36. C
37. D
38. A
39. B
40. A

Practice Test Questions Set 2

THE QUESTIONS BELOW ARE NOT THE SAME AS YOU WILL FIND ON THE TACHS - THAT WOULD BE TOO EASY! And nobody knows what the questions will be and they change all the time. Below are general questions that cover the same subject areas as the TACHS. So, while the format and exact wording of the questions may differ slightly, and change from year to year, if you can answer the questions below, you will have no problem with the TACHS.

For the best results, take these practice test questions as if it were the real exam. Set aside time when you will not be disturbed, and a location that is quiet and free of distractions. Read the instructions carefully, read each question carefully, and answer to the best of your ability.

Use the bubble answer sheets provided. When you have completed the practice questions, check your answer against the Answer Key and read the explanation provided.

Do not attempt more than one set of practice test questions in one day. After completing the first practice test, wait two or three days before attempting the second set of questions.

Section I – Reading
Questions: 50
Time: 45 minutes

Section II - Language
Questions: 50
Time: 30 minutes

Section III – Mathematics
Questions: 50
Time: 40 Minutes

Section IV - Ability
Questions: 40
Time: 30 Minutes

Reading Answer Sheet

Language Answer Sheet

	A	B	C	D	E		A	B	C	D	E
1	○	○	○	○	○	26	○	○	○	○	○
2	○	○	○	○	○	27	○	○	○	○	○
3	○	○	○	○	○	28	○	○	○	○	○
4	○	○	○	○	○	29	○	○	○	○	○
5	○	○	○	○	○	30	○	○	○	○	○
6	○	○	○	○	○	31	○	○	○	○	○
7	○	○	○	○	○	32	○	○	○	○	○
8	○	○	○	○	○	33	○	○	○	○	○
9	○	○	○	○	○	34	○	○	○	○	○
10	○	○	○	○	○	35	○	○	○	○	○
11	○	○	○	○	○	36	○	○	○	○	○
12	○	○	○	○	○	37	○	○	○	○	○
13	○	○	○	○	○	38	○	○	○	○	○
14	○	○	○	○	○	39	○	○	○	○	○
15	○	○	○	○	○	40	○	○	○	○	○
16	○	○	○	○	○	41	○	○	○	○	○
17	○	○	○	○	○	42	○	○	○	○	○
18	○	○	○	○	○	43	○	○	○	○	○
19	○	○	○	○	○	44	○	○	○	○	○
20	○	○	○	○	○	45	○	○	○	○	○
21	○	○	○	○	○	46	○	○	○	○	○
22	○	○	○	○	○	47	○	○	○	○	○
23	○	○	○	○	○	48	○	○	○	○	○
24	○	○	○	○	○	49	○	○	○	○	○
25	○	○	○	○	○	50	○	○	○	○	○

Mathematics Answer Sheet

	A	B	C	D	E		A	B	C	D	E
1	○	○	○	○	○	26	○	○	○	○	○
2	○	○	○	○	○	27	○	○	○	○	○
3	○	○	○	○	○	28	○	○	○	○	○
4	○	○	○	○	○	29	○	○	○	○	○
5	○	○	○	○	○	30	○	○	○	○	○
6	○	○	○	○	○	31	○	○	○	○	○
7	○	○	○	○	○	32	○	○	○	○	○
8	○	○	○	○	○	33	○	○	○	○	○
9	○	○	○	○	○	34	○	○	○	○	○
10	○	○	○	○	○	35	○	○	○	○	○
11	○	○	○	○	○	36	○	○	○	○	○
12	○	○	○	○	○	37	○	○	○	○	○
13	○	○	○	○	○	38	○	○	○	○	○
14	○	○	○	○	○	39	○	○	○	○	○
15	○	○	○	○	○	40	○	○	○	○	○
16	○	○	○	○	○	41	○	○	○	○	○
17	○	○	○	○	○	42	○	○	○	○	○
18	○	○	○	○	○	43	○	○	○	○	○
19	○	○	○	○	○	44	○	○	○	○	○
20	○	○	○	○	○	45	○	○	○	○	○
21	○	○	○	○	○	46	○	○	○	○	○
22	○	○	○	○	○	47	○	○	○	○	○
23	○	○	○	○	○	48	○	○	○	○	○
24	○	○	○	○	○	49	○	○	○	○	○
25	○	○	○	○	○	50	○	○	○	○	○

Ability Answer Sheet

	A	B	C	D	E		A	B	C	D	E
1	○	○	○	○	○	26	○	○	○	○	○
2	○	○	○	○	○	27	○	○	○	○	○
3	○	○	○	○	○	28	○	○	○	○	○
4	○	○	○	○	○	29	○	○	○	○	○
5	○	○	○	○	○	30	○	○	○	○	○
6	○	○	○	○	○	31	○	○	○	○	○
7	○	○	○	○	○	32	○	○	○	○	○
8	○	○	○	○	○	33	○	○	○	○	○
9	○	○	○	○	○	34	○	○	○	○	○
10	○	○	○	○	○	35	○	○	○	○	○
11	○	○	○	○	○	36	○	○	○	○	○
12	○	○	○	○	○	37	○	○	○	○	○
13	○	○	○	○	○	38	○	○	○	○	○
14	○	○	○	○	○	39	○	○	○	○	○
15	○	○	○	○	○	40	○	○	○	○	○
16	○	○	○	○	○						
17	○	○	○	○	○						
18	○	○	○	○	○						
19	○	○	○	○	○						
20	○	○	○	○	○						
21	○	○	○	○	○						
22	○	○	○	○	○						
23	○	○	○	○	○						
24	○	○	○	○	○						
25	○	○	○	○	○						

Section I – Reading

Part I - Vocabulary

Directions: Choose the word that is closest in meaning to the underlined word.

1. She has been to some very dangerous places. She is an <u>intrepid</u> explorer.

   a. Brave
   b. Timid
   c. Timorous
   d. Cowardly

2. He wasn't especially generous. All the servings were very <u>judicious</u>.

   a. Abundant
   b. Careful
   c. Sparing
   d. Careless

3. She presented a pretty good case up to now, but the latest evidence tends to <u>negate</u> everything he has said.

   a. Disagree
   b. Reinforce
   c. Improve
   d. None of the above

4. It is boring and I would rather not go, but the ceremony is <u>obligatory</u>.

   a. Mandatory
   b. Optional
   c. Adaptable
   d. None of the above.

5. We used that operating system 20 years ago, now it is <u>obsolete</u>.

   a. Functional
   b. Disused
   c. Obese
   d. None of the Above.

6. His bad manners really <u>rankle</u> me.

   a. Annoy
   b. Obsucate
   c. Enliven
   d. None of the above.

7. We don't want to hear the whole thing. Just the <u>salient</u> facts please.

   a. Irrelevant
   b. Erroneous
   c. Relevant
   d. Trivial

8. She works in a cubicle answering the phone all day. Her doctor says she is too <u>sedentary</u>.

   a. Inactive
   b. Active
   c. Morbid
   d. None of the Above.

9. We cannot reveal the source. It was posted by anonymous.

    a. Unidentified
    b. Author
    c. Someone
    d. Nobody

10. I have never seen anyone so rude. His behavior was atrocious.

    a. Monstrous
    b. Perfect
    c. Unwarranted
    d. Suspicious

11. I still don't know exactly. That isn't conclusive evidence.

    a. Undeterred
    b. Unrelenting
    c. Unfortunate
    d. Definitive

12. His investment scheme duped many serious investors, who lost money.

    a. Helped
    b. Vindicated
    c. Fooled
    d. Reproved

13. When we go to a party, we always designate a driver.

    a. Feign
    b. Exploit
    c. Dote
    d. Appoint

14. Choose the best definition of specious.

    a. Logical
    b. Illogical
    c. Emotional
    d. 2 species

15. Choose the best definition of proscribe.

    a. Welcome
    b. Write a prescription
    c. Banish
    d. Give a diagnosis

16. Fill in the blank.

When Craig's dog was struck by a car, he rushed his pet to the _____.

    a. Emergency room
    b. Doctor
    c. Veterinarian
    d. Podiatrist

17. Select another word for the underlined word in the sentence below.

She never made a mistake - her performance was always impeccable.

    a. Charming
    b. Flattering
    c. Perfect
    d. Impervious

18. Select the synonym of boisterous.

    a. Loud
    b. Soft
    c. Gentle
    d. Warm

19. Select the adjective that means hidden, secret, disguised.

    a. Accustomed
    b. Covert
    c. Hide
    d. Carriage

20. Select the verb that means straightforward, open and sincere.

    a. Lawful
    b. Candid
    c. True
    d. Lawful

Part III - Reading Comprehension

Questions 21 - 24 refer to the following passage.

Passage 1 - The Crusades

In 1095 Pope Urban II proclaimed the First Crusade with the intent and stated goal to restore Christian access to holy places in and around Jerusalem. Over the next 200 years there were 6 major crusades and numerous minor crusades in the fight for control of the "Holy Land." Historians are divided on the real purpose of the Crusades, some believing that it was part of a purely defensive war against Islamic conquest; some see them as part of a long-running conflict at the frontiers of Europe; and others see them as confident, aggressive, papal-led expansion attempts by Western Christendom. The impact of the crusades was profound, and judgment of the Crusaders ranges from laudatory to highly critical. However, all agree that the Crusades and wars waged during those crusades were brutal and often bloody. Several hundred thousand Roman Catholic Christians joined the Crusades, they were Christians from all over Europe.

Europe at the time was under the Feudal System, so while the Crusaders made vows to the Church they also were beholden to their Feudal Lords. This led to the Crusaders not only fighting the Saracen, the commonly used word for Muslim at the time, but also each other for power and economic gain in the Holy Land. This infighting between the Crusaders is why many historians hold the view that the Crusades were simply a front for Europe to invade the Holy Land for economic gain in the name of the Church. Another factor contributing to this theory is that while the army of crusaders marched towards Jerusalem they pillaged the land as they went. The church and feudal Lords vowing to return the land to its original beauty, and inhabitants, this rarely happened though as the Lords often kept the land for themselves. A full 800 years after the Crusades, Pope John Paul II expressed his sorrow for the massacre of innocent people and the lasting damage the Medieval church caused in that area of the World.

21. What is the tone of this article?

    a. Subjective

    b. Objective

    c. Persuasive

    d. None of the Above

22. What can all historians agree on concerning the Crusades?

    a. It achieved great things

    b. It stabilized the Holy Land

    c. It was bloody and brutal

    d. It helped defend Europe from the Byzantine Empire

23. What impact did the feudal system have on the Crusades?

a. It unified the Crusaders

b. It helped gather volunteers

c. It had no effect on the Crusades

d. It led to infighting, causing more damage than good

24. What does Saracen mean?

a. Muslim

b. Christian

c. Knight

d. Holy Land

Questions 25 - 28 refer to the following passage.

ABC Electric Warranty

ABC Electric Company warrants that its products are free from defects in material and workmanship. Subject to the conditions and limitations set forth below, ABC Electric will, at its option, either repair or replace any part of its products that prove defective due to improper workmanship or materials.

This limited warranty does not cover any damage to the product from improper installation, accident, abuse, misuse, natural disaster, insufficient or excessive electrical supply, abnormal mechanical or environmental conditions, or any unauthorized disassembly, repair, or modification.

This limited warranty also does not apply to any product on which the original identification information has been altered, or removed, has not been handled or packaged correctly, or has been sold as second-hand.

This limited warranty covers only repair, replacement, refund or credit for defective ABC Electric products, as provided above.

25. I tried to repair my ABC Electric blender, but could not, so can I get it repaired under this warranty?

a. Yes, the warranty still covers the blender

b. No, the warranty does not cover the blender

c. Uncertain. ABC Electric may or may not cover repairs under this warranty

26. My ABC Electric fan is not working. Will ABC Electric provide a new one or repair this one?

  a. ABC Electric will repair my fan
  b. ABC Electric will replace my fan
  c. ABC Electric could either replace or repair my fan can request either a replacement or a repair.

27. My stove was damaged in a flood. Does this warranty cover my stove?

  a. Yes, it is covered.
  b. No, it is not covered.
  c. It may or may not be covered.
  d. ABC Electric will decide if it is covered

28. Which of the following is an example of improper workmanship?

  a. Missing parts
  b. Defective parts
  c. Scratches on the front
  d. None of the above

Questions 29 – 32 refer to the following passage.

Passage 2 - Women and Advertising

Only in the last few generations have media messages been so widespread and so readily seen, heard, and read by so many people. Advertising is an important part of both selling and buying anything from soap to cereal to jeans. For whatever reason, more consumers are women than are men. Media message are subtle but powerful, and more attention has been paid lately to how these message affect women.
Of all the products that women buy, makeup, clothes, and other stylistic or cosmetic products are among the most popular. This means that companies focus their advertising on women, promising them that their product will make her feel, look, or smell better than the next company's product will. This competition has resulted in advertising that is more and more ideal and less and less possible for everyday women. However, because women do look to these ideals and the products they represent as how they can potentially become, many women have developed unhealthy attitudes about themselves when they have failed to become those ideals.

In recent years, more companies have tried to change advertisements to be healthier for women. This includes featuring models of more sizes and addressing a huge outcry against unfair tools such as airbrushing and photo editing. There is debate about what the right balance between real and ideal is, because fashion is also considered art and some changes are made to purposefully elevate fashionable products and signify that they are creative, innovative, and the work of individual people. Artists want their freedom protected as much as women do, and advertising agencies are often caught in the middle.

Some claim that the companies who make these changes are not doing enough. Many people worry that there are still not enough models of different sizes and different ethnicities. Some people claim that companies use this healthier type of advertisement not for the good of women, but because they would like to sell products to the women who are looking for these kinds of messages. This is also a hard balance to find: companies do need to make money, and women do need to feel respected.
While the focus of this change has been on women, advertising can also affect men, and this change will hopefully be a lesson on media for all consumers.

29. The second paragraph states that advertising focuses on women

    a. to shape what the ideal should be
    b. because women buy makeup
    c. because women are easily persuaded
    d. because of the types of products that women buy

30. According to the passage, fashion artists and female consumers are at odds because

    a. there is a debate going on and disagreement drives people apart
    b. both of them are trying to protect their freedom to do something
    c. artists want to elevate their products above the reach of women
    d. women are creative, innovative, individual people

31. The author uses the phrase "for whatever reason" in this passage to

    a. keep the focus of the paragraph on media messages and not on the differences between men and women
    b. show that the reason for this is unimportant
    c. argue that it is stupid that more women are consumers than men
    d. show that he or she is tired of talking about why media messages are important

32. This passage suggests that

    a. advertising companies are still working on making their messages better
    b. all advertising companies seek to be more approachable for women
    c. women are only buying from companies that respect them
    d. artists could stop producing fashionable products if they feel bullied

Questions 33 - 36 refer to the following passage.

FDR, the Treaty of Versailles, and the Fourteen Points

At the conclusion of World War I, those who had won the war and those who were forced to admit defeat welcomed the end of the war and expected that a peace treaty would be signed. The American president, Franklin D. Roosevelt, played an important part in proposing what the agreements should be and did so through his Fourteen Points.
World War I had begun in 1914 when an Austrian archduke was assassinated, leading to a domino effect that pulled the world's most powerful countries into war on a large scale. The war catalyzed the creation and use of deadly weapons that had not previously existed, resulting in a great loss of soldiers on both sides of the fighting. More than 9 million soldiers were killed.

The United States agreed to enter the war right before it ended, and many believed that its decision to become finally involved brought on the end of the war. FDR made it very clear that the U.S. was entering the war for moral reasons and had an agenda focused on world peace. The Fourteen Points were individual goals and ideas (focused on peace, free trade, open communication, and self reliance) that FDR wanted the power nations to strive for now that the war had concluded. He was optimistic and had many ideas about what could be accomplished through and during the post-war peace. However, FDR's fourteen points were poorly received when he presented them to the leaders of other world powers, many of whom wanted only to help their own countries and to punish the Germans for fueling the war, and they fell by the wayside. World War II was imminent, for Germany lost everything.

Some historians believe that the other leaders who participated in the Treaty of Versailles weren't receptive to the Fourteen Points because World War I was fought almost entirely on European soil, and the United States lost much less than did the other powers. FDR was in a unique position to determine the fate of the war, but doing it on his own terms did not help accomplish his goals. This is only one historical example of how the United State has tried to use its power as an important country, but found itself limited because of geological or ideological factors.

33. The main idea of this passage is that

a. World War I was unfair because no fighting took place in America

b. World War II happened because of the Treaty of Versailles

c. the power the United States has to help other countries also prevents it from helping other countries

d. Franklin D. Roosevelt was one of the United States' smartest presidents

34. According to the second paragraph, World War I started because

   a. an archduke was assassinated
   b. weapons that were more deadly had been developed
   c. a domino effect of allies agreeing to help each other
   d. the world's most powerful countries were large

35. The author includes the detail that 9 million soldiers were killed

   a. to demonstrate why European leaders were hesitant to accept peace
   b. to show the reader the dangers of deadly weapons
   c. to make the reader think about which countries lost the most soldiers
   d. to demonstrate why World War II was imminent

36. According to this passage, it can be understood that the word catalyzed means

   a. analyzed
   b. sped up
   c. invented
   d. funded

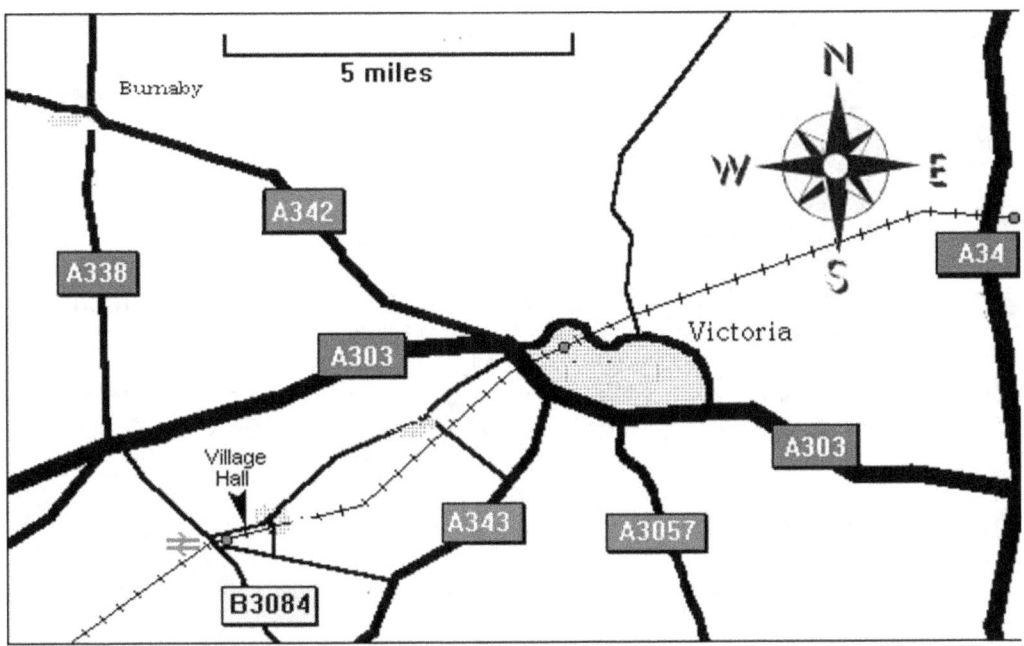

37. Approximately how far is Victoria to Burnaby?

    a. About 10 miles
    b. About 5 miles
    c. About 15 miles
    d. About 20 miles

38. How is the Village Hall from Victoria?

    a. About 10 miles
    b. About 5 miles
    c. About 15 miles
    d. About 20 miles

Questions 39 - 42 refer to the following passage.

Chocolate Chip Cookies

3/4 cup sugar
3/4 cup packed brown sugar
1 cup butter, softened
2 large eggs, beaten
1 teaspoon vanilla extract
2 1/4 cups all-purpose flour
1 teaspoon baking soda
3/4 teaspoon salt
2 cups semisweet chocolate chips
If desired, 1 cup chopped pecans, or chopped walnuts.
Preheat oven to 375 degrees.

Mix sugar, brown sugar, butter, vanilla and eggs in a large bowl. Stir in flour, baking soda, and salt. The dough will be very stiff.

Stir in chocolate chips by hand with a sturdy wooden spoon. Add the pecans, or other nuts, if desired. Stir until the chocolate chips and nuts are evenly dispersed.

Drop dough by rounded tablespoonfuls 2 inches apart onto a cookie sheet.

Bake 8 to 10 minutes or until light brown. Cookies may look underdone, but they will finish cooking after you take them out of the oven.

39. What is the correct order for adding these ingredients?

a. Brown sugar, baking soda, chocolate chips
b. Baking soda, brown sugar, chocolate chips
c. Chocolate chips, baking soda, brown sugar
d. Baking soda, chocolate chips, brown sugar

40. What does sturdy mean?

a. Long
b. Strong
c. Short
d. Wide

41. What does disperse mean?

a. Scatter
b. To form a ball
c. To stir
d. To beat

42. When can you stop stirring the nuts?

a. When the cookies are cooked.
b. When the nuts are evenly distributed.
c. When the nuts are added.
d. After the chocolate chips are added.

Questions 43 - 46 refer to the following passage.

Passage 5 - Frankenstein

Great God! What a scene has just taken place! I am yet dizzy with the remembrance of it. I hardly know whether I shall have the power to detail it; yet the tale which I have recorded would be incomplete without this final and wonderful catastrophe. I entered the cabin where lay the remains of my ill-fated and admirable friend. Over him hung a form which I cannot find words to describe—gigantic in stature, yet uncouth and distorted in its proportions. As he hung over the coffin, his face was concealed by long locks of ragged hair; but one vast hand was extended, in color and apparent texture like that of a mummy. When he heard the sound of my approach, he ceased to utter exclamations of grief and horror and sprung towards the window. Never did I behold a vision so horrible as his face, of such loathsome yet appalling hideousness. I shut my eyes involuntarily and endeavored to recollect what were my duties with regard to this destroyer. I called on him to stay.

He paused, looking on me with wonder, and again turning towards the lifeless form of his creator, he seemed to forget my presence, and every feature and gesture seemed instigated by the wildest rage of some uncontrollable passion.

"That is also my victim!" he exclaimed. "In his murder my crimes are consummated; the miserable series of my being is wound to its close! Oh, Frankenstein! Generous and self-devoted being! What does it avail that I now ask thee to pardon me? I, who irretrievably destroyed thee by destroying all thou lovedst. Alas! He is cold, he cannot answer me."

His voice seemed suffocated, and my first impulses, which had suggested to me the duty of obeying the dying request of my friend in destroying his enemy, were now suspended by a mixture of curiosity and compassion. I approached this tremendous being; I dared not again raise my eyes to his face, there was something so scaring and unearthly in his ugliness. I attempted to speak, but the words died away on my lips. The monster continued to utter wild and incoherent self-reproaches. At length I gathered resolution to address him in a pause of the tempest of his passion.

"Your repentance," I said, "is now superfluous. If you had listened to the voice of conscience and heeded the stings of remorse before you had urged your diabolical vengeance to this extremity, Frankenstein would yet have lived."

43. Who is the "ill-fated and admirable friend" who is lying in the coffin?

    a. Frankenstein's monster
    b. Frankenstein
    c. Mary Shelley
    d. Unknown

44. Why is the speaker 'suspended" from following through on his duty to destroy the monster?

    a. The way the monster looks
    b. The monster's remorse
    c. Curiosity and compassion
    d. Fear the monster might kill him too

45. How does Frankenstein's monster destroy Frankenstein?

    a. By killing Frankenstein
    b. By letting himself be the monster everyone sees him as
    c. By destroying everything Frankenstein loved
    d. All of the above

46. When the Speaker says the monster's repentance is "superfluous," what does he mean?

a. That it is unnecessary and unused because Frankenstein is already dead and cannot hear him

b. That he accepts the repentance on behalf of Frankenstein

c. That the monster does not actually feel remorseful

d. That his repentance is unneeded because he did not do anything wrong

Questions 47 - 50 refer to the following passage.

Lowest Price Guarantee

Get it for less. Guaranteed!

ABC Electric will beat any advertised price by 10% of the difference.

1) If you find a lower advertised price, we will beat it by 10% of the difference.

2) If you find a lower advertised price within 30 days* of your purchase we will beat it by 10% of the difference.

3) If our own price is reduced within 30 days* of your purchase, bring in your receipt and we will refund the difference.

*14 days for computers, monitors, printers, laptops, tablets, cellular & wireless devices, home security products, projectors, camcorders, digital cameras, radar detectors, portable DVD players, DJ and pro-audio equipment, and air conditioners.

47. I bought a radar detector 15 days ago and saw an ad for the same model only cheaper. Can I get 10% of the difference refunded?

a. Yes. Since it is less than 30 days, you can get 10% of the difference refunded.

b. No. Since it is more than 14 days, you cannot get 10% of the difference re-funded.

c. It depends on the cashier.

d. Yes. You can get the difference refunded.

48. I bought a flat-screen TV for $500 10 days ago and found an advertisement for the same TV, at another store, on sale for $400. How much will ABC refund under this guarantee?

a. $100

b. $110

c. $10

d. $400

49. What is the purpose of this passage?

   a. To inform
   b. To educate
   c. To persuade
   d. To entertain

Questions 50 refers to the following passage.

Passage 6 - What Is Mardi Gras?

Mardi Gras is fast becoming one of the South's most famous and most celebrated holidays. The word Mardi Gras comes from the French and the literal translation is "Fat Tuesday." The holiday has also been called Shrove Tuesday, due to its associations with Lent. The purpose of Mardi Gras is to celebrate and enjoy before the Lenten season of fasting and repentance begins.

What originated by the French Explorers in New Orleans, Louisiana in the 17th century is now celebrated all over the world. Panama, Italy, Belgium and Brazil all host large scale Mardi Gras celebrations, and many smaller cities and towns celebrate this fun loving Tuesday as well. Usually held in February or early March, Mardi Gras is a day of extravagance, a day for people to eat, drink and be merry, to wear costumes, masks and to dance to jazz music.

The French explorers on the Mississippi River would be in shock today if they saw the opulence of the parades and floats that grace the New Orleans streets during Mardi Gras these days. Parades in New Orleans are divided by organizations. These are more commonly known as Krewes.

Being a member of a Krewe is quite a task because Krewes are responsible for overseeing the parades. Each Krewe's parade is ruled by a Mardi Gras "King and Queen." The role of the King and Queen is to "bestow" gifts on their adoring fans as the floats ride along the street. They throw doubloons, which is fake money and usually colored green, purple and gold, which are the colors of Mardi Gras. Beads in those color shades are also thrown and cups are thrown as well. Beads are by far the most popular souvenir of any Mardi Gras parade, with each spectator attempting to gather as many as possible.

50. The purpose of Mardi Gras is to

   a. Repent for a month.
   b. Celebrate in extravagant ways.
   c. Be a member of a Krewe.
   d. Explore the Mississippi.

Section II - Language

Part I - Spelling, Capitalization, Punctuation, and Usage

1. Elaine promised to bring the camera _____ at the mall yesterday.

   a. by me
   b. with me
   c. at me
   d. to me

2. Last night, he _____ the sleeping bag down beside my mattress.

   a. lay
   b. laid
   c. lain
   d. has laid

3. I would have bought the shirt for you if

   a. I had known you liked it.
   b. I have known you liked it.
   c. I would know you liked it.
   d. I know you liked it.

4. Many believers still hope _____ proof of the existence of ghosts.

   a. two find
   b. to find
   c. to found
   d. to have been found

5. Choose the sentence with the correct grammar.

   a. The court summons was placed on his desk
   b. The court summons are placed on his desk
   c. The court summons were placed on his desk
   d. None of the above

6. To _____, Anne was on time for her math class.

   a. everybody's surprise
   b. every body's surprise
   c. everybodys surprise
   d. everybodys' surprise

7. As an added bonus, we got to see the orchestra warm up.

What part of this sentence is redundant?

   a. Added
   b. Bonus
   c. Warm up
   d. None of the above

8. If he _____ the textbook like he was supposed to, he would have known what was on the test.

   a. will have read
   b. shouldn't have read
   c. would have read
   d. had read

9. Following the tornado, telephone poles _____ all over the street.

   a. laid
   b. lied
   c. were lying
   d. were laying

10. In Edgar Allen Poe's _____ Edgar Allen Poe describes a man with a guilty conscience.

   a. short story, "The Tell-Tale Heart,"
   b. short story The Tell-Tale Heart,
   c. short story, The Tell-Tale Heart
   d. short story. "the Tell-Tale Heart,"

11. Billboards are considered an important part of advertising for big business, _____ by their critics.

   a. but, an eyesore;
   b. but, " an eyesore,"
   c. but an eyesore
   d. but-an eyesore-

12. I can never remember how to use those two common words, "sell," meaning to trade a product for money, or _____ meaning an event where products are traded for less money than usual.

   a. sale-
   b. "sale,"
   c. "sale
   d. "to sale,"

13. Choose the sentence with the correct grammar.

   a. Neither the teacher nor the students is left in class.
   b. Neither the teacher nor the students was left in class.
   c. Neither the teacher nor the students are left in class.
   d. None of the above.

14. The class just finished reading _____ a short story by Carl Stephenson about a plantation owner's battle with army ants.

   a. -"Leinengen versus the Ants,"
   b. Leinengen versus the Ants,
   c. "Leinengen versus the Ants,"
   d. Leinengen versus the Ants

15. After the car was fixed, it _____ again.

   a. ran good
   b. ran well
   c. would have run well
   d. ran more well

16. "Where does the sun go during the _____ asked little Kathy.

   a. night,"
   b. night"?,
   c. night,?"
   d. night?"

17. Choose the correct spelling.

   a. conscentious
   b. conscientios
   c. conscientious
   d. consceintious

18. I have finished studying for today.

What type of sentence is this?

   a. Imperative
   b. Interrogative
   c. Exclamatory
   d. Declarative

19. Which of the following sentences contains a redundant phrase?

   a. I haven't seen her for ages.
   b. My suitcase is books all the way to Amsterdam.
   c. The end result was very disappointing.
   d. None of the above.

20. Choose the correct sentence.

a. Their only employee with a nose ring is a young man named Daniel.

b. Their only employee is a young man named Daniel with a nose ring.

c. Their only employee is a young man with a nose ring named Daniel.

d. A and C are correct.

21. Choose the sentence with the correct grammar.

a. Everyone are to wear a black tie.

b. Everyone have to wear a black tie.

c. Everyone has to wear a black tie.

d. None of the above.

22. Choose the correct spelling.

a. leisuire
b. lesure
c. lesure
d. leisure

23. Choose the correct spelling.

a. pigeone
b. pigoen
c. pigeon
d. pidgeon

24. Choose the correct spelling.

a. odyessy
b. odeyssey
c. odysey
d. odyssey

25. Choose the sentence with the correct grammar.

a. The salmon has been cooked.
b. The salmon have been cooked.
c. Both of the above.
d. None of the above.

26. This is absolutely incredible ____

a. !
b. .
c. :
d. ;

27. Watch out for the broken glass ____

a. .
b. ?
c. ,
d. !

28. I still don't know exactly. That isn't _____ evidence.

a. Undeterred
b. Unrelenting
c. Unfortunate
d. Conclusive

29. He walked all the way downtown.

What is the simple subject of this sentence?

a. He
b. Walked
c. Downtown
d. All the way

30. He could manipulate the coins in his fingers very

    a. Brazenly

    b. Eloquently

    c. Boisterously

    d. Deftly

Part II - Paragraphs

Leg Surgery

The main reason many young women opt for surgery, despite the pain, inconvenience and cost, is the height discrimination in an increasingly competitive job market. [1] Almost all firms put certain height criteria for the candidates who apply. [2] For example, for an air stewardess position, women must be no more than 163 cm tall; whereas for jobs in foreign affairs, Chinese diplomats are required to match their foreign counterparts. [3] Height concerns also effect routine citizenship privileges such as driving licenses, which require a height of at least 157 cm to be eligible for taking the test in some places. [4]

The urge to undergo surgery is becoming increasingly popular among Chinese males as well. [5] "It offers me a 10 cm increase in my height, which can dramatically change my future," says Jing Yong, an interpreter working in Hong Kong. [6] "This will allow me better opportunities in the competitive job market here," adds the young multilingual who couldn't make it to the foreign ministry for being below 168 cm. [7]
Even parents approve of the idea, being fully aware of all the complexity and they are willing to finance such a labyrinth surgery. [8] "It's something that will give her confidence and achieve her goals in life. [9] Her height used to bother her tremendously, now this can change that," comments Swee Jing's father by her bedside as she is recovering from the eighteen-months process that involves elongating her tibia and fibula by placing two rods that will stimulate the extra growth of the bones. [10] They too are hopeful about the possibilities the surgery would affect the life of their daughter. [11]

31. Which sentence in the second paragraph is least relevant to the main idea of the first paragraph?

    a. 2

    b. 3

    c. 4

    d. 5

32. Which sentence is not consistent with the author's purpose?

a. 3
b. 6
c. 9
d. 12

33. Which of the following sentences, if inserted after sentence 7, would best illustrate the main idea of the passage?

a. This is the main reason I am willing to undergo this surgery

b. This artificial way of gaining height is turning out to be a new trend among the new generation in height conscious China.

c. Height is a very big problem for Chinese people, particularly for those who wish to go abroad and carry the flag of China there.

d. Young people like Yong will have to spend the rest of their lives with a fake pair of legs though.

34. Which of the following changes are needed in sentence 8?

a. Even parents approve of the idea, being fully aware of all the sophistications and they are willing to finance such a labyrinth surgery.

b. Even parents approve of the idea, being fully aware of all the complications and they are willing to finance such a sophisticated surgery.

c. Even parents approve of the idea, being fully aware of all the complexity and they are willing to finance such a sophisticated surgery.

d. Even parents approve of the idea, being fully aware of all the complexity and they are willing to finance such a sophisticated surgery.

My Friend Luke

My forty-year old friend Luke is possibly the sweetest, shyest person enjoying his life on the entire Earth. [1] He is somewhat short, skinny and upright; has a thin moustache and a thinner trace of hair covering his head. [2] And since he has problems seeing distant things, he wears glasses that are small, thick and frameless; the round coffee-brown colored glasses give him a cool appearance uniquely suited to his personality. [3] Which I doubt belongs to any other person. [4]

There are traits in him seldom found in others. [5] While in a crowd, he walks sideways so as not to trouble others. [6] Instead of requesting a space to move ahead, he glides past to one side of the person blocking in his way. [7] If the gap turns out to be so narrow that it does not permit his bony frame to pass, he waits patiently for the person to move out of the way. [8] He is panicked by street dogs and neighbors' cats and in order to avoid them, he crosses to the other side of the street every now and then. [9]

Luke never speaks, as he thinks speaking is a waste of energy; something he is vehemently dedicated to saving. [10] Whenever he does, in order not to interrupt anybody, he speaks with a very soft, low tone – in a way no one ever notices him speaking in the first place. [11] Quite ironically, when he gets a rare chance to speak, he never succeeds in speaking more than two words before being interrupted by others. [12]

35. What sentence from the passage is an example of a sentence fragment?

    a. 4
    b. 5
    c. 6
    d. 7

36. Which sentence in the second paragraph is least relevant to the main idea of the second paragraph?

    a. 6
    b. 7
    c. 8
    d. 9

37. Which of the following sentences should be modified to reduce redundancy?

    a. 2
    b. 3
    c. 4
    d. 5

Spiderman

Spiders have always fascinated Johnson. [1] Ever since his childhood visit to his grandfather's farm in Vancouver where he first saw them in a large web that almost covered the gate of the granary warehouse, he looked for spiders everywhere he visited. [2] He would search for spider webs even in the high rise apartments such as the one he lives in now. [3] He would find them there too. [4] Hanging between two walls near one corner of the store room, a magnificent piece of art left half woven and still being worked on. [5]

It is not the life of the spiders itself that attracted Johnson, rather their art. [6] He likes their delicate webs. [7] The amazing shape and sizes of the webs. [8] The symmetry, the balance, the intricate design and the detailed network fascinates him. [9] He wanders how they manage to create something unique like this with such a little brain that they have. [10] That is why he likes to catch them in action, while they are weaving. [11]

When he opened the store room this week, he saw the huge web in the left corner touching the roof. [12] That has been there for almost six months now and it lay there as it were last month. [13] No strands added. [14] It took on a grayish shade from the dust it gathered over the weeks, making it obvious that Binny has stopped working on it. [15] Hanging here and there in the web are some dry mosquitoes that were spared by the monster that owns the trap. [16]

In the far left, on the wall adjacent to the door, Johnson is trying to build a web out of string and glue -without much success! [17] "Incredible, you little genius!" Johnson murmurs to himself. [18]

In the far left, on the wall adjacent to the door, Johnson is trying to build a web out of string and glue -without much success! ^{17} "Incredible, you little genius!" Johnson murmurs to himself. ^{18}

38. What sentence from the passage is an example of a sentence fragment?

    a. 2
    b. 3
    c. 4
    d. 5

39. Which of the following changes would focus attention on the main idea of the second paragraph?

    a. He finds the webs to be magnificent piece of art.
    b. He is more interested in the web that they weave.
    c. He enjoys the webs that they weave.
    d. He wanders about the webs that they weave.

40. Which of the following are needed in the sentence 10?

    a. He wonders how they manage to create something so unique with such a tiny brain.
    b. He ponders how they manage to create something unique like this with such a tiny brain.
    c. He imagines how they manage to create something unique like this with such a tiny brain.
    d. He questions how they manage to create something unique like this with such a little brain that they have.

Section IV – Math

1. The sum of the digits of a 2-digit number is 12. If we switch the digits, the number we get will be greater than the initial one by 36. Find the initial number.

    a. 39
    b. 48
    c. 57
    d. 75

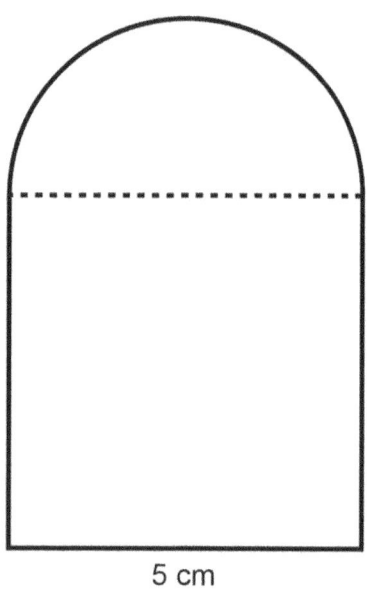

5 cm

Note: figure not drawn to scale

2. What is the perimeter of the above shape, assuming the bottom portion is square?

    a. 17.5 π cm
    b. 20 π cm
    c. 15 π cm
    d. 25 π cm

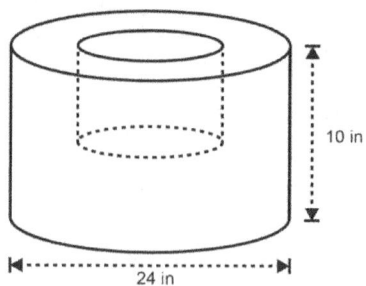

Note: figure not drawn to scale

3. What is the volume of the above solid made by a hollow cylinder that is half the size (in all dimensions) of the larger cylinder?

    a. 1440 π in^3
    b. 1260 π in^3
    c. 1040 π in^3
    d. 960 π in^3

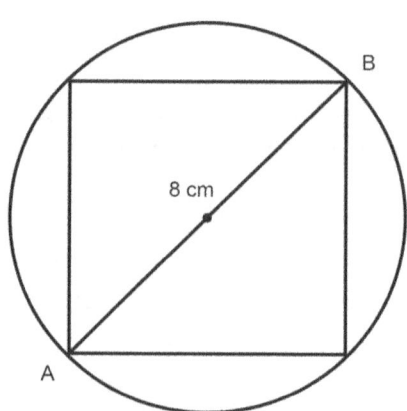

Note: figure not drawn to scale

4. What is area of the circle?

    a. 4 π cm^2
    b. 12 π cm^2
    c. 10 π cm^2
    d. 16 π cm^2

5. John jogs around a 75-meter diameter track 7 times. How much linear distance did he cover?

   a. 1250 meters
   b. 1450 meters
   c. 1650 meters
   d. 1725 meters

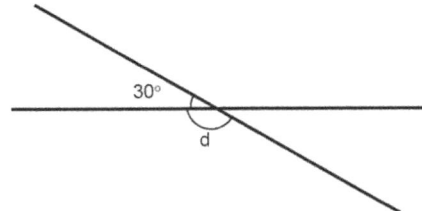

6. What is the indicated angle above?

   a. 150°
   b. 330°
   c. 60°
   d. 120°

7. On a circular jogging track with a circumference of 1.2 km, John, Tony and David walk at the rate of 120, 100 and 75 meters per minute respectively. If they all start walking in the same direction, how long will it take until they are together again?

   a. 200 minutes
   b. 220 minutes
   c. 240 minutes
   d. 260 minutes

8. On a scaled map, city A is 12.4 cm away from city B. If the scale is 1 cm = 5 km then what is the actual distance between these two cities?

   a. 12.4 km
   b. 48.4 km
   c. 58 km
   d. 62 km

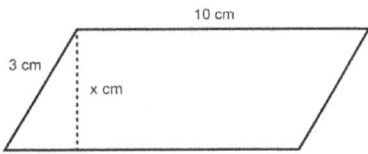

Note: figure not drawn to scale

9. What is the perimeter of the parallelogram above?

   a. 12 cm
   b. 26 cm
   c. 13 cm
   d. (13+x) cm

10. Estimate 2009 x 108.

   a. 110,000
   b. 2,0000
   c. 21,000
   d. 210,000

11. The playing times for three songs on a compact disc are as follows: 4 minutes 56 seconds for song A, 2 minutes 30 seconds for song B, 10 minutes 16 seconds for song C. What is the average playing time for the three songs?

    a. 17 minutes 42 seconds
    b. 6 minutes 7 seconds
    c. 6 minutes
    d. 5 minutes 54 seconds

12. John is a barber and receives 40% of the amount paid by his customers, and all the tips. If a customer pays $8.50 for a haircut and leaves a tip of $1.30, how much money does John receive?

    a. $3.92
    b. $4.70
    c. $5.30
    d. $6.40

13. The length of a rectangle is 5 in. more than its width. The perimeter of the rectangle is 26 in. What is the width and length of the rectangle?

    a. Width 6 in., Length 9 in.
    b. Width 4 in., Length 9 in.
    c. Width 4 in., Length 5 in.
    d. Width 6 in., Length 11 in.

14. Calculate $(3a + 4b) * d$ when $A = 2$, $b = 4$ and $d = 8$

    a. 40
    b. 150
    c. 112
    d. 176

15. $c = 4$, $n = 5$ and $x = 3$. Calculate $2cnx/2n$

    a. 12
    b. 50
    c. 8
    d. 21

16. Simplify $3\ 1/2\ /\ 2\ 4/5$

    a. 1 1/4
    b. 2 1/4
    c. 1 1/3
    d. 2 1/3

17. Solve $2b/3 + 3a/5 - 2$, where $b = 9$ and $a = 10$

    a. 5
    b. 10
    c. 20
    d. 9

18. Simplify $(1/3 + 2/6) - (3/4 - 1/3)$

    a. 1/4
    b. 5/11
    c. 3/7
    d. 2/9

19. Simplify $(4/5 - 3/10) + (2/3 - 3/9) =$

    a. 4/11
    b. 5/6
    c. 7/15
    d. 9/11

20. Translate the following into an equation: 2 + a number divided by 7.

    a. (2 + X)/7
    b. (7 + X)/2
    c. (2 + 7)/X
    d. 2/(7 + X)

21. If a = 12 and b = 8, solve 6b - a + 2a

    a. 12/9
    b. 18
    c. 16
    d. 12

22. Simplify 3 2/3 - 1 2/8

    a. 3/5
    b. 3/5
    c. 2 5/12
    d. 1 5/12

23. Simplify 7 2/5 – 4 3/10

    a. 3 1/10
    b. 3 2/5
    c. 4 1/5
    d. 3 7/10

24. Solve for x. -5 – 5x = 8x + 8

    a. 6
    b. 3
    c. 1
    d. 2

25. Solve 2 1/3 x 1 3/7 x 3/4

    a. 2 1/2
    b. 9
    c. 3 2/3
    d. 2 2/5

26. Simplify 7 4/5 – 4 2/3

    a. 4 2/5
    b. 3 2/15
    c. 3 7/15
    d. 4 3/5

27. Solve for x. 12x - 8 = 3x + 10

    a. 6
    b. 4
    c. 2
    d. 3

28. Simplify (3/5 - 2/5) + (3/4 – 2/8)

    a. 18/45
    b. 7/11
    c. 14/20
    d. 12/19

29. Solve for a. 6a + 4 = 28 + 2a

    a. 4
    b. 8
    c. 2
    d. 6

30. Simplify (3/4 - 1/4) - (3/5 – 2/5)

    a. 9/20
    b. 4/15
    c. 7/15
    d. 11/20

31. Solve for x. 6 + 9x = 12 + 7x

  a. 5
  b. 2
  c. 4
  d. 3

32. Simplify 6 2/5 / 2 2/7

  a. 2 1/4
  b. 1 1/5
  c. 2 4/5
  d. 2 2/3

33. Solve for a. -6 + 7a = 9 + 4a

  a. 3
  b. 5
  c. 2
  d. 6

34. A square lawn has an area of 62,500 square meters. What is the cost of building fence around it at a rate of $5.5 per meter?

  a. $4000
  b. $4500
  c. $5000
  d. $5500

35. The following numbers are the ages of people on a bus – 3, 6, 27, 13, 6, 8, 12, 20, 5, 10. Calculate their average of their ages.

  a. 11
  b. 6
  c. 9
  d. 110

36. A farmer wants to plant 65,536 trees in such a way that number of rows must be equal to the number of plants in a row. How many trees will he plant in a row?

  a. 1684
  b. 1268
  c. 668
  d. 256

37. How much pay does Mr. Johnson receive if he gives half of his pay to his family, $250 to his landlord, and has exactly 3/7 of his pay left after these expenses?

  a. $3600
  b. $3500
  c. $2800
  d. $1750

38. A boy has 4 red, 5 green and 2 yellow balls. He chooses two balls randomly. What is the probability that one is red and other is green?

  a. 2/11
  b. 19/22
  c. 20/121
  d. 9/11

39. Simplify 5 1/2 – 5 3/7

  a. 1/10
  b. 1/14
  c. 1/7
  d. 2/7

40. What is -3 - (-7) - (+5)?

a. -6
b. 6
c. 3
d. -1

41. Solve 3 3/4 x 4/5 x 1 3/4

a. 3 3/4
b. 4 1/3
c. 6
d. 5 1/4

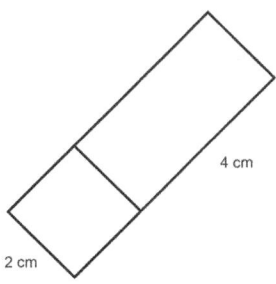

Note: figure not drawn to scale

42. Assuming the smaller shape is a square, what is the perimeter of the above shape?

a. 12 cm
b. 16 cm
c. 6 cm
d. 20 cm

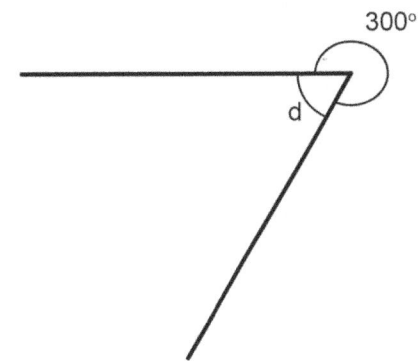

43. What is the measurement of the indicated angle?

a. 45°
b. 90°
c. 60°
d. 50°

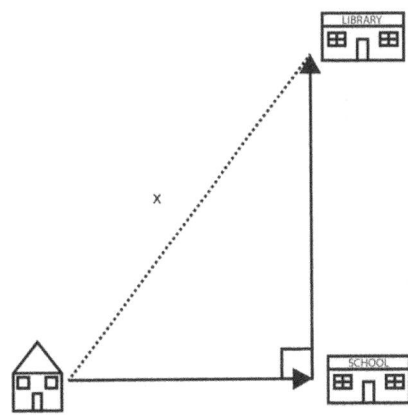

Note: figure not drawn to scale

44. Every day starting from his home Peter travels due east 3 kilometers to the school. After school he travels due north 4 kilometers to the library. What is the distance between Peter's home and the library?

a. 15 km
b. 10 km
c. 5 km
d. 12 ½ km

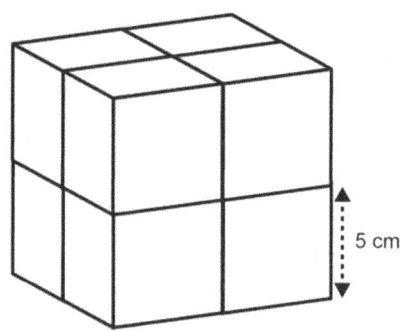

Note: figure not drawn to scale

45. Assuming the figure above is made of cubes, what is the volume?

    a. 125 cm³
    b. 875 cm³
    c. 1000 cm³
    d. 500 cm³

46. Solve √121

    a. 11
    b. 12
    c. 21
    d. None of the above

47. Write 51.738 to the nearest 100th.

    a. 51.735
    b. 51.7
    c. 51.73
    d. 51.74

48. What number is 8 less than 5 squared?

    a. 22
    b. 17
    c. 19
    d. 21

49. What is 25 more than 6/8 of 64?

    a. 73
    b. 85
    c. 55
    d. 62

50. 1/10 of what number is 5 times 10?

    a. 150
    b. 500
    c. 250
    d. 400

Section III - Ability

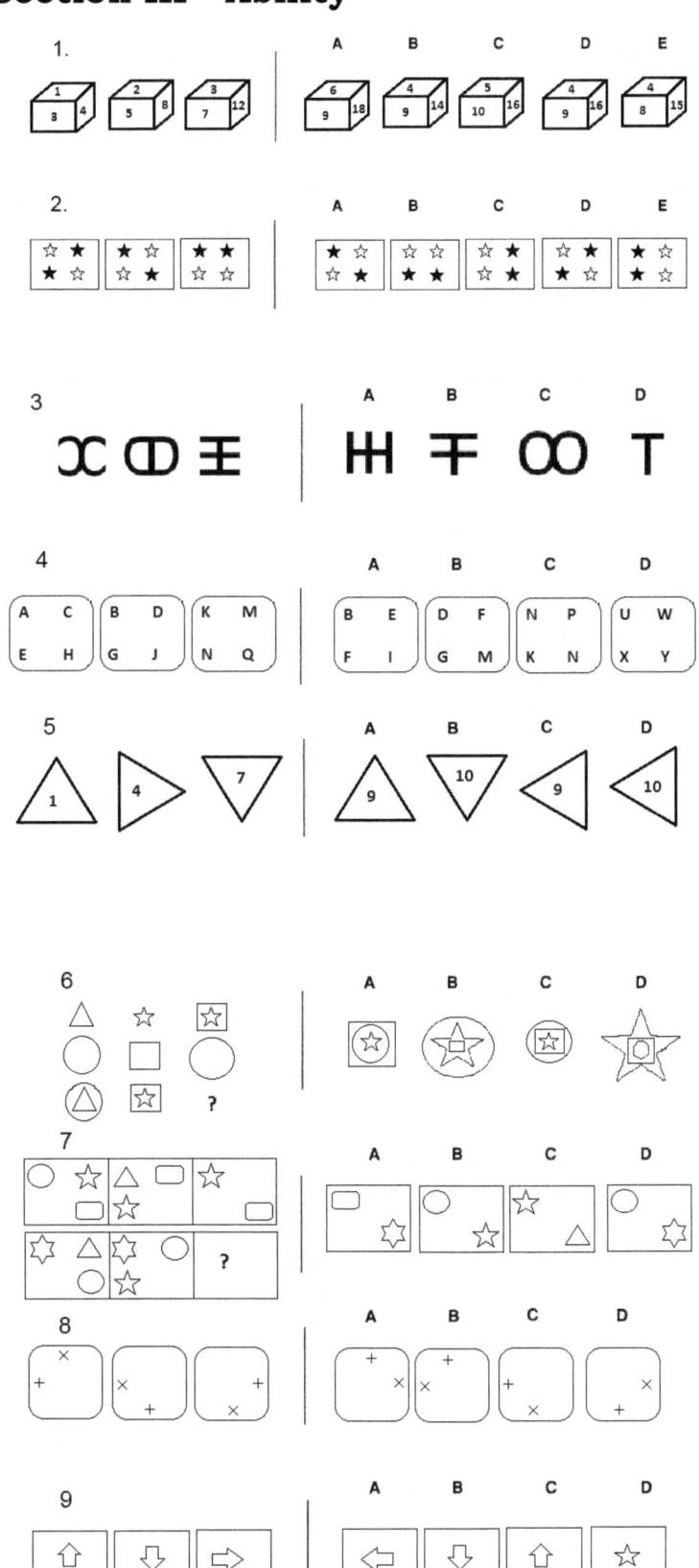

10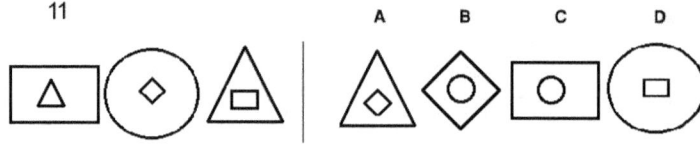

11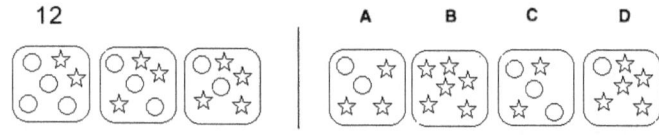

12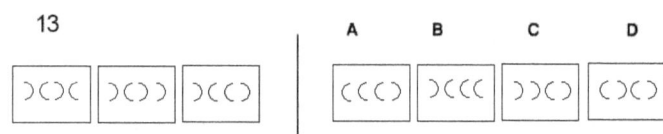

13

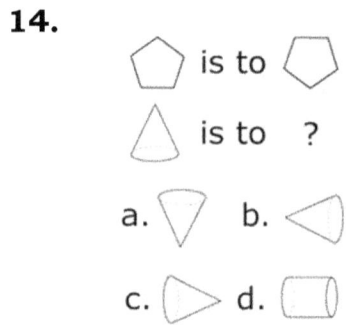

14. ⬠ is to ⬠
    △ is to ?

    a. ▽ b. ◁
    c. ▷ d. ⌭

15. △ is to ▷
    ⌭ is to ?

    a. ▷ b. □
    c. ⬠ d. ⌭

16. ⬜ is to △
    △ is to ?

    a. △ b. □
    c. ⬠ d. ⌭

Practice Test Questions 2

17. 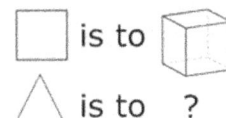 is to ?

   a. △ (cone) b. ▲ (pyramid)

   c. ⬠ (pentagon) d. ⬭ (cylinder)

18. ⬠ is to ⬡

   ⬡ is to ?

   a. ☐ b. ⬯ (octagon)

   c. ⬠ d. ⬡

19. ⁛⁛⁛ is to ⁛⁛

   ⁛⁛⁛ is to ?

   a. ⁛⁛ b. ⁛⁛⁛

   c. ⁚⁚ d. ⁚⁚⁚

20. 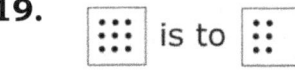 is to ?

   a. ▷ b. ⌒

   c. ▷ d. ⌒

21. 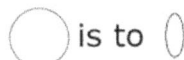 is to ?

   a. ☐ b. ▯

   c. ▭ d. ☐

22. ⁛⁛ is to ⁛⁛

   ⁛⁛ is to ?

   a. ⁛⁛ b. ⁛⁛

   c. ⁛⁛ d. ⁛⁛

23. When folded along the dotted lines, which shape will you get?

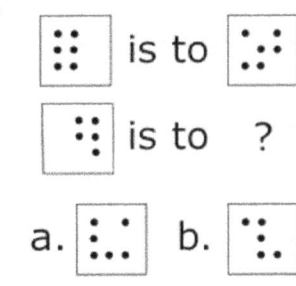

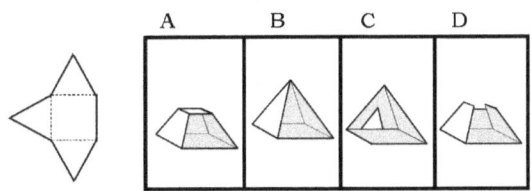

24. When folded, what pattern is possible?

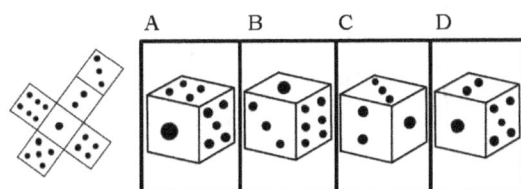

25. When folded into a loop, what will the strip of paper look like?

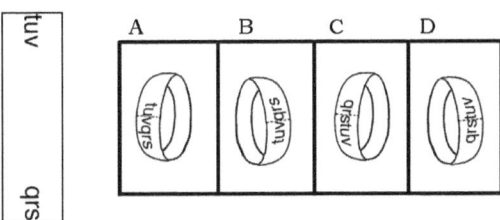

26. Which of the choices is the same pattern at a different angle?

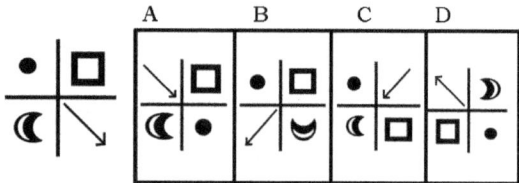

30. Which of the choices is the same pattern at a different angle?

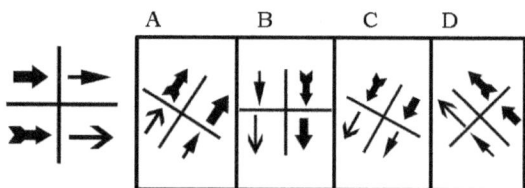

27. When put together, what 3-dimensional shape will you get?

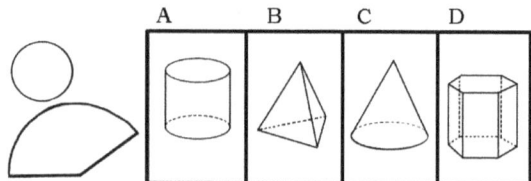

31. When put together, what 3-dimensional shape will you get?

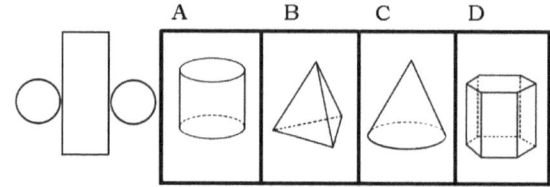

28. When folded, what pattern is possible?

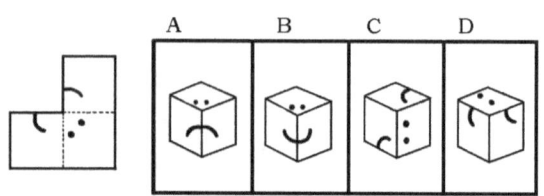

32. When folded into a loop, what will the strip of paper look like?

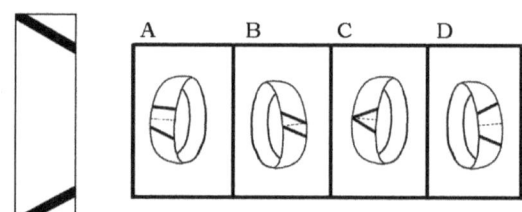

29. When folded, what pattern is possible?

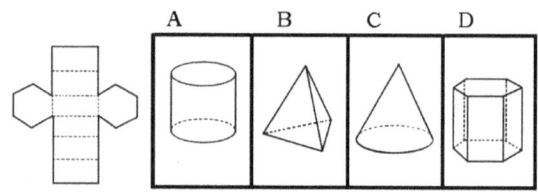

33. Which of the choices is the same pattern at a different angle?

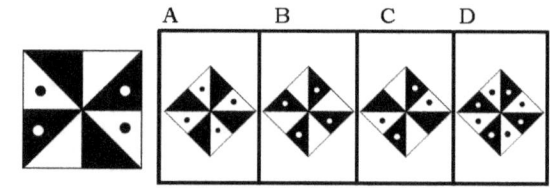

Practice Test Questions 2

34. When put together, what 3-dimensional shape will you get?

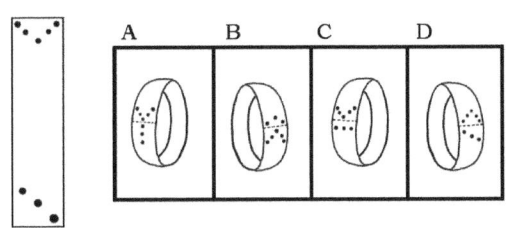

38. When folded, what pattern is possible?

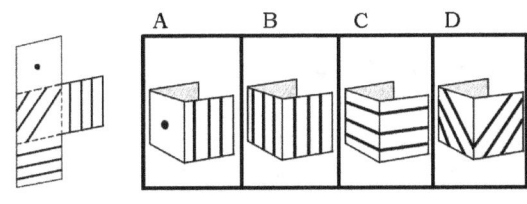

35. When folded into a loop, what will the strip of paper look like?

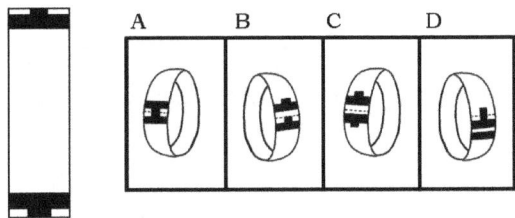

39. Which of the choices is the same pattern at a different angle?

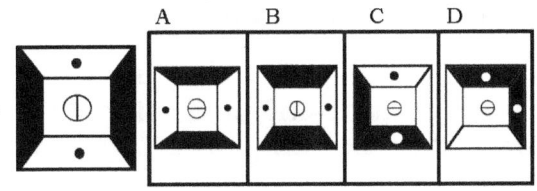

36. Which of the choices is the same pattern at a different angle?

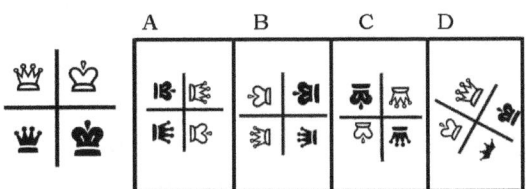

40. Which of the choices is the same pattern at a different angle?

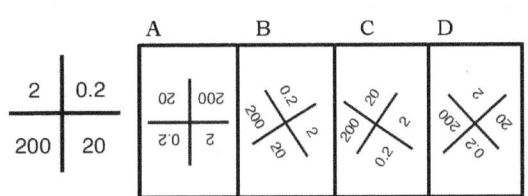

37. When folded into a loop, what will the strip of paper look like?

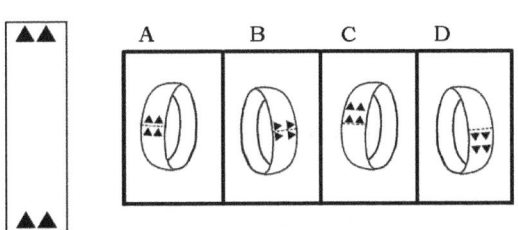

Answer Key

Section I Reading

Part I - Vocabulary

1. A
Intrepid: Fearless; bold; brave.

2. B
Judicious: Having, or characterized by, good judgment or sound thinking.

3. A
Negate: To deny the existence, evidence, or truth of; to contradict.

4. A
Obligatory: Imposing obligation, morally or legally; binding: an obligatory promise.

5. B
Obsolete: no longer in use; gone into disuse; disused or neglected.

6. A
Rankle: To cause irritation or deep bitterness.

7. C
Salient: Worthy of note; pertinent or relevant.

8. A
Sedentary: Not moving; relatively still; staying in the vicinity.

9. A
Anonymous: Of unknown name; whose name is withheld.

10. A
Atrocious: very bad; abominable or disgusting

11. D
Conclusive: Providing an end to something; decisive.

12. C
Dupe: To swindle, deceive, or trick.

13. D
Designate: appointed; chosen.

14. B
Specious: adj. Seemingly well-reasoned or factual, but actually fallacious or insincere; strongly held but false.

15. C
Proscribe: v. To forbid or denounce.

16. C
Veterinarian: n. A person qualified to treat diseased or injured animals.

17. C
Impeccable: adj. Perfect, without faults, flaws or errors.

18. A
Boisterous: adj. Noisy, energetic, and cheerful; rowdy.

19. B
Covert: adj. Partially hidden, disguised, secret, surreptitious.

20. B
Candid: adj. Straightforward, open and sincere.

Part II – Reading Comprehension

21. B
We can infer an important part of the respiratory system are the lungs. From the passage, "Molecules of oxygen and carbon dioxide are passively

exchanged, by diffusion, between the gaseous external environment and the blood. This exchange process occurs in the alveolar region of the lungs."

Therefore, a primary functions for the respiratory system is the exchange of oxygen and carbon dioxide, and this process occurs in the lungs. We can therefore infer that the lungs are an important part of the respiratory system.

22. C
The process by which molecules of oxygen and carbon dioxide are passively exchanged is diffusion.

This is a definition type question. Scan the passage for references to "oxygen," "carbon dioxide," or "exchanged."

23. A
The organ that plays an important role in gas exchange in amphibians is the skin.

Scan the passage for references to "amphibians," and find the answer.

24. A
The three physiological zones of the respiratory system are Conducting, transitional, respiratory zones.

25. B
This warranty does not cover a product that you have tried to fix yourself. From paragraph two, "This limited warranty does not cover ... any unauthorized disassembly, repair, or modification. "

26. C
ABC Electric could either replace or repair the fan, provided the other conditions are met. ABC Electric has the option to repair or replace.

27. B
The warranty does not cover a stove damaged in a flood. From the passage, "This limited warranty does not cover any damage to the product from improper installation, accident, abuse, misuse, natural disaster, insufficient or excessive electrical supply, abnormal mechanical or environmental conditions."

A flood is an "abnormal environmental condition," and a natural disaster, so it is not covered.

28. A
A missing part is an example of defective workmanship. This is an error made in the manufacturing process. A defective part is not considered workmanship.

29. B
The first paragraph tells us that myths are a true account of the remote past.

The second paragraph tells us that, "myths generally take place during a primordial age, when the world was still young, prior to achieving its current form."

Putting these two together, we can infer that humankind used myth to explain how the world was created.

30. A
This passage is about different types of stories. First, the passage explains myths, and then compares other types of stories to myths.

31. B
From the passage, "Unlike myths, folktales can take place at any time and any place, and the natives do not usually consider them true or sacred."

32. B

This passage describes the different categories for traditional stories. The other choices are facts from the passage, not the main idea of the passage. The main idea of a passage will always be the most general statement. For example, choice A, Myths, fables, and folktales are not the same thing, and each describes a specific type of story. This is a true statement from the passage, but not the main idea of the passage, since the passage also talks about how some cultures may classify a story as a myth and others as a folktale.

The statement, from choice B, Traditional stories can be categorized in different ways by different people, is a more general statement that describes the passage.

33. B

Choice B is the best choice, categories that group traditional stories according to certain characteristics.

Choices A and C are false and can be eliminated right away. Choice D is designed to confuse. Choice D may be true, but it is not mentioned in the passage.

34. D

The best answer is D, traditional stories themselves are a part of the larger category of folklore, which may also include costumes, gestures, and music.

All the other choices are false. Traditional stories are part of the larger category of Folklore, which includes other things, not the other way around.

35. A

There is a distinct difference between a myth and a legend, although both are folktales.

36. D

This question tests the reader's summarization skills. The other answers A, B, and C focus on portions of the second paragraph that are too narrow and do not relate to the specific portion of text in question. The complexity of the sentence may mislead students into selecting one of these answers, but rearranging or restating the sentence will lead the reader to the correct answer. In addition, A makes an assumption that may or may not be true about the intentions of the company, B focuses on one product rather than the idea of the products, and C makes an assumption about women that may or may not be true and is not supported by the text.

37. B

This question tests reader's attention to detail. If a reader selects A, he or she may have picked up on the use of the word "debate" and assumed, very logically, that the two are at odds because they are fighting; however, this is simply not supported in the text. C also uses very specific quotes from the text, but it rearranges them and gives them false meaning. The artists want to elevate their creations above the creations of other artists, thereby showing that they are "creative" and "innovative." Similarly, D takes phrases straight from the texts and rearranges and confuses them. The artists are described as wanting to be "creative, innovative, individual people," not the women.

38. A

This question tests reader's vocabulary and summarization skills. This phrase, used by the author, may seem flippant and dismissive if readers focus on the word "whatever" and misinterpret it as a popular, colloquial terms. In this way, the answers B and C may mislead the reader to selecting one of them by including the terms "unimportant" and "stupid," respectively. D is a similar misreading, but doesn't make sense when the phrase is at the beginning of the passage and the entire passage is on media messages. A is literally and contextually appropriate, and the reader can understand that the author would like to keep the introduction focused on the topic the passage is going to discuss.

39. A
This question tests a reader's inference skills. The extreme use of the word "all" in choice B suggests that every single advertising company are working to be approachable, and while this is not only unlikely, the text specifically states that "more" companies have done this, signifying that they have not all participated, even if it's a possibility that they may some day. The use of the limiting word "only" in choice C lends that answer similar problems; women are still buying from companies who do not care about this message, or those companies would not be in business, and the passage specifies that "many" women are worried about media messages, but not all. Readers may find choice D logical, especially if they are looking to make an inference, and while this may be a possibility, the passage does not suggest or discuss this happening. Choice A is correct based on specifically because of the relation between "still working" in the answer and "will hopefully" and the extensive discussion on companies struggles, which come only with progress, in the text.

40. B
The time limit for radar detectors is 14 days. Since you made the purchase 15 days ago, you do not qualify for the guarantee.

41. B
Since you made the purchase 10 days ago, you are covered by the guarantee. Since it is an advertised price at a different store, ABC Electric will "beat" the price by 10% of the difference, which is,

500 – 400 = 100 – difference in price

100 X 10% = $10 – 10% of the difference

The advertised lower price is $400. ABC will beat this price by 10% so they will refund $100 + 10 = $110.

42. C
The purpose of this passage is to persuade.

43. A
We can infer that an important purpose of the circulatory system is that of fighting diseases.

44. B
Humans have a closed circulatory system.

45. C
Besides blood, the heart and the blood vessels form the cardiovascular system.

46. B
The digestive system, along with the circulatory system, helps provide nutrients to keep the human heart pumping.

47. C
This question tests the reader's summarization skills. The entire passage is leading up to the idea that the president of the US may not have had grounds to assert his Fourteen Points when other countries had lost

so much. A is pretty directly inferred by the text, but it does not adequately summarize what the entire passage is trying to communicate. B may also be inferred by the passage when it says that the war is "imminent," but it does not represent the entire message, either. The passage does seem to be in praise of FDR, or at least in respect of him, but it does not in any way claim that he is the smartest president, nor does this represent the many other points included. C is then the obvious answer, and most directly relates to the closing sentences which it rewords.

48. C
This question tests the reader's attention to detail. The passage does state that A and B are true, and while those statements are in proximity to the explanation for why the war started, they are not the actual reason given. D is a mix up of words used in the passage, which says that the largest powers were in play but not that this fact somehow started the war. The passage does make a direct statement that a domino effect started the war, supporting C as the correct answer.

49. A
This question tests the reader's understanding of functions in writing. Throughout the passage, it states that leaders of other nations were hesitant to accept generous or peaceful terms because of the grievances of the war, and the great loss of life was chief among these. While the passage does touch on the devastation of deadly weapons (B), the use of this raw, emotional fact serves a much larger purpose, and the focus of the passage is not the weapons. While readers may indeed consider who lost the most soldiers (C) when so many countries were involved and the inequalities of loss are mentioned in the passage, there is no discussion of this in the passage. D is related to A, But A is more direct and relates more to the passage.

50. B
This question tests the reader's vocabulary skills. A may seem appealing to readers because it is phonetically similar to "catalyzed," but the two are not related in any other way. C makes sense in context, but if plugged in to the sentence creates a redundancy that doesn't make sense. D does also not make sense contextually, even if the reader may consider that funds were needed to create more weaponry, especially if it was advanced.

Section II - Language

Part I - Spelling, Capitalization, Punctuation and Usage

1. D
The preposition "to" is correct. 'To' here means give.

2. A
"Lie" means to recline, and does not take an object. "lay" means to place and does take an object.

3. A
Past unreal conditional. Takes the form,
[If ... Past Perfect ..., ... would have + past participle ...]

4. B
This sentence is in the present tense, so "to find" is correct.

5. A
Always use the singular verb form for nouns like politics, wages, mathemat-

ics, innings, news, advice, summons, furniture, information, poetry, machinery, vacation, scenery etc.

6. A
Possessive pronouns ending in 's' take an apostrophe before the 's': one's; everyone's; somebody's, nobody else's, etc.

7. A
A bonus is an extra feature, so added is redundant.

8. D
When talking about something that didn't happen in the past, use the past perfect (if I had done).

9. C
"Lie" means to recline, and does not take an object. "Lay" means to place and does take an object. Peter lay the books on the table (the books are the direct object), or the telephone poles were lying on the road (no direct object).

10. A
Titles of short stories are enclosed in quotation marks.

11. C
No additional punctuation is required here.

12. B
Here the word "sale" is used as a "word" and not as a word in the sentence, so quotation marks are used.

13. C
If one of the subjects linked by "either," "or," "nor" or "neither" is in plural form, then the verb should also be in plural, and the verb should be close to the plural subject.

14. C
Titles of short stories are enclosed in quotation marks, and commas always go inside quotation marks.

15. B
"Ran well" is correct. "Ran good" is never correct.

16. D
Commas and periods always go inside quotation marks. Question marks that are part of a quote also go inside quotation marks; however, if the writer quotes a statement as part of a larger question, the question mark is placed after the quotation mark.

17. C
Conscientious is the correct spelling.

18. D
This is a declarative sentence.

19. C
A result is something that occurs at the end, so an 'end result' is redundant.

20. D
Both A and C are correct.

> a. Their only employee with a nose ring is a young man named Daniel.

> c. Their only employee is a young man with a nose ring named Daniel.

21. C
Use a singular verb with either, each, neither, everyone and many.

22. D
Leisure is the correct spelling.

23. C
Pigeon is the correct spelling.

24. D
Odyssey is the correct spelling.

25. C
Nouns like deer, sheep, swine, salmon etc can take a singular or plural verb depending if they are used in

their singular or plural form.

26. A
Use an exclamation mark to end an exclamatory sentence, that is, at the end of a statement showing strong emotion.

27. D
Use an exclamation mark after an imperative sentence if the command is urgent and forceful.

28. D
Conclusive ADJECTIVE providing an end to something; decisive.

29. A
'He' is the simple subject of this sentence.

30. D
Deftly: VERB. Quick and skillful.

Part II - Paragraphs

1. A
Sentence 4 is a fragment. "Which I doubt belongs to any <u>other</u> person."

This sentence is an extension of the sentence preceding it. It does not complete the thought when alone, and is thus a sentence fragment.

2. A
Sentence 3 sentence is not consistent with the author's purpose. "For example, for an air stewardess position, girls have to be no more than 163 cm tall; whereas for jobs in foreign affairs, Chinese diplomats are required to match their foreign counterparts."

The passage talks about the people who want to increase their height by undergoing a surgery and points out the minimum height requirements for getting a job that they wish to work in. However, the expression "no more than 163 cm tall" is a statement about a maximum not a minimum. In addition, the sentence refers to Chinese diplomats who must 'match' the height of their foreign counterparts, which could be taller, and hence require surgery, or could be shorter and not require surgery.

3. B
The following sentence, if inserted after sentence 7, would best illustrate the main idea of the passage, "This artificial way of gaining height is turning out to be a new trend among the new generation in height conscious China."

The paragraph discusses about the application of leg surgery among Chinese young people to increase their height. This is best reflected in the sentence suggested in choice B which also contributes to the cohesion of the second paragraph as well as allowing a smooth transition between the second and third paragraph.

4. B
Suggested changes to sentence 8, "Even parents approve of the idea, being fully aware of all the complications and they are willing to finance such a sophisticated surgery."

The usage of vocabulary is incorrect in this sentence. The word "complexity" is an adjective noun used to describe detailed aspects of a given subject which is less relevant in this case. The word "labyrinth" is also incorrect in this context. The correct counterpart for "complexity" in this case would be "complications" which takes into account the length of the surgery itself and the agony, sacrifice and the commitment associated with it, all in one. Also the word "sophisticated," as suggested in choices B and C in the place of "labyrinth" is more appropriate as it hints about the details of the surgery. Choice B offers both changes.

5. A
Sentence 4 is a fragment. "Which I doubt belongs to any other person."

This sentence is an extension of the sentence preceding it. It does not complete the thought when alone and is thus a sentence fragment.

6. D
Sentence 9 is the least relevant to the main idea of the second paragraph. "He is panicked by street dogs and neighbors' cats and to avoid them, he crosses to the other side of the street every now and then."

The second paragraph mainly talks about Luke's odd behavior while in a moving in a crowd, but sentence 9 shifts the subject to his strategy when he encounters cats and dog in the streets.

7. C
Sentence 4 contains a redundant phrase. "Which I doubt any other person belongs to other than him."

In this sentence the second "other" is redundant. It can be omitted.

8. D
Sentence 5 is a fragment. "Hanging in between two sides of the wall near one corner of the store room which they rarely open, a magnificent piece of art left half woven and still being worked on."

This sentence does not express a complete thought since it does not have a verbal clause. A possible revision would be: "Hanging between two walls near one corner of the store room , lies a magnificent piece of art left half woven and still being worked on."

9. B
The following changes to sentence 7 would focus attention on the main idea of the second paragraph, "He is more interested in the web that they weave."

The style of the original sentence lacks cohesion with the passage. Choice B uses a relative comparison with the words "more interested in." The other choices offer changes which does not differ greatly from the original sentence.

10. A
Suggested changes to sentence 10 are, "He wonders how they manage to create something unique like this with such a little brain that they have."

The change in this case is related to the use of the word "wander" which is inappropriate in this case. "Wonder" is the correct word in this case.

Section III – Mathematics

1. B
Let XY represent the initial number, X + Y = 12, YX = XY + 36, only b = 48 satisfies both equations.

2. A
The problem is to find the perimeter of a shape made by merging a square and a semi circle. Perimeter = 3 sides of the square + 1/2 circumference of the circle.
= (3 x 5) + ½(5 π)
= 15 + 2.5 π
Perimeter = 17.5 π cm

3. B
Volume = Volume of large cylinder - Volume of small cylinder
(Volume of cylinder = area of base x height)
Volume = (π 12²x 10) - (π 6²x 5),
1440π - 180π
Volume = 1260π in³

4. D
We have a circle given with diameter 8 cm and a square located within the circle. We are asked to find the area of the circle for which we only need to know the length of the radius that is the half of the diameter.

Area of circle = πr² ... r = 8/2 = 4 cm

Area of circle = π * 4²

= 16π cm² ... As we notice, the inner square has no role in this question.

5. C
In one trip around the track, he covers the distance equal to the circumference of the circular path.
Circumference of the path = 75 × π = 235.65 meters.
Distance covered in 7 times around = 235.65 × 7 = 1650 meters.

6. A
The angles opposite both angles 30° & angle d are respectively equal to vertical angles.
2(30° + d) = 360°
2d = 360° - 60°
2d = 300°
d = 150°

7. C
The length of the track = 1.2 km = 1200 meters.
John will complete 1 round in 1200/120 = 10 minutes.
Tony will complete 1 round in 1200/100 = 12 minutes.
David will complete 1 round in 1200/75 = 16 minutes.
The Least Common Multiple of these is 240. Therefore, they will be together after 240 minutes.

8. D
1 cm = 5 km so 12.4 cm will be = 12.4 × 5 = 62 km.

9. B
Perimeter of a parallelogram is the sum of the sides.

Perimeter = 2(l + b)
Perimeter = 2(3 + 10), 2 x 13
Perimeter = 26 cm

10. D
2009 X 108 is 216,972, or approximately 210,000.

11. D
First, convert everything to seconds.
Song A = 240 + 56 = 296 sec.
Song B = 120 + 30 = 150 sec.
Song C = 600 + 16 = 616 sec.
Total = 296 + 150 + 616 = 1062. Average will be 1062/3 = 354.
In hours, 354/60 = 5 minutes, 54 seconds.

12. B
8.50 * .4 = 3.40 + 1.30 = $4.70

13. B
Formula for perimeter of a rectangle is 2(L + W)
p=26, so 2(L+W) = p

The length is 5 inches more than the width, so
2(w+5) + 2w = 26
2w + 10 + 2w = 26
2w + 2w = 26 - 10
4w = 18
W = 16/4 = 4 inches
L is 5 inches more than w, so
L = 5 + 4 = 9 inches.

14. D
Substitute the known variables, (3 x

2) + (4 x 4) x 8 =, 6 + 16 x 8, 24 x 8 = 176

15. A
2cnx = 2(4 x 5 x 3)/(2 X 5) = (2 x 60)/(2 x 5) = 120/10 = 12

16. A
First change all the terms to fractions, therefore, we get 7/2 / 14/5, to divide we need to invert the second fraction, 7/2 x 5/14, and then we cancel out to reduce to the lowest terms, 1/2 x 5/2 = 5/4, convert back to proper fraction to get 1 1/4

17. B
Substitute known variables, 2 x 9/3 + 3 x 10/5 – 2 =, 18/3 + 30/5 – 2 =, 6 + 6 -2 =, 12 - 2 = 10

18. A
First solve the fraction in each bracket separately, therefore (1/3 + 2/6) - (3/4 - 1/3) = (find common denominator) (2+2/6) – (9- 4/12) = (4/6) – (5/12) = (find common denominator again) 8/12 – 5/12 =, 8 - 5/12 = 3/12 = 1/4.

19. B
(4/5 - 3/10) + (2/3 – 3/9) =, (find a common denominator) (8-3/10) + (6-3/9) =, (5/10) + (3/9) = 1/2 + 1/3, (find a common denominator) 3+2/6 = 5/6

20. A
2 + a number divided by 7.
(2 + X) divided by 7.
(2 + X)/7

21. D
Substitute with known variables, (6 x 8) – 12 + (2 x 12) =, 48 – 12 + 24, do the additions first, 48 – (12 + 24) =, 48 – 36 = 12

22. C
Subtract the whole numbers and then subtract the fractions, therefore 3 2/3 - 1 2/8 = (3-1) (2/3 – 2/8) = find common denominator to subtract the fractions, (2) (16-6)/24 = 2 10/24, reduce to lowest terms, 2 5/12

23. A
Subtract the whole numbers and then subtract the fractions, therefore (7-4) (2/5 – 3/10) = 3 (4-3/10) = 3 1/10

24. C
-5 – 5x = 8x + 8, bring same terms to same side of the equation changing the negative or positive signs when they cross over, therefore -5x - 8x = 8 + 5, = -13x = 13, x = 1.

25. A
First, convert all the terms to fractions and then cancel out. Therefore, 7/3 x 10/7 x 3/4 = 1/3 x 10/1 x 3/4, 1 x 5 x 1/2, 5 x 1/2 = 2 1/2

26. B
Subtract the whole numbers and then subtract the fractions, therefore (7 - 4) (4/5 – 2/3) = 3 (12 - 10/15) = 3 2/15

27. C
12x – 8 = 3x + 10, bring same terms to same side of the equation changing the negative or positive signs when they cross over, therefore 12x -3x = 10 + 8, 9x = 18, x = 2

28. C
(3/5 - 2/5) + (3/4 – 2/8) =, (3-2/5) + (6-2/8) =, 1/5 + 4/8 =, (find a common denominator) 8+20/40 = 28/40
= 14/20

29. D
6a + 4 = 28 + 2a, solve for a. Bring same terms to same side of the equation changing the negative or positive

signs when they cross over, therefore 6a − 2a = 28 - 4, 4a = 24, a = 24/4 = 6

30. D
(3-1/4) − (3-2/5) =, 3/4 - 1/5 =. 15-4/20 = 11/20

31. D
6 + 9x = 12 + 7x, bring same terms to same side of the equation changing the negative or positive signs when they cross over, therefore 9x − 7x = 12 − 6, 2x = 6, x = 6/2, x = 3

32. C
First change all the terms to fractions, therefore, we get 32/5 / 16/7, to divide we need to invert the second fraction, 32/5 x 7/16, and then we cancel out to reduce to the lowest terms, 2/5 x 7/1 = 14/5, convert back to proper fraction to get 2 4/5

33. B
-6 + 7a = 9 + 4a, bring same terms to same side of the equation changing the negative or positive signs when they cross over, therefore 7a − 4a = 9 + 6 = 3a = 15, a = 15/3, a = 5

34. D
As the lawn is square, the length of one side will be= √62500 = 250 meters. Therefore, the perimeters will be 250 × 4 = 1000 meters. The total cost will be 1000 × 5.5 = $5500.

35. A
First add all the numbers 3 + 6 + 27 + 13 + 6 + 8 + 12 + 20 + 5 + 10 = 110. Then divide by 10 (the number of data provided) = 110/10 = 11

36. D
Let x be number of rows, and number of trees in a row. So equation becomes X^2 = 65536, X = 256.

37. B
We check the fractions in the question and see that there is a "half" (that is 1/2) and 3/7. So, we multiply the denominators of these fractions to decide how to name the total money. We say that Mr. Johnson has 14x at the beginning; he gives half of this, meaning 7x, to his family. $250 to his landlord. He has 3/7 of his money left. 3/7 of 14x is equal to:

14x * (3/7) = 6x

So,

Spent money is: 7x + 250

Unspent money is: 6x

Total money is: 14x

We write an equation: total money = spent money + unspent money

14x = 7x + 250 + 6x

14x - 7x - 6x = 250

x = 250

We are asked to find the total money that is 14x:

14x = 14 * 250 = $3500

38. A
The probability that the 1st ball drawn is red = 4/11. The probability that the 2nd ball drawn is green = 5/10. The combined probability will then be 4/11 X 5/10 = 20/110 = 2/11.

39. B
(5-5) (1/2 − 3/7) = (7-6/14) = 1/14

40. D
-(-) becomes + and -(+) becomes -, therefore, -3 - (-7) - (+5) = -3 + 7 − 5, -4 + 5 = -1

41. D
First, convert all the terms to fractions and then cancel out. Therefore, 15/4 x 4/5 x 7/4 = 3/4 x 4/1 x 7/4, 3/4 x 1/1 x 7/1, 21/4 = 5 1/4

42. B
We see that there is a square with side 2 cm and a rectangle adjacent to it, with one side 2 cm (common side with the square) and the other side 4 cm. The perimeter of a shape is found by summing up all sides surrounding the shape, not adding the ones inside the shape. Three 2 cm sides from the square, and two 4 cm sides and one 2 cm side from the rectangle contribute the perimeter.

So, the perimeter of the shape is: 2 + 2 + 2 + 4 + 2 + 4 = 16 cm.

43. C
The sum of angles around a point is 360°
d + 300 = 360°
d = 60°

44. C
We see that two legs of a right triangle form by Peter's movements and we are asked to find the length of the hypotenuse. We use the Pythagorean Theorem:

Pythagorean Theorem:
$(Hypotenuse)^2 = (Perpendicular)^2 + (Base)^2$
$h^2 = a^2 + b^2$

Given: $3^2 + 4^2 = h^2$
$h^2 = 9 + 16$
$h = \sqrt{25}$
$h = 5$

45. C
The large cube is made up of 8 smaller cubes with 5 cm sides. The volume of a cube is found by the third power of the length of one side.
Volume of the large cube = Volume of the small cube•8

$= (5^3) \cdot 8 = 125 \cdot 8$

$= 1000 \text{ cm}^3$

There is another solution for this question. Find the side length of the large cube. There are two cubes rows with 5 cm length for each. So, one side of the large cube is 10 cm.

The volume of this large cube is equal to $10^3 = 1000 \text{ cm}^3$

46. A
$\sqrt{121} = 11$

47. D
The number is 51.738. The last digit is greater than 5, so it is removed and 1 is added to the next number to the left. Answer = 51.74.

48. B
5 X 5 = 25 – 8 = 17

49. A
6/8 of 64 = 48 + 25 = 73

50. B
5 X 10 = 50
1/10Z = 50
Z = 500

Section IV - Ability

1. D
The numbers on top are increasing by one, the number on the front are increasing by 2 and the numbers on the right are multiple of 4.

2. B
Two black stars are placed in the opposite direction to the previous.

3. B
These are back to back letters in ascending alphapbetical order.

4. C
In the upper row, one letter is missing, and in the bottom row, two letters are missing.

5. D
The triangle rotates clockwise and the numbers increase by three.

6. C
The first shape should be inside the second shape.

7. D
The third box contains two shapes which are present in both of the first two boxes.

8. A
The shape rotates counter-clockwise.

9. A
The arrow inside the box is the inverse of the previous one.

10. C
The number of points increases with each figure.

11. B
The larger, exterior figure is the smaller interior figure.

12. D
The number of stars increases by one, and the number of circles decreases by one.

13. C
The half circles rotate 180 degrees from right to left.

14. A
The relation is the same figure rotated.

15. D
The relation is the same figure rotated.

16. B
The relation is a 3-dimensional figure to a 2-dimensional figure.

17. B
The relation is a 2-dimensional figure to a 3-dimentional figure.

18. B
The relation is a n-sided figure to an n+1 sided figure.

19. C
The first figure has 9 cots in a square and the second figure has 6 dots, which is 1/3 removed.

20. C
The relation is a 3-dimentional figure to a rotated 2-dimentional figure.

21. C
The relation is the same figure with the bottom half removed.

22. B
Each square has the same number of dots inside. Six in the top figures and 5 in the given figure.

23. B
24. A
25. D
26. D
27. C
28. B
29. D
30. C
31. A
32. C
33. C
34. D
35. A
36. B
37. A
38. C
39. A
40. A

Conclusion

CONGRATULATIONS! You have made it this far because you have applied yourself diligently to practicing for the exam and no doubt improved your potential score considerably! Getting into a good school is a huge step in a journey that might be challenging at times but will be many times more rewarding and fulfilling. That is why being prepared is so important.

Good Luck!

FREE Ebook Version

Download a FREE Ebook version of the publication!

Suitable for tablets, iPad, iPhone, or any smart phone.

Go to: http://tinyurl.com/mtysrpw

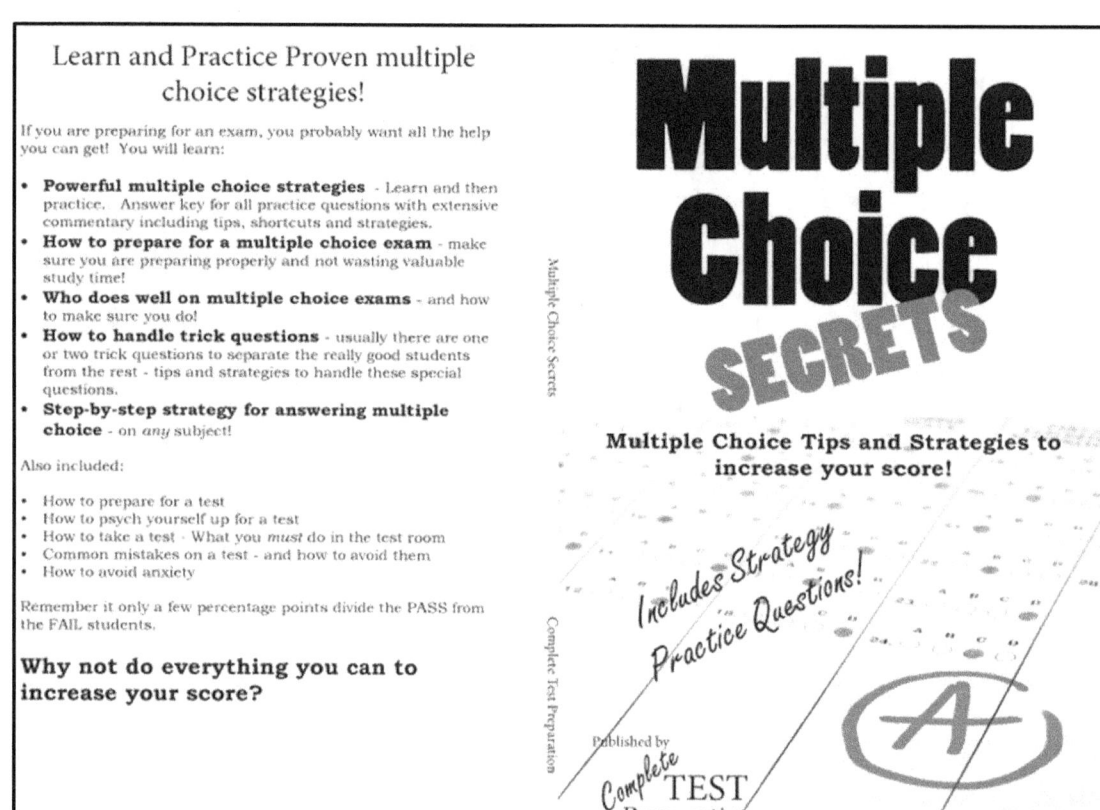

Learn to increase your score using time-tested secrets for answering multiple choice questions!

This practice book has everything you need to know about answering multiple choice questions on a standardized test!

You will learn 12 strategies for answering multiple choice questions and then practice each strategy with over 45 reading comprehension multiple choice questions, with extensive commentary from exam experts!

Maybe you have read this kind of thing before, and maybe feel you don't need it, and you are not sure if you are going to buy this Book.

Remember though, it only a few percentage points divide the PASS from the FAIL students.

Even if our multiple choice strategies increase your score by a few percentage points, isn't that worth it?

www.multiple-choice.ca